Teaching Manual for

Written on Our Hearts

Teaching Manual for

Written on Our Hearts: The Old Testament Story of God's Love

Third Edition

Student text
by Mary Reed Newland

Saint Mary's Press®

The publishing team included Steven C. McGlaun, development editor; Lorraine Kilmartin, reviewer; prepress and manufacturing coordinated by the production departments of Saint Mary's Press.

Cover image by Brian Singer-Towns, Saint Mary's Press

Printed in the United States of America

1241

ISBN 978-0-88489-992-1

Happy are those
 who do not follow the advice of the wicked,
or take the path that sinners tread,
or sit in the seat of scoffers;
but their delight is in the law of the LORD,
 and on his law they meditate day and night.
They are like trees
 planted by streams of water,
which yield their fruit in its season,
 and their leaves do not wither.
In all that they do, they prosper.

(Ps. 1:1–3)

Contents

Epilogue

Appendices

Acknowledgments

Introduction for the Teacher

The Narrative Approach of This Course

The Scriptures as Sacred Stories

When family gathers for Thanksgiving or Christmas dinner, we wait for the stories to begin. An uncle or an aunt tells about the hard days of the Great Depression. Our father's or grandfather's face takes on a sober stare as he relates his story about going off to war in the Pacific. A teenage cousin is urged to speak about her induction into the National Honor Society. Stories whirl around the table and in the memories of everyone present, providing sustenance. The holiday meal nourishes everyone's body; the stories nourish a sense of family identity.

A family's stories form the myth by which the family members know themselves. The term *myth* in this context does not, of course, carry the reduced meaning of myth as an empty, false story or an illusion. Rather, myth is a story that reveals an inner truth. In a family where stories of the past are shared, myth is the glue that holds the family together.

Joseph Campbell, in *The Power of Myth* (p. 31), claims that myths have four functions:

1. *A mystical function.* Myths open us to "realizing what a wonder the universe is, and what a wonder you are, and experiencing awe before this mystery."
2. *A cosmological function.* Myths show us "what the shape of the universe is, but . . . in such a way that the mystery again comes through."
3. *A sociological function.* Myths support and validate a particular social order.
4. *A pedagogical function.* Myths show us "how to live a human lifetime under any circumstances."

Human beings need myths to live by; myths join us with God, Creation, and the human family.

The Old Testament (called by Jews the Hebrew Scriptures or, simply, the Bible) provides myths for Jews and Christians as a religious family. The biblical stories shed light on our identity, outline our relationship with God, and show us how to live with mystery and all of life's ups and downs. They nourish our faith, hope, and love. Robert Alter describes the Old Testament in this way:

> As odd as it may sound at first, I would contend that prose fiction is the best general rubric for describing biblical narrative. Or, to be more precise, . . . we can speak of the Bible as *historicized* prose fiction. . . .

Let me hasten to say that in giving such weight to fictionality, I do not mean to discount the historical impulse that informs the Hebrew Bible. The God of Israel, as so often has been observed, is above all the God of history: the working out of His purposes in history is a process that compels the attention of the Hebrew imagination, which is thus led to the most vital interest in the concrete and differential character of historical events. The point is that fiction was the principal means which the biblical authors had at their disposal for realizing history. (*The Art of Biblical Narrative*, pp. 23 and 32)

Through stories, the biblical narrators explained their experiences of God's action in their life. They told these stories to unify and inspire, to coax and warn the people of Israel.

Stories: Interesting and Accessible

The authors of the Old Testament told stories, and Jesus himself taught in stories, for good reason: stories are interesting and accessible. Teachers know that if they want to hold students' attention, a story does the trick. Great speakers know the same thing, and they practice at being good storytellers. Why do stories work so well? Because they are interesting. They put flesh and bone on abstract ideas. The story of Ruth and Naomi puts the concepts of devotion and love on their own two feet and shows what these virtues look like in the flesh. Listening to a volleyball champion talk about her games is far more informative and interesting than studying diagrams in a book or listening to an audiotape about how to serve.

Stories tap the imagination. Religious stories tap the religious imagination. John H. Westerhoff comments:

The Scripture contains the sacred myths of the Christian community. They ought not be reduced to rational discourse. The Bible is poetry plus, not science minus. . . . For too long we have attempted to understand reality solely through reason and have forgotten the importance of symbolic narrative, metaphor, and sacred story. Christianity is a historical, but also a metaphorical, religion. (*Aesthetic Dimensions of Religious Education*, p. 23)

Because stories are metaphorical and symbolic narrative, they engage the imagination. When the imagination is engaged, interest cannot be far behind.

Stories are accessible. Jesus certainly understood this: "With many such parables he spoke the word to [the crowd], as they were able to hear it; he did not speak to them except in parables, but he explained everything in private to his disciples" (Mark 4:33–34). The greatest teacher who ever lived realized that parables—stories—made his teachings accessible to everyone, not just the learned elite.

In the student text for this course, a strong narrative element is used for the above-mentioned reasons. The biblical stories are interesting and accessible, particularly when introduced to young readers by a storyteller like Mary Reed Newland, the author of the text.

Mature Themes in the Scriptural Stories

The stories of the Old Testament are filled with murder and mayhem, suffering and sex, betrayal and infidelity—not the stuff of children's books. The first story after the Creation narrative is one of crime and punishment: Adam and Eve sin, and God banishes them from Eden. In the next episode of Genesis, we read of fratricide: Cain brutally murders his brother, Abel.

Few of the biblical stories have ideal endings. After the many agonies of leading the Israelites out of slavery, Moses cannot enter the Promised Land. At one point the prophet Elijah begs God to kill him. After Job lands on a dunghill, suffers with horrible sores, and loses all his property, he is still not sure why he has to suffer.

Also, consider the violent curses that are hurled in the Psalms; for instance:

Pour out your indignation upon them,
  and let your burning anger overtake them.
May their camp be a desolation;
  let no one live in their tents.

(69:24–25)

Consider the delight in this psalm:

I pursued my enemies and overtook them;
  and did not turn back until they were consumed.
I struck them down, so that they were not able to rise;
  they fell under my feet.

(18:37–38)

If we heard our students or other adults talking like that, we would probably call the police, or at least a counselor. It takes a good deal of perspective to understand such passages in their context.

In other words, extensive experience and maturity help considerably when reading the Old Testament. By the time we reach adulthood, we might more fully understand the burning anger and bitterness that the psalmist poured out. We might better comprehend the anguish of Moses or Elijah or Job because we are more likely to have experienced great disappointment, despair, and suffering.

Although the Old Testament is taught in many high schools in the ninth grade—and the student text for this course is certainly usable at that level—older students are much more likely to understand and appreciate the biblical stories. Each year of life adds to the students' base of experience. For that reason Saint Mary's Press recommends that this course be taught at the tenth- or eleventh-grade level.

In any case, the marvelous stories of the Old Testament can inspire and challenge all of us, no matter what age. In them we can see God's faithful love working in the lives of fallible, scared, courageous, and sometimes humorous human beings. This course, by telling the stories and explaining key concepts, opens up the richness of the Old Testament to students and teachers alike.

Drawing Out the Meaning of Stories

Mary Reed Newland was a premier storyteller, and she used her skills and experience as a storyteller to write the student text for this course. She sought to open up the Jewish experience of God's faithful action in history by doing what the people of Israel themselves did—telling a story first and then discussing its meaning. Mary Newland believed that knowing the Bible would lead to loving it, and that knowing the Bible meant, first and foremost, knowing its stories. (In order to become most familiar with these stories, your students should each have their own copy of the Bible, which they can feel free to write in and personalize with highlighting, reflections, and questions.)

The following three steps describe how we learn through telling and hearing stories.

1. Experience. The learning process begins with a significant experience, which is formed into a story or a history. For example, a young woman's volleyball team captures the state championship despite all sorts of adversity. When the woman comes home, her parents and siblings say: "Tell us all about the game. What did the scout from the university say to you? What did it feel like to win the game?" And so on. In formulating the story she tells, the young woman gives her own coloring to the events, adding her personal realizations and emotions. Observers of the game and ensuing celebration would tell a different story than the young woman because their experience of the event would be different. Nevertheless, for the hearer of the account, the story serves as a vicarious experience of the actual event. A story is a way of experiencing something.

The people of Israel learned in a way similar to how the family of the volleyball player did, indeed as we all do. The Israelites heard the stories of God's saving deeds among their people, and those stories were vicarious experiences for them. For instance, God (working through Moses and Aaron) led the people out of Egypt. God saved them from slavery. Time and time again, God showed mercy to the people. Eventually they reached the Promised Land. Thus every year at Passover, Jews all over the world retell the story of their ancestors, and the telling of the story becomes a way of reliving the experience. The story of the Exodus gives both Jews and Christians a sense of who they are and how God's actions have affected their lives.

Mary Newland used the Bible itself as a model for her approach to the student text. Her first concern in writing was to tell the biblical stories as clearly and concisely as possible, focusing on the main events. Then she directed the reader to the relevant scriptural passages. This approach enables students to vicariously experience the events of the stories.

One way to build on the storytelling dimension of the Old Testament is to regularly read, or have the students read, passages aloud in class, to get a sense of the oral tradition out of which the Bible originated.

2. Reflection and analysis. After our initial real-life or vicarious experience of something, often we reflect on or analyze what happened. We ponder the story. We compare our version of events with the versions of reliable sources who can broaden our understanding and perspective. The young woman on the winning volleyball team will undoubtedly talk to her teammates and her coach about the game and the season. They all will read the newspaper reports. If a video of the championship game was made, they will watch it, noting mistakes and good plays.

This process of reflection and analysis also happened with the biblical stories. The stories of the Bible began as oral traditions, not written accounts. Over time, each story became nuanced or colored by successive tellers. By the time the books of the Bible were written and compiled, long years of reflection and analysis had been integrated into the fabric of the stories. Because the Bible is the living Word of God, biblical scholars and devout people continue to add to our understanding and appreciation of the history of God's Chosen People.

3. Application. Finally, our experiences and the reflection and analysis that follow them permit us to apply what we have learned to our life. This application is a personal decision. Based on their analysis of the game, the volleyball players might try to improve their serves or spikes. So too through reflection on their collective stories, the people of Israel learned how to live righteously in God's eyes.

The textbook for this course provides students with many opportunities to apply their learnings from the biblical stories to their own way of life. And after all, a new and better way of living is the intended fruit of reading God's Word. John Shea, in *Stories of Faith,* comments:

> [The biblical stories] are stories meant to disclose aspects of our relationship to God and through that relationship our commitments to each other. The stories of scripture were remembered and today remain memorable because they are similar enough to our own lives for us to see ourselves, yet different enough from our lives for us to see new possibilities. They tell us what we want to know and more. They come close to home and yet are an invitation to journey. . . . The traditional stories, both historical and fictional, reflect concerns and conflicts present in our lives and suggest ways of dealing with them. (P. 89)

The Bible lives today as we live out its lessons in our actions. The stories of Abraham, Hagar, Moses, Ruth, David, Jeremiah, and all the other great figures of the Old Testament give us models for our own life, models who were imperfect and flawed like us but were nonetheless totally loved by God.

The Contents of This Course

The Old Testament, which contains the roots of not only Judaism but also Christianity, is closely tied to the history of the biblical Jews. So in order to understand the Old Testament and its import in the lives of today's Christians, we need to understand the history of, and the challenges to, the people of Israel.

The text for this course aims to help students comprehend the wealth of the Judeo-Christian spiritual tradition and challenges them to grow in their appreciation of God, themselves, and other people. Valuing the Old Testament as a source of living wisdom—the Word of God—comes about in part when students understand how these Scriptures were written and in what contexts they inspired and were heard by the ancestors of our tradition.

An Exile Lens

The text takes the position, as do many mainstream biblical scholars, that most of the Scriptures of the Old Testament reached their final form during or around the time of the Babylonian exile. Thus the exile experience became the lens through which the ancient Jews perceived their stories. Their history made sense in light of what was happening to them during the exile, and vice versa: what was happening to them in exile made sense to them because of their history.

At many points in the student text the students are reminded of the exile "lens" as the way the Israelites interpreted their experience and found God's past messages and deeds particularly significant. These reminders to the readers are not inserted simply to help the students become more attuned to scholarly issues in biblical criticism. Rather, awareness of the exile lens enables young people to see that their own condition of "exile," in the various contemporary forms they may experience it, can heighten their own openness to God's Word. The exile perspective of the text aims ultimately at affecting the level of spirituality, not just knowledge.

Goals and Objectives

This course has the following goals and objectives:

Goal 1. That the students read the Old Testament and understand it
Objective. The student text lists and provides commentary on key passages to be read from the Old Testament.

Goal 2. That the students know and appreciate the major themes and issues in the Old Testament
Objectives. The text and teaching manual do the following:
- provide commentary, analysis, and reflection on the major sections of the Old Testament
- include maps, timelines, and illustrations of important places and events
- offer group activities, questions for discussion, map exercises, background information, research and art projects, role-play situations, ideas for guest speakers, interview suggestions, case studies, writing projects, and debate topics—all designed to deepen the students' understanding of the Old Testament
- provide review questions and test questions that may be used to check the students' knowledge

Goal 3. That the students reflect on how biblical truths may be incorporated into their own lives
Objective. Through review questions, personal reflection exercises, prayer services, writing activities, and group discussions, the students have opportunities to consider their values and actions in light of insights from the Old Testament.

Goal 4. That the students develop a deeper understanding of how God has worked in human history and still works in the present
Objectives. The text and teaching manual do the following:
- help the students encounter the stories of people who have been touched by God and have responded in heroic, simple, inspiring, or dramatic ways
- emphasize that despite all the failings and sins of the Chosen People, God continually saved them by calling them to repentance
- show the Old Testament as the tradition out of which Jesus came and proclaimed his message
- ask the students to respond—through the prayer services and the writing of reflections—to ways God has been present to them in their own life story

These goals will be best met if the Bible, the student text, and this teaching manual are used together.

Meeting these goals does not necessarily, or even ideally, mean covering all the material in the text. The approach of this text and teaching manual is to offer material on every book of the Old Testament and to point out the most important passages of each book. However, you must select from this material according to the needs and capabilities of your students. For ideas on selecting content from the text, see the note on pages 16 to 17 of this manual.

An Outline of Major Concepts

The following list of major concepts corresponds to the major sections in each chapter of the student text. This teaching manual is also organized according to these major concepts. This list serves as an outline of the course contents.

Chapter 1
The Old Testament: The Story of God's Boundless Love
A. The Bible: A Time Capsule from God
B. Interpreting the Scriptures
C. A God Who Acts in History
D. What Are the Scriptures of the Old Testament?

Chapter 2
Beginnings: Stories of God's Creation and Promises
A. Stories of the Origins
B. Abraham: The Father of Biblical Faith
C. Jacob: A Man Named Israel
D. Joseph: Treachery, Triumph, and Forgiveness

Chapter 3
Freedom: The Exodus and the Covenant of Sinai
A. The Exodus: Freed from Slavery
B. The Covenant of Sinai: An Offering from God
C. Sealing the Covenant

Chapter 4
The Law: Living Out the Covenant
A. Leviticus: Holiness and Ritual
B. Numbers: Priestly Regulations and Inspiring Stories
C. Deuteronomy: The Law and Love

Chapter 5
The Land: Finding Hope for the Future in God's Gift
A. Making Sense of the Past
B. Joshua: Sweeping into the Promised Land
C. Judges: Saving Israel from Itself
D. Ruth: An Israelite Foreigner with a Great Destiny

Chapter 6
The Kings: Becoming a Nation
A. Stories of Transition to Nationhood
B. Samuel: Anointer of Kings
C. Saul and David in Conflict
D. King David: Nation Builder
E. King Solomon: Temple Builder

Chapter 7
The Prophets: Crying Out the Word of God
A. The Kingdom Breaks Up
B. Elijah and Elisha in the North
C. Amos and Hosea in the North
D. Isaiah in the South: The Greatest Writing Prophet
E. Micah in the South: Sympathy from the Bottom of Society

We now turn to the "how" of this course—the ways you can use the student text and teaching manual to accomplish the course goals.

Lesson Planning for This Course

Tools for Teaching

During the brief explanation given here, you may find it helpful to periodically glance at one of the chapters in the text and its corresponding chapter in this manual to see examples of the teaching tools described.

Note: It is unlikely that a class—even a class of advanced students—will be able to cover every biblical figure, story, event, and book described in the student text. For instance, in studying the judges (chapter 5), you may need to focus on some of the judges' stories and leave out others. Or you may choose to assign the scriptural readings for only one or two judges and then have the students simply read Mary Newland's brief accounts of the other judges. If your students are assigned to read all the scriptural readings suggested in the text, they will probably find the course burdensome. Therefore, pick and choose from among the readings. This is possible throughout the course. For example, when several minor prophets are covered in a major concept, you may choose to focus on only one. Naturally, you will want to pay the most attention to key figures such as Isaiah, Jeremiah, and Ezekiel, but even for those major prophets, you will probably need to select from the assigned readings about them.

Teacher Prayers

At the beginning of each chapter in the teaching manual there is a brief prayer and reflection for teachers. This is intended to help you approach your teaching prayerfully, aware that you are acting as God's instrument, a witness of faith to your students.

Use of the teacher prayers offered here is optional—perhaps you have found another way to bring faith and prayer into your work. If you choose to use the prayers offered, here are several suggestions for their use:
- The prayer can be used at the beginning and end of each chapter you teach, as suggested.
- You may choose to use a prayer from a given chapter each day that you teach that chapter.
- Perhaps there is one prayer in the manual that captures you, and you wish to use it as your reflection every day throughout the course.
- In addition to private prayer, you may also wish to gather periodically with the team of teachers for this course and spend a few minutes in shared prayer. This will strengthen you as a team and support you individually.

However you pray, entering the classroom with a prayerful heart will have a far-reaching effect on your students and the entire school-faith community.

Major Concepts

As mentioned earlier in this introduction, each chapter of the textbook and teaching manual is organized according to the major concepts of that chapter. The major concepts for a given chapter of the text correspond roughly to the major, largest headings within the chapter. Thus the major concepts are the organizing principle for teaching the material. In the chapters of the manual, these concepts are given as concise summaries of the significant ideas conveyed by the chapter. Most chapters have three to five such major concepts, and these serve as a helpful tool for planning your schedule and organizing your teaching of the course.

The major concepts in a given chapter are listed and described at the beginning of that chapter in the teaching manual, with references to numbers in the *Catechism of the Catholic Church* for each concept. This opening description of concepts can serve as a chapter summary for your purposes. Then each concept for the chapter is treated in turn. That is, the title of each major concept is repeated, with a reference to the related student text pages. Then review questions and activities on that concept are provided.

Review Questions

The review questions that end each section of the chapter in the student text are repeated in the teaching manual, and a suggested answer is provided for each question. The intent of the review questions is simply to check whether the students have retained the basic information for a given concept. The questions do not require full comprehension or assimilation of the material, as more analytical or reflective kinds of questions would. Students who can accurately answer the review questions demonstrate basic comprehension. It is hoped that by using other course methods, they will go beyond that level to analysis, reflection, and application.

Student Text Activities

Sidebar activities appear in the student text corresponding with student text material on that page or spread. These activities are repeated for you in this manual. Your students will not be able to do all the activities in the span of a semester, the time normally allotted for this course. So you will need to select from these activities to fit the needs of your class. Even if you do not assign a given text activity, however, the students' reading of the activity along with the regular text material can have the positive effect of helping them see the text material in a new light—perhaps a more personalized light. The text activities should be viewed not as burdensome assignments but as intriguing reflection starters that may or may not be assigned as homework or class activities.

Almost all the text activities require the students to respond in writing. This is done intentionally, to remove the teacher's burden of requiring written work for every activity. You may decide not to require written work for most, or even all, of the activities, and you may tell the students that they can accomplish the activity in some way other than by writing.

However, a typical method of using text activities is to assign them as written homework or class work. This use of the activities as written assignments will work most effectively if it is combined with some other processing of the students' reflections or findings in class. Here are some ways of using these activities:

1. Paired exchanges. Have each student exchange her or his written reflections with another student (if you judge that the material generated by the activity is appropriate and that the students will be comfortable sharing it). Direct the students to read their partner's reflections and then to discuss them. Afterward a whole-class discussion could draw insights from students who volunteer their thoughts from the paired discussions. However, caution the students that they should not bring up what their partner said unless the partner gives the okay.

2. Quiet collection of thoughts, followed by a discussion. Ask the students to think about the question or task presented in the activity for a few quiet minutes, rather than having them write their thoughts. Giving them a few moments to collect their thoughts before asking for class involvement in discussion often yields a more fruitful discussion than would off-the-cuff remarks. The follow-up discussion to the quiet time could be done in pairs, small groups, or with the whole class.

3. Brainstorming. Brainstorm answers to the question in the text activity with the whole class. For example, an activity may call for the students to recall times when they have experienced something similar to what is in the student text. Sometimes the most effective way to generate examples like this is to have students call them out to you without discussion as you write them on the chalkboard. Once the whole list is out, you can go back and ask for elaboration on the ones that you think would be most helpful to discuss. Always treat the students' own accounts with respect, helping them reflect on their experience by the way you ask them clarifying questions or affirm them in your comments on what they have related.

4. Skits or role-plays. Some activities that call for examples from the students' experiences can be extended into skits or role-plays. Of course, to pull this off, you must have willing students who are comfortable with letting their experiences be the subject of dramatization. If you are portraying a dilemma or a "what would you do?" incident, either the student who offered the example or another student could play the principal role and try to resolve the situation. At times, activities call for the students to write imaginary dialogs between two persons. These, too, could be read aloud by two students to heighten their impact.

5. Fishbowl discussions. When a text activity calls for reflection on an issue that is likely to generate controversy or at least differing opinions, an effective way to discuss the issue is with a "fishbowl." In this type of discussion or debate, a small group of students discusses a topic in a circle while the rest of the class observes from outside the circle.

Try to make sure that the small group is made up of students with a variety of opinions on the issue. Leave one chair in the circle empty and tell the rest of the class that if someone outside the circle wants to make a comment or a point, the person can occupy that chair, make the comment, and then vacate the chair for others to do the same. This method can sustain interest in the discussion by enabling limited participation by potentially everyone in the class. But it also avoids the pitfalls of a controversial large-group discussion, which can get out of hand.

6. Journal writing. A journal is a written record of a person's inner dialog—the thoughts, feelings, questions, impressions, and connections that come to mind over a period of time. For this course it is strongly recommended that each student keep a journal, with the expectation that he or she will write in it almost every day. The students can write in response to assigned reflection activities from the text or from the additional activities suggested in this manual. Besides using their journals to respond to assignments, they can use them simply to record their thoughts on and reactions to daily life. Generally speaking, the more one writes in a journal, the more effective the journal keeping is. If the students truly give themselves to journal keeping, they will find that it generates as well as records their inner dialog.

7. Test questions. Text activities can often check for deeper levels of comprehension than review questions can. (In many cases, these activities require personal reflection, analysis, evaluation, application of the material to one's personal life, etc.) Because of this, you may choose to incorporate some text activities into your quizzes and tests as, for example, essay questions. In doing so, however, remember that these activities generally require subjective responses from the students, responses that cannot be as easily judged for accuracy as can answers to review questions and objective test questions. (Sample test questions, both objective and essay, are given in appendix 1 of this manual.)

Additional Activities

For each major concept, you will find one or more additional activities. These are most often classroom activities that suggest small-group or large-group discussion. They occasionally require handouts that must be photocopied and then distributed to the students. These handouts appear at the end of the respective chapters in the manual.

Please refer to appendix 2 for additional teaching suggestions.

One attractive but potentially frustrating feature of this teaching manual is that, generally, more classroom strategies are offered than you can use in your teaching. Each chapter of this manual is set up like a smorgasbord from which you will need to select those activities that best meet the needs of your class. The need to make such decisions is a major reason for presenting here a method of planning and scheduling your teaching of the entire course.

A Method of Planning and Scheduling

This section suggests a method for developing your overall course schedule, as well as for deciding how you will teach individual major concepts. This basic approach to lesson planning consists of the following five steps:

   1. **Identify the total number of class periods available for this course.** If you are teaching the course within one full semester, you may have eighteen weeks or so to work with. However, each semester in a school calendar includes vacation or holidays, special school functions, test days, and so on. For purposes of planning, therefore, only sixteen of the eighteen weeks in a semester may actually be available for teaching. This results in a total of about eighty class periods in a typical semester. Naturally you will need to adjust this estimate based on the variables of your school calendar. If you are teaching the course over an entire academic year, you may have about 160 class periods actually available for teaching the material.

   2. **Assess for the entire course the approximate number of class periods needed for each major concept.** To assist you in this step, the major concepts are listed at the beginning of each chapter of this manual. It may be immediately apparent that some concepts will have to be treated briefly, perhaps in one class period or less. Other concepts may require several class periods. You may even decide to skip certain major concepts or even whole chapters. All such preliminary decisions should be made at this stage of planning.
   The primary objective here is to take a broad view of the course to ensure that you will cover all that you intend to cover. Consciously planning to eliminate parts of the student text from study is one thing; simply running out of time at the end of the course is another. This step of the planning method should help you avoid such surprises.

   3. **Divide the course into approximately two-week blocks of time.** In advance of each two-week block, make more specific decisions regarding which major concepts to present during that block. Determine how many and which class periods will be devoted to each of those concepts. At this point in the process, you will be ready to begin more immediate plans for your teaching. Note, however, that planning in two-week blocks does not include planning for audiovisuals. You will need to order these well in advance if you are relying on national distributors or even a diocesan resource office for films and videotapes.

   4. **For each major concept to be taught during a given two-week block, select the pages of the student text that you will cover and the teaching strategies from this manual that you will use, keeping in mind the number of class periods devoted to that concept.** You may encounter a situation in which you have two class periods available for teaching a major concept, but this manual and the student text offer enough material and strategies to fill several periods. How do you decide what to do?

In such cases always begin by asking: What approaches have the students responded well to in the past? What kinds of strategies seem ineffective with them? What am I comfortable doing in class? Which strategies just feel right to me? And of course: How much time is required by each available strategy? How much time do I have?

5. After each class period, briefly evaluate for future reference your experience with the strategies selected. Ongoing evaluation may be one of the most talked about and least practiced virtues of effective teaching. We are usually so caught up with preparing for our next task that we simply do not take the time to look back on classes we have successfully completed—or maybe only survived! The task of ongoing evaluation can seem so tedious and time-consuming that we feel oppressed by it before even attempting it.

In this planning process, the step of evaluation is so simple that it can quickly and consistently be included in your teaching. For further explanation see point 6 of the next section.

A Lesson Planning Chart

On page 23, you will find a copy of the lesson planning chart for this course that includes examples of how the chart can be used. A blank copy of the chart is provided on page 24.

Here is an explanation of how to use the chart:

1. In the first column, write the number or date of the class period. That is, you may wish to number your class periods for the semester from, say, one to eighty. Or you may prefer to specify each session by the date on which you will teach it. (*Note:* You may want to complete the chart in pencil rather than pen, knowing that you will have to make at least minor adjustments, given the students' response to the material, missed class periods, etc.)

2. In the second column, state the major concept to be taught during the class period. Use an abbreviation of the concept title listed in this manual.

3. Identify the relevant pages of the student text to be covered in class or assigned in advance as homework reading. List these in the third column. You may be teaching one concept for several class periods, so you will want to identify the specific pages of the student text for each of those periods. (This point may become clearer when you read point 5, below.)

4. Now you are ready to specify the teaching strategies, or activities, that you will use during the class. Use the activity titles along with page references from this manual to complete the column headed "Activities." Also describe briefly any modifications or additions you made to a text activity. For instance, write "Activity as brainstormed with whole class" or "Activity descriptions in paired exchange, with whole-class discussion following."

5. In the column titled "Homework Assignment," specify the student text pages to be read, the text activities to be completed, or any other task that you want to assign as homework.

6. Finally, after teaching each class, briefly jot down in the last column your evaluation of the class, particularly concentrating on the strategies you identified in the column "Activities." You will likely develop a shorthand of your own for this. Perhaps you might simply state, "Effective as described in manual; repeat next time." In another case you might write, "Too much material; drop activity." These statements, brief as they are, may be all you need to refresh your memory when teaching the course in the future.

Lesson Planning Chart

Date, Class	Major Concept	Text Pages	Activities	Homework Assignment	Evaluation
Mon. 9/28	Ch. 2: B, Abraham	39–40 (was homework)	Discuss "'Spiritually, We Are All Semites'" (tm p. 57). Do activity on tx p. 39 and discuss.	Read pp. 40–42. Do activity on tx p. 42.	Some students had difficulty identifying a person who left all behind. They expressed doubt that people would really do this. It led to an interesting discussion about risk, sacrifice, and following God.
Tues. 9/29	Abraham	40–42	Two student reports on "The Bedouin Lifestyle" (tm p. 57). Then do "The Continuing Obligation of Hospitality" (tm pp. 57–58) and discuss the students' responses to activity on tx p. 42.	Read pp. 42–47. Do activity on tx p. 44.	Students liked the bedouin reports. The "Hospitality" activity led to an intense discussion of obligation to homeless people.
Wed. 9/30	Abraham	42–47	Students share their reflections from their homework (activity on tx p. 44). Go over the review questions on p. 47 of the text.	Read pp. 47–49, up to "A Strange Encounter." Do "A Summary of Abraham's Role" (tm p. 58).	Needed a follow-up activity to activity on tx p. 44.
Thurs. 10/1	Ch. 2: C, Jacob	47–49	Work on activity on tx p. 48 in pairs. Have the students first reflect on and share experiences from their own life, then write a story or skit that depicts an example.	Read pp. 49–51. Do activity on tx p. 50.	The students were shy about sharing their experiences with one another—better to leave as personal reflection. The stories and skits were great!
Fri. 10/2	Jacob	49–51	Go over the homework (activity on tx p. 50). Do "World Happenings" (tm p. 59). Go over the review questions on p. 51 of the text.	Read pp. 51–53, up to "The Brothers on Joseph's Turf." Do activity on tx p. 52.	Discussion about issues of young people didn't go far—students expressed that they are tired of talking about the problems and issues of young people. The map activity went well.

Lesson Planning Chart

Date, Class	Major Concept	Text Pages	Activities	Homework Assignment	Evaluation

Teaching Strategies

CHAPTER 1

The Old Testament:
The Story of God's Boundless Love

Major Concepts

A. **The Bible: A Time Capsule from God.** The Bible is the word of the living God. The Old Testament and the New Testament together tell the Story of God's love for us. The Bible can be thought of as a sort of time capsule from God—a collection of ancient stories, history, poetry, and wisdom—that helps us see and understand God's boundless love for us and his longing for our happiness. The Old Testament declares how God created the world out of love, offered hope of salvation when humans rejected that love, formed a covenant with the Israelites, and promised that the whole world would be saved through them. The New Testament affirms that God sent Jesus to bring salvation to all the world, the Holy Spirit renews Christ's followers as they carry on his mission, and Christ will come at the end of time to complete God's Reign of justice and peace. The Scriptures were inspired by God, which means he ensured that they contain all the truth necessary for our salvation. In creating the Bible, God collaborated with humans by inspiring biblical writings and by guiding the Church as it selected which writings would be collected in the Bible. *See* the *Catechism,* nos. 54–64 (a sketch of Israel's salvation history); 101–124 (sacred Scriptures); 128–130 (the unity of the Old and New Testaments); 430–432, 457–458, 727–730 (Jesus); 702–706, 731–741 (the Holy Spirit).

B. **Interpreting the Scriptures.** We study the Bible to discover the authors' original intent in writing scriptural texts, in order to appreciate what God is saying to us through those texts today. Like the Scriptures, the Church's Tradition comes from God's revelation. The Church's Tradition is the oral preaching of Jesus' followers that has been handed down to the bishops and expressed in the Church's doctrines, teaching, and worship. The Church uses Scripture scholarship and Church Tradition to guide us as we interpret the Scriptures' meaning. The deeper intent of Scripture study is to know and love God more deeply. Study of the Old Testament is essential for Christians not only because it points to the New Testament but also because we encounter God in it. *See* the *Catechism,* nos. 76–84 (the relationship between Church Tradition and the Scriptures); 109–120 (interpretation of the Scriptures); 128–130 (the unity of the Old and New Testaments).

C. **A God Who Acts in History.** The history and the Scriptures of ancient Israel are intertwined. The Bible recounts salvation history, or the Story of God's actions and the people's responses over many centuries. The bibli-

1

cal period was from about 1850 BC, when God promised that Abraham's descendants would reveal the one God to the world, until about AD 100, when the canon of the Hebrew Scriptures was defined. Through the Israelites' exodus from slavery in Egypt to the founding of the nation of Israel, from its split to its exile and its oppression by several empires, God remained with the Chosen People. Christians see Jesus as the Messiah long awaited by the Jews. After the Jews were dispersed throughout the world in AD 70, Jewish religious leaders agreed on an official set of scriptures to guide Jewish religious life and ensure Jews' sense of identity. *See* the *Catechism,* nos. 54–64, 705–710 (a sketch of Israel's salvation history); 436–439 (Jesus as the Messiah); 839–840 (the Church's relationship with the Jews); 1961–1964 (the Law); 2580 (the Temple).

D. **What Are the Scriptures of the Old Testament?** The Hebrew Scriptures told the Jews in their own language how to live a faithful life and provided reassurance that God loved them. Because Christianity's religious roots are in Judaism, the Hebrew Scriptures have always been part of the Scriptures of Christianity. The Catholic canon of the Old Testament consists of forty-six books, including a few more texts than those in the Protestant and Jewish canon. The Old Testament is divided into four main sections: the Pentateuch, the historical books, the wisdom books, and the prophetic books. The Pentateuch (or Torah) is the heart of Israel's story and, for Jews, the primary scriptural authority in matters of faith and practice. *See* the *Catechism,* nos. 64 (prophets); 120 (the canon); 121–123, 702, 2569–2584 (the Old Testament); 2585–2589 (the Psalms).

Opening Teacher Prayer

Call to prayer. Be still within and without. Center yourself in the assurance of God's boundless love.

Read. Psalm 111

Reflect. In the past week, how have you experienced the work of God's hands? In what ways have you experienced God's love through the Bible?

Hold in your heart. "Holy and awesome is his name" (Ps. 111:9).

Pages 8–12

Concept A: The Bible: A Time Capsule from God

Review Questions: The Bible: A Time Capsule from God

Question. In what sense can the Bible be thought of as a time capsule from God?

Answer. The Bible can be thought of as a sort of time capsule from God—a collection of ancient stories, history, poetry, and wisdom—that helps us see and understand God's boundless love for us and his longing for our happiness.

Question. Give a brief outline of the great Story of God's love as told in the Bible.

Answer. (1) God created the world and humankind out of infinite love. (2) God offered a promise of salvation when humans rejected that love. (3) God formed a covenant with Israel, the Chosen People, and promised that the world would be saved through them. (4) God molded Israel during the ups and downs of its history, challenging and comforting the people. (5) God sent Jesus, the divine Son and Messiah, as the human expression of his love and the fulfillment of his promises to Israel. (6) By his life, death, and Resurrection, Jesus brought salvation to all the world. (7) God the Father and Jesus Christ sent the Holy Spirit to sustain Christ's followers, who carry on his mission until the end of time. Then Christ will return in glory as Lord of all, and God's universal Reign of justice and peace will finally be complete.

Question. What does it mean to say that the Scriptures are the Word of God? What does it mean to say that they are inspired by God? Explain how the Bible can be thought of as the result of a collaboration of God and human beings.

Answer. It means that God ensured the Scriptures contain all the truth that is necessary for our salvation: the truth about our relationship to God and all creation and the destiny meant for us, union with God forever. The Bible was created by a kind of collaboration of God with human beings in that God inspired the biblical writers and guided the Church as it selected which writings would be collected in the Bible.

 ## Text Activities: The Bible: A Time Capsule from God

- List five *facts* about your family. Then list five *truths* about them. How have you come to understand these truths?
- Promise is a major theme throughout the Bible. What is the most important promise you ever made? Write about what that promise has meant to you and what difficulties, if any, you have faced in keeping it.

 ## Additional Activities: The Bible: A Time Capsule from God

A Time Capsule from God

Review with the students the idea of the Bible being a time capsule from God. Ask them to reflect on what they would put in a time capsule to be opened by their great-grandchildren that would reflect the students' hopes for them and the love they have for them. Invite the students to share what they would include and why. Explore with them how the Bible is one way God shares his love with us as well as his desire for us to have true happiness.

1

Comparing the Old Testament with the New Testament

1. Instruct your students to thumb through the Old Testament and to note the number of pages it has. Tell them to find the table of contents and to count the number of books in the Old Testament.

2. Then have the students thumb through the New Testament and note the number of its pages. Tell them to count the number of books in the New Testament.

3. Pose these questions for discussion:
- ♦ What is immediately apparent about the relative sizes of the Old Testament and the New Testament?
- ♦ Why is the Old Testament so much longer?

The purpose of the exercise is to give the students an initial feel for the Old Testament. Point out that these Scriptures were written by many people over many centuries. On the other hand, the New Testament was written by a few people during a period of about fifty years.

4. As an additional step, encourage the students to simply sit and explore the Bible for a while to discover the kinds of things that are in it. Tell them to write down interesting things they find, questions that arise, insights, and so on. Have them share their findings in small groups or with the entire class. This activity is just intended to get them looking at what's inside (for some students, it may be their first time holding or looking through a Bible). Later in this chapter, an activity is offered in which the students explore in more detail the features of the Bible and learn about citations.

Attitudes Are Important

We live in an era when many people value passive entertainment more than disciplined activity like serious study. Thus expecting students to willingly spend time studying the Bible may be seen by some as asking a great deal. To cultivate in your students a positive attitude toward scriptural study, lead the following activity, which investigates the formation and importance of attitudes.

1. Tell your students to bring to class a souvenir or another object that has special significance for them—for example, a straw hat from Mexico, a ring, an old pair of tennis shoes. Also have them write and bring to class a paragraph or so describing what significance the object holds for them.

2. At the next class meeting, ask the students to pair off. Explain that the partners in each pair are to show their significant objects to each other—without any comments about why the objects are important. Each partner is to write a paragraph describing why the *other person's object* might be important to *that person*.

3. Next, direct the partners to take turns focusing on the significance of their objects. One partner should read her or his paragraph on why the other person's object might be important to that person. Then the owner of the object should read her or his own explanation of why the object holds significance. The partners should then focus on the second object in a similar fashion.

4. When all the pairs have finished sharing, lead a discussion of the activity, using these questions:

- ◆ How well did your partner's perceptions about the significance of your object match your own feelings? [For an example, ask several pairs to read their paragraphs about the same objects.]
- ◆ Why can two people react so differently to the same object? [The owner has much more experience of the object and the circumstances surrounding its history; in short, the owner's attitude is unique.]
- ◆ How are our attitudes formed? [By all the experiences we have and by how we respond to those experiences.]

5. With comments like the following, explain the relationship between this exercise and the students' study of the Old Testament:

- ◆ Each of us brings to this course a variety of attitudes—perhaps some of them negative. We can be victims of these negative attitudes; that is, we can let them close our minds to this learning opportunity. Or we can overcome the negativity and open ourselves to a new learning experience. Vital to our getting the most out of this course is an openness to the truths offered by the stories of Moses, Ruth, Jeremiah, Esther, Job, and the many other characters of the Old Testament.
- ◆ An object—no matter how expensive or inexpensive it is, no matter how new or old it is—can have significance for us, but only if our attitude toward the object gives it significance. If an object is seen by someone who has no involvement with it or no appreciation of its history, it might be perceived as useless, ugly, or insignificant. Only involvement and understanding make things valuable to us.
- ◆ So our attitude toward the Old Testament, our willingness to invest time and energy in coming to know it, determines how much we will appreciate and value these sacred texts. An open mind is essential.

Scrolls and Scroll Making

The sidebar "The Treasured Scrolls" on page 10 of the student text describes how the ancients made the scrolls on which the sacred Scriptures were written. Assign one or more students to look into the scroll-making process in more detail and to report their findings to the class. Understanding the difficulties in the ancient process of writing texts can help increase modern people's respect and appreciation for their spiritual ancestors who left a written heritage.

Some creative or ambitious students may even want to try making scrolls themselves and then writing on them, as a visual for the classroom. The easiest, most practical way to demonstrate scroll making is to use two cardboard tubes from paper towel packages as the ends of a scroll and continuous-form computer paper as the "parchment."

1

 Pages 13–17

Concept B: Interpreting the Scriptures

 ## Review Questions: Interpreting the Scriptures

Question. How does Scripture scholarship help us get in touch with the intended meanings of the scriptural texts?
Answer. Scholars delve into the history, archaeology, literary forms, and culture surrounding the development of the texts to help us understand their intended meanings.

Question. What is the relationship of the Scriptures to the Church's Tradition?
Answer. Like the Scriptures, the Church Tradition comes from God's revelation—his self-communication with us. While the Sacred Scriptures were written down, the Church's Tradition is the oral preaching of Jesus' followers, the Apostles, that has been handed down to the bishops and expressed in the Church's doctrines, teachings, and worship.

Question. Why do Christians need to understand both the Old Testament and the New Testament?
Answer. They cannot understand the New Testament and Jesus without understanding the Old Testament. Also, the Old Testament has permanent value in itself because we encounter God, its inspiration, in it.

 ## Text Activity: Interpreting the Scriptures

• Spend some time exploring your Bible. Find a passage in the Old Testament that you think is beautiful, powerful, or inspiring. Write out the passage and explain why you chose it. What does it have to say to you (what is the *truth* it offers you)?

 ## Additional Activities: Interpreting the Scriptures

Getting into the Bible

Some of your students may not be familiar with reading the Bible, pronouncing biblical names, finding scriptural references, using footnotes, and so on; others may need a review. The following suggestions can help your students become comfortable with the Bible:

1. Personalized Bibles. Have each of the students personalize his or her Bible by covering it with paper of his or her choosing and tastefully decorating it, incorporating his or her name.

2. Contents and abbreviations. To get into the mechanics of reading the Bible, point out to the students the table of contents and the list of abbreviations (for both the Old Testament and the New Testament) that can be found at the front of every Christian edition of the Bible. Tell them to insert a bookmark there or to clip those pages of their Bible for quick reference. Mention that the abbreviations vary somewhat across different versions of the Bible: for instance, Genesis is abbreviated Gen. in some versions and Gn. in others. (See suggestion 8, below, for more on the versions of the Bible.)

3. Pronunciations. Point out the pronunciations in the index of the student text. To make sure that the students can pronounce the names of all the books of the Bible, lead a choral-type drill or chant so that they end up pronouncing each name five or six times. Students who like rap music might even want to make up a rap song using the names of the books of the Bible (or later in the course, the names of the patriarchs, the kings, the prophets, etc.). The emphasis should be on pronouncing names accurately, not on memorizing a list.

4. The structure of the books. Outline for your students the structure of the books of the Bible—that is, the fact that each book is divided into chapters and each chapter into verses. Also point out that some books have the same name but different numbers (e.g., 1 Samuel and 2 Samuel, also written as I Samuel and II Samuel, which are referred to as the First Book of Samuel and the Second Book of Samuel).

5. Sources of information. Explain that each book of the Bible is often prefaced by a valuable introduction giving information about the book's author, the period in which it was written, who it was written for, and its significance. Recommend that the students read this material as well as the footnotes to each assigned passage. Questions that arise while we read the Scriptures are often answered in the introduction to a given book or in the footnotes. Show the students how to find the footnotes, explain the symbols used, and so on.

Handout **1–A**

6. Scriptural references. Most students need to learn how to look up scriptural references, or citations; do not assume that they know how to do this. To familiarize your class with the process, distribute handout 1–A, "How to Find a Scriptural Reference." With the students, go over the information on the first page of the handout. Then assign (either for small-group work in class or for homework) the matching exercise on the second page. The students are asked to look up each scriptural reference and write the letter of the corresponding summary in the appropriate blank.

7. Highlighter. If the Bibles are owned by the students, encourage the students to use a highlighter pen to mark the passages they are assigned to read. This will eliminate time spent in back-and-forth checking and will result in a Bible nicely marked up for later reference to significant passages. Let them know it is all right to write notes or questions or reflections in the Bible—God would approve of a well-used Bible!

8. Differences in versions. Explain that various versions of the Bible offer different translations. Choose a few students to look up passages in two or three versions, reporting to the class on the differences among the versions and whether they prefer any one version. Also, let the students know that the Catholic Bible includes some books that are not in the Protestant Bible: Wisdom, Sirach (Ecclesiasticus), Judith, Tobit, Baruch, 1 and 2 Maccabees, parts of Esther, and parts of Daniel.

1

The Bible and Catholic Attitudes

Before Vatican Council II, few Catholics read and studied the Bible. To explore past attitudes about scriptural study, ask your students to interview their parents (or even their grandparents or other older persons, who are more likely to have grown up before Vatican Council II) about what place scriptural study held in their early religious education. Older Catholics will probably have memories quite different from those of older Protestants. Each student should prepare a brief written report on the interview and should be prepared to comment on his or her findings in class.

Why Different Sources Tell Different Stories

Handout **1–B**

Some students have a hard time understanding why the Old Testament, if it is from God, has different sources and why those sources offer such varied and at times contradictory versions of the same events. Handout 1–B, "Writing a Family History," may help those students and enhance others' understanding of how the various sources contributed to the finished product of the Old Testament.

Distribute the handout, read aloud the quote by Anthony Gilles, and direct the students to answer the questions that follow the quote. Then ask them to volunteer their answers for discussion with the whole class. Finally, close with comments along the following lines:

◆ The Old Testament was put together over a long period of time. Like a family history that goes back for centuries, the Scriptures were formulated out of oral and written accounts composed and edited by many people throughout the years. The scriptural composers perceived God's actions in history in slightly different ways, depending on who they were and what their experiences had been. This difference in perception is natural, and it represents the human dimension of the Scriptures. It actually makes the Scriptures more interesting and more complete—like a family history that draws from the experiences of many family members and branches of the family tree. Just as we know that family members will at times differ in their versions or interpretations of what happens over the years, we can expect that this was so in the gradual formulation of the Scriptures.

Ten Commandments for Studying the Bible

Handout **1–C**

Handout 1–C, "Ten Commandments for Studying the Bible," offers guidelines for reading, interpreting, and meditating on the Bible. Give a copy to each student as a reference for the course and perhaps post these "commandments" prominently in your classroom (you could enlarge them on a photocopier). Read through the handout with your students and explain each guideline.

(These guidelines have been adapted from "Ten Commandments for Catholic Bible Study Groups," by Matthias Neuman, in *PACE* 16, October 1985, pages 20–24. The article is included in its entirety in appendix 4 of this manual.)

Pages 18–24

Concept C: A God Who Acts in History

Review Questions: A God Who Acts in History

Question. List the events in salvation history as given in the timeline of biblical history in this chapter.
Answer.
Abraham and Sarah arrive in Canaan.
Jacob's descendants settle in Egypt.
Moses leads the Exodus from Egypt.
Joshua invades Canaan.
The Judges lead the Israelite tribes in Canaan.
Saul is named the first king of Israel.
David unites the kingdom and takes Jerusalem as its capital.
Solomon rules the kingdom and builds the Temple.
The kingdom divides into Israel and Judah.
The Assyrians capture Samaria, ending the kingdom of Israel.
The Babylonians take Jerusalem. The exile of Judah begins.
Cyrus of Persia frees the Jews to return to Judah.
The people of Judah rebuild the Temple.
Nehemiah becomes governor of Judah and starts a renewal.
Ezra brings the Torah to Jerusalem.
The Greeks conquer the Holy Land.
The Maccabees revolt against the Greek rulers.
The Romans conquer the Holy Land.
Jesus is born.
Jesus is crucified.
The Romans destroy the Jerusalem Temple.

Question. How do Christians see Jesus Christ in relation to the promises made by God to Israel?
Answer. Christians see Jesus as the long-awaited Messiah—the fulfillment of all God's promises to Israel and the Savior of the world.

Question. Summarize Catholic teaching on Judaism.
Answer. Christians are forever linked with the Jewish people, who were the first to hear the Word of God. God's Covenant and special relationship with the Jews still stand, "for the gifts and the calling of God are irrevocable" (Rom. 11:29). Like Christians, Jews work toward and await in hope the coming of God's Reign of peace and justice. But whereas Judaism looks for an unknown messiah to come, Christianity recognizes Jesus Christ as the Messiah, who has already come and who will return in glory.

Text Activities: A God Who Acts in History

• Do you find it easy or challenging to trust that God is taking care of you? Write a paragraph or two explaining your thoughts on this. If you wish, offer an example of a time you felt deep trust in God, or a time you faltered in your trust.

1

- List five experiences you have had of being a stranger or of being *with* strangers: for example, moving to a new city or trying to communicate with a foreigner. Next to each experience, write the emotions you felt.
- In your own words, write a paragraph explaining the meaning of Martin Buber's statement.

Additional Activities: A God Who Acts in History

The Bible Comes from the Jews

The sidebar entitled "Still the Chosen People: Catholic Teaching on Judaism" on page 19 of the student text discusses the relationship between Judaism and Christianity. To extend this discussion with your class, you could pose questions such as the following:

◆ Is it possible to be anti-Jewish and still be a Christian?
◆ Could Christianity exist without its Jewish background, especially the Hebrew Scriptures?
◆ Do you think of Jesus as a Jew, a Christian, or a Catholic?

A Geographical Perspective on Ancient History

A fascinating aspect of studying biblical history is the opportunity to put that history into perspective with what we know about the rest of the ancient world.

Handout **1–D**

To foster a sense of what was happening in the rest of the world at various times in biblical history, the student text includes occasional sidebars about concurrent happenings around the world—including the parts of the world that were unknown to the people of the Near East. The students will have a better sense of these worldwide developments if they work with the outlined map of the world that is provided on handout 1–D, "World Map." At the outset of the course, distribute copies of the outlined map to the students. Direct them to look up (in an atlas or an encyclopedia) and fill in the names of the following land areas and waterways. Most of these areas and waterways will be referred to in the sidebars of the text at some point in the course.

1. *Continents and subcontinents.* North America, Central America, South America, Greenland, Europe, Africa, Asia, New Guinea, Australia
2. *Countries and regions.* Egypt, Greece, India, Iraq, China, the Near East, the Sudan, Mexico, Peru, England, the Bering Strait, Turkey, the Saharan region
3. *Major waterways.* The Pacific Ocean, the Atlantic Ocean, the Mediterranean Sea, the Nile River

As the course proceeds and the text refers to these areas and bodies of water, have your students take out the filled-in maps and locate where the relevant happenings took place.

The Near East: Ancient and Modern

Handout **1–E**

The map on page 20 of the student text shows the lands of the ancient Near East. Direct the students to revise the map on handout 1–E, "The Near East Today," by drawing in (with dotted lines) the boundaries of the countries that presently occupy the same part of the world. They can consult an up-to-date atlas or encyclopedia in their work. The activity can help the students relate the ancient Near East to countries they may hear about in the news.

A Graphic Display of Israel's Ups and Downs

A portrayal of Jewish history along a straight timeline is surely less descriptive than the chart on page 38, "The Ups and Downs of Israel's History." This chart shows the ups and downs of Israel's history, according to the Bible and what we know of events in the ancient world. The last part of the chart represents the future—beyond history. In reviewing concept C with your students, copy the timeline onto the chalkboard or photocopy it onto an overhead transparency.

Note for the students that the ups and downs of Jewish history, in the sense of national victories and defeats, did not necessarily correspond with their spiritual ups and downs. That is, they were often closest to God in times of defeat, and their national victories frequently led them to forget their dependence on God. For example, the exile in Babylon was a low period from a national standpoint, but it was a time of tremendous growth in terms of the people's spiritual development and identity as God's people.

Family Stories and Family Identity

1. Ask your students to write down one story that is often told in their family about them or about some incident that is important to their family. Then tell them to write answers to these questions:
   a. Why is this story told over and over in your family?
   b. How do you feel when the story is told?
   c. Can a family have a sense of who they are as a family without stories such as this one?

2. Use question c to begin a discussion about how stories help to give us a sense of who we are.

3. Before your students hand in their assignment, invite them to pair off and share their stories.

The Ups and Downs of Israel's History

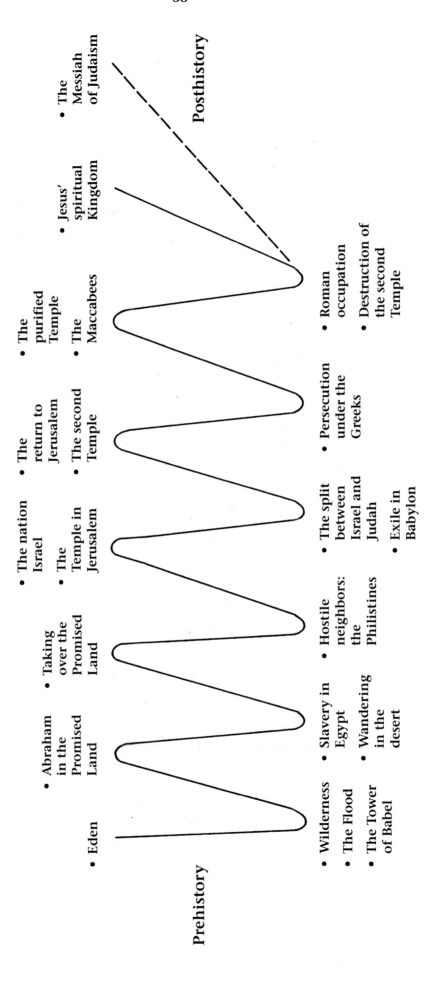

Prehistory

- Eden

- Abraham in the Promised Land

- Taking over the Promised Land

- The nation Israel
- The Temple in Jerusalem

- The return to Jerusalem
- The second Temple

- The purified Temple
- The Maccabees

- Jesus' spiritual Kingdom

- The Messiah of Judaism

Posthistory

- Wilderness
- The Flood
- The Tower of Babel

- Slavery in Egypt
- Wandering in the desert

- Hostile neighbors: the Philistines

- The split between Israel and Judah
- Exile in Babylon

- Persecution under the Greeks

- Roman occupation
- Destruction of the second Temple

Concept D:
What Are the Scriptures of the Old Testament?

Review Questions:
What Are the Scriptures of the Old Testament?

Question. How many books are in the Catholic canon of the Old Testament? Into what main sections are they divided?

Answer. Forty-six, divided into these major sections: the Pentateuch, the historical books, the wisdom books, and the prophetic books

Question. Name three books in each of the main sections of the Old Testament.

Answer. [Any three from each of the following sections are correct.]

- *The Pentateuch.* Genesis, Exodus, Leviticus, Numbers, and Deuteronomy
- *The historical books.* Joshua, Judges, Ruth, 1 and 2 Samuel, 1 and 2 Kings, 1 and 2 Chronicles, Ezra, Nehemiah, Tobit, Judith, Esther, and 1 and 2 Maccabees
- *The wisdom books.* Job, Psalms, Proverbs, Ecclesiastes, Song of Songs, Wisdom, and Sirach (or Ecclesiasticus)
- *The prophetic books.* Isaiah, Jeremiah, Lamentations, Baruch, Ezekiel, Daniel, Hosea, Joel, Amos, Obadiah, Jonah, Micah, Nahum, Habakkuk, Zephaniah, Haggai, Zecariah, and Malachi

Additional Activities:
What Are the Scriptures of the Old Testament?

Writing a Letter to a Faraway Friend

1. For homework, ask that the students each write a letter of one or more pages to a friend or relative who lives far away. They should bring their letter with a stamped and addressed envelope to class.

2. When the students bring the letters to class, ask the following questions, in order to reveal the importance of letters:
- In general, what sort of information did you put in your letter?
- What is the reason for writing a letter to a friend or relative?
- How do you feel when you get a letter?
- What images are triggered in your imagination when you receive a letter from someone who is far away?

1

3. Explain to the students that the point of the exercise has been to reinforce their understanding of the purposes behind the Old Testament. In a way the Scriptures were letters from home to all the Jews dispersed throughout the world. The letters told them in their own language how best to deal with unfamiliar surroundings. Most important, the Scriptures told them that they were valued, they were loved by God, and they had a rich heritage as the Chosen People.

4. Encourage the students to mail their letters after school. Or collect the letters and mail them yourself.

An Interview: Being a Stranger

In considering the need that the Jews of the Dispersion had for the Hebrew Scriptures, arrange for your students to conduct a class interview of a refugee or an immigrant to this country. The interview may help them see the difficulties of being a stranger in a strange land. Some questions your students could pose during the interview are the following:
◆ What have been the most difficult aspects of adjusting to life here?
◆ Do you feel a need to stay in contact with your homeland?
◆ How do you keep a sense of your identity as a person from [name the person's homeland] while also identifying with the people from this country?

Note: In a class period before the interview, you may want to let the students develop questions they would like to pose to the visitor; this could be done in small groups. Have them turn in the questions so you can ensure they are appropriate.

Closing Prayer

This chapter's closing prayer focuses the students on the Word of God as a source of growth and life for those who are receptive to that word.

1. In advance, ask the students each to choose and write down a brief passage (one or two sentences) from a designated section of the Old Testament—a passage that they just happen to like or one that expresses something important to them. One group or row should pick their passages from Psalms 1 through 50; a second group, from Psalms 51 through 100; a third group, from Psalms 101 through 150; a fourth group, from the Book of Proverbs; and a fifth group, from the Book of Wisdom. Each student should prepare to read aloud her or his brief passage.

Also, before the prayer begins, instruct your students to put bookmarks at Psalm 1 and Psalm 103. Ask one student to be the reader of Luke 8:4–15, the parable of the sower and the seed.

2. Open the prayer with a reminder such as the following:

◆ As we begin our prayer, let us first remember that God is present in this room, in each of us, and in the Word of God that we will hear today. Let us be receptive to God's presence in our midst.

3. Pray together Psalm 1.

4. Have the preselected student read Luke 8:4–15 to the rest of the class.

5. Offer this prayer or one of your own:

◆ Creator God, help us be the good soil that receives your Word and lets it spring up and grow in us. Prepare us to nourish the seeds that are planted during this course, so that they can take root in our life.

6. Invite each student to read his or her passage from Psalms, Proverbs, or Wisdom. Pause for a moment of reflection between each passage.

7. Then ask the students to hold their Bibles open in their hands as you continue with this blessing:

◆ We thank you for giving us your Word, for communicating it to us in the lives and events, great deeds, and even weaknesses of the people chosen as your own. Bless these Bibles, which we will come to know much better during this course. May we treat them with reverence and a sense of anticipation, knowing that the stories of your people of long ago are also our own stories. We ask this in the name of Jesus. Amen.

8. In closing pray together Psalm 103:1–8. Or play a recording of "Bless the Lord," by Stephen Schwartz, from the sound track of the film *Godspell* (Bell Records, 1970). The song is based on Psalm 103.

 ## Closing Teacher Prayer

Call to prayer. Be still within and without. Center yourself in God's loving embrace.

Reflect. What have you learned in the process of teaching this chapter? Was it a learning of the head or the heart? Does this reveal God more fully to you? How? What effect could this learning have on your life?

1

What gift did you receive from your students? Which students do you feel are especially in need of God's tender care today?

Pray.
Loving God,
I declare my need for you.
You are nearer than my heartbeat,
closer than my next breath.
Gracious God,
may I always remember that
I am a cherished creature
and you are Creator. Amen.

(Bergan and Schwan, *Taste and See: Prayer Services for Gatherings of Faith*)

How to Find a Scriptural Reference

- The Bible is composed of books.
- Each book is composed of chapters.
- Each chapter is composed of verses.

A scriptural reference provides all the information you need to find a particular passage. Take, for example, the reference **Genesis 1:31.**

- The name of the book comes first. Here the name is Genesis (often abbreviated Gen.).
- The chapter number appears directly after the name of the book. The example gives the number 1, meaning chapter 1.
- The last number, separated from the chapter number by a colon, indicates the verse. The example refers to verse 31. (In some versions of the Bible, a comma, rather than a colon, separates the verse number from the chapter number.)

Look up **Gen. 1:31.** What does it say? Write it down on a separate piece of paper.

Scriptural references generally contain more detailed information. Here are some examples:

- Gen. 1:1–8 means Genesis, chapter 1, verses 1 through 8.
- Gen. 1:3,6,9 means Genesis, chapter 1, verses 3, 6, and 9. (Notice the comma between separate verses from the same chapter.)
- Gen. 2:8–10,18–25 means Genesis, chapter 2, verses 8 through 10 and verses 18 through 25.
- Gen. 1—3 means Genesis, chapters 1 through 3. (Notice the long dash between chapter numbers. For clarity, your textbook does not use long dashes in scriptural references. In your book, Gen. 1—3 would be written Genesis 1:1–31; 2:1–25; 3:1–24, listing all the verses. But you will encounter dashes in your Bible's footnotes and in future scriptural study.)
- Gen. 1:31—2:3 means Genesis, chapter 1, verse 31, through chapter 2, verse 3.

- Distinct references to different chapters are separated by a semicolon. Gen. 1; 3 means Genesis, chapters 1 and 3 (but not chapter 2). Similarly, Gen. 2:4–7,14; 3:1–3,8 means Genesis, chapter 2, verses 4 through 7 and verse 14, then chapter 3, verses 1 through 3 and verse 8.
- A long verse may be broken up into parts. To designate the first part of a verse, the letter *a* is used; for the second part of the verse, *b* is used. Gen. 1:9a means Genesis, chapter 1, the first part of verse 9.
- Some books of the Bible share the same name. For instance, 1 Samuel and 2 Samuel mean "the First Book of Samuel" and "the Second Book of Samuel." (Sometimes these are written I Samuel and II Samuel.) Notice that the number of the book comes before the name of the book. So 2 Sam. 1:11–12 means the Second Book of Samuel, chapter 1, verses 11 through 12.

Look up **Exod. 5:22—6:1,11; 7:6.** What does it say? Write it down on a separate piece of paper.

Matching

In your Bible look up each scriptural reference from the left-hand column. Then match the reference with its summary on the right, writing the letter of the summary in the blank next to the reference.

_____ **1.** Ruth 1:16–18	**a.** Jerusalem's destruction
_____ **2.** Dan. 3:13–24	**b.** a pledge to stay with Naomi
_____ **3.** Josh. 3:14–17	**c.** the anointing of Saul, Israel's first king
_____ **4.** Prov. 28:15	**d.** choosing life
_____ **5.** Gen. 12:1–3	**e.** how to build an ark
_____ **6.** Ps. 51:3–4	**f.** the Ten Commandments
_____ **7.** Exod. 11:4–7	**g.** the fate of Egypt's firstborn
_____ **8.** 1 Sam. 9:26b—10:1a	**h.** a wicked ruler
_____ **9.** Deut. 30:15,19b	**i.** the prayer of a guilty person
_____ **10.** Eccles. 3:1–8	**j.** crossing the Jordan River
_____ **11.** Gen. 6:14–16	**k.** thirsting for God
_____ **12.** Ps. 63:2–4	**l.** a time for everything
_____ **13.** Exod. 20:1–17	**m.** Abram's call to a new land
_____ **14.** Jer. 52:12–14	**n.** fidelity in a fiery furnace

Writing a Family History

Read the following passage, which compares the composition of the Old Testament to the writing of a family history. Then answer the questions that follow.

Suppose you were commissioned by your relatives to write a family history. How would you proceed? You would probably go back and collect as many bits and pieces of information as you could before you started writing. You would talk to Grandma, who would tell you stories about her childhood. She might even remember stories about her grandmother's childhood—which could extend back as far as 150 years. Next, you would look at Aunt Kate's old diaries and Uncle Herman's letters, particularly the ones he wrote home during World War II. You might even use an old recipe for a section on your family's favorite dish. Or you might look up newspaper clippings in the town where your Grandpa was born.

All of these materials are sources. Some of them are oral and some written. You are the one who has to weave them together into the family history. Perhaps you write your first draft in longhand. Next Cousin Ernie comes along and types it, correcting your grammar and syntax as he does so. Then, to top it off, rich Uncle Dave decides the manuscript is so valuable to the family that he wants to have it printed [and then bound] in a leather cover. He even hires an editor to make it read as though it were a professionally written history.

The important thing to notice here is that the starting point for the finished product . . . was the original sources you collected. The Old Testament was written in pretty much the same way. As the family history of God's chosen people, it owes its existence to the sources on which it is based. (From *The People of the Book*, by Anthony E. Gilles [Cincinnati: Saint Anthony Messenger Press, 1981], pages 3–4. Copyright © 1983 by Anthony E. Giles. Used with permission of the author.)

1. Suppose you are about to write a history of your family, going back several generations. List as many sources as you can think of that you might use. (You may want to ask your parents for help on coming up with possible sources.)

_____

_____

_____

_____

_____

_____

_____

_____

2. For what event in your family history might you find different versions among members or branches of the family? Why?

_____

_____

_____

_____

_____

_____

3. Which family history would you prefer (circle one)?
   a. one that is perfectly consistent but written from only one person's point of view
   b. one that has some inconsistencies but represents the experiences of many parts of your family

Ten Commandments for Studying the Bible

1. Christians treasure the Bible because it is the Word of God.

2. Catholics believe that the Bible is inspired by the Holy Spirit, meaning that a special truth from God can be found in its writings.

3. The revealed truth of the Bible is found in what the various writers expressed about the meaning of faith itself.

4. Thou shalt not believe every historical, biographical, and scientific detail in the Bible.

5. Thou shalt not take one passage from the Bible and make it an absolute.

6. Thou shalt not be surprised at finding conflicting opinions in the Bible.

7. Thou shalt learn something about the history and the literary background of the various books of the Bible.

8. Thou shalt read the Bible regularly to stimulate and nourish personal faith.

9. The Bible serves as a "religious conscience" for the Christian Church and the individual believer.

10. The Bible does not remove the responsibility of the reader to make conscientious and responsible decisions about faith.

(Adapted from by "Ten Commandments for Catholic Study Groups," Matthias Neuman, in *PACE* 16, October 1985, pages 20–24)

World Map

Your teacher will provide you with the names of major land areas and waterways. Write each name in its appropriate place on the map below, consulting an up-to-date atlas or encyclopedia as needed. Then keep the map for future reference during this course.

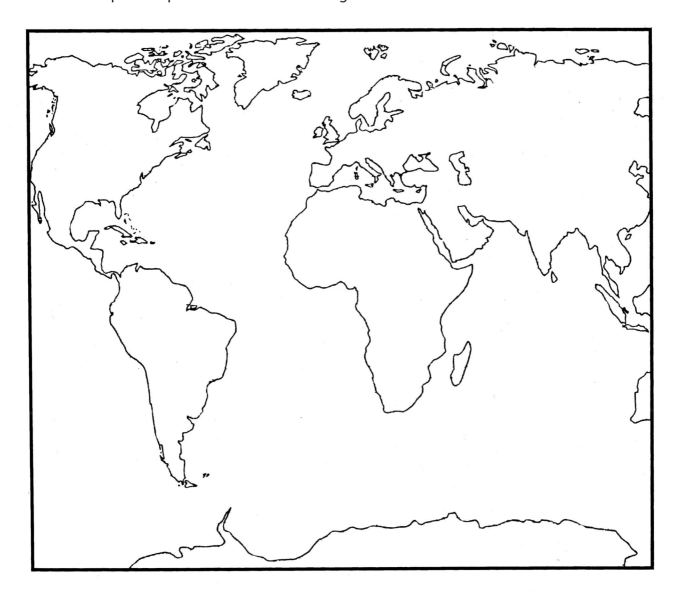

The Near East Today

This map shows the lands of the Near East as they were known in ancient times. Using an up-to-date atlas or encyclopedia for reference, draw in (with dotted lines) the political boundaries of the countries that exist in the Near East today. Write in the names of those countries.

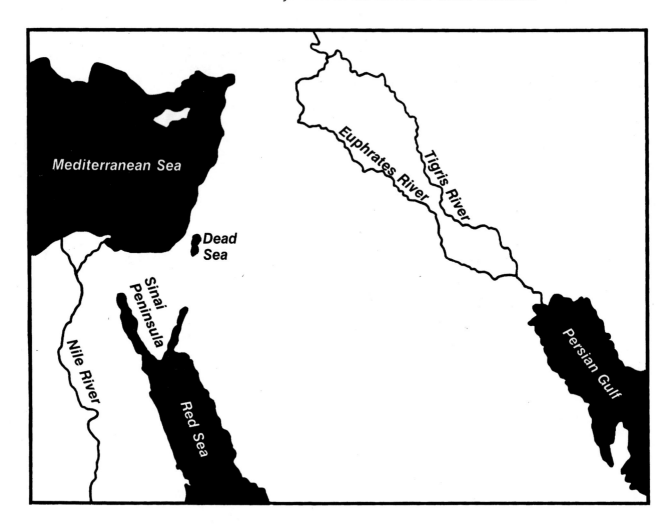

Beginnings: Stories of God's Creation and Promises

Major Concepts

A. **Stories of the Origins.** The first eleven chapters of Genesis portray the one God bringing forth goodness out of chaos and creating humankind in God's own image. Catholics believe the Creation story does not contradict the theory of evolution. Genesis also describes how sin entered the world through Adam and Eve's attempt to be equal to God. The stories of Cain and Abel, Noah and the Flood, and the Tower of Babel illustrate how sin continued to spread. God extended the first covenant to Noah because he obeyed God's Word. *See* the *Catechism,* nos. 54, 374–379 (humans in Paradise); 55, 311, 385–390, 396–409 (the Fall and Original Sin); 56–58 (the covenant with Noah); 159 (faith and science); 269 (the omnipotence of God); 279–297, 299–301, 337–339, 355, 373, 1700 (the goodness of God's Creation); 280, 288, 293–294 (God creates out of love); 301 (God sustains Creation); 345–349, 2168–2172 (the Sabbath); 401–402, 1865–1869, 2259, 2317 (sin's ripple effect); 458 (God's love shown in Jesus); 1730–1739, 1749, 1853 (human freedom); 2569 (Noah and prayer).

B. **Abraham: The Father of Biblical Faith.** God calls Abraham to leave everything behind and go to an unknown land, where his many descendants would become a great nation. Responding obediently, Abraham becomes the father of biblical faith for Jews, Christians, and Muslims. Abraham has a son, Ishmael, with his concubine, Hagar, because his wife, Sarah, seemed to be barren. But God's plan for Abraham to conceive a son with Sarah prevails, and Isaac is born. Later Abraham is tested when God asks him to sacrifice Isaac. An angel stays Abraham's hand at the last moment, confirming that God forbids human sacrifice. *See* the *Catechism,* nos. 59–61 (the call of Abraham); 64, 489 (Sarah); 144–146, 165, 1080–1081, 1819, 2570–2572 (the faith of Abraham); 201 (the one God); 422, 2619 (the fulfillment of a promise); 705–706, 709, 762, 1222, 1716 (the promise to Abraham); 841 (Abraham and the Muslims); 1150 (circumcision); 2260–2261 (human sacrifice is forbidden); 2390 (the biblical ideal of monogamy); 2572 (Abraham's test).

C. **Jacob: A Man Named Israel.** The stories about Isaac and Rebekah's son Jacob show how God remains faithful to the promise to Abraham and his descendants. Because Rebekah believes God wants Jacob to be Isaac's principal heir, she helps Jacob in a deception that gains him what should have been his brother Esau's birthright. Jacob flees to Haran, where he stays for many years before returning to the Promised Land. On his way back, he meets a mysterious stranger who, after wrestling with him all night, gives Jacob the name Israel. Jacob initiates his family into the worship of the God of Israel, carrying on the blessing God gave to Abraham and Isaac. *See* the *Catechism,* nos. 63 (Israel); 2573 (Jacob, ancestor of the twelve tribes, wrestles with an angel).

D. **Joseph: Treachery, Triumph, and Forgiveness.** Joseph's resentful brothers sell him into slavery in Egypt, where he becomes governor. During a severe famine, his brothers come to Egypt to buy grain, but do not recognize Joseph, who insists that his brother Benjamin be brought to him. An anguished Jacob sacrifices Benjamin for the sake of his people. Eventually Joseph reveals his true identity and reconciles with his brothers. Like so many other stories in Genesis, Joseph's tale shows how our all-powerful God works with sinful human beings to save the world. *See* the *Catechism,* nos. 312–314 (God brings good out of wrongdoing).

Opening Teacher Prayer

Call to prayer. Be still within and without. Be aware that you are the focus of God's creative love. Center yourself in that love.

Read. Psalm 104

Reflect. Recall memories and moments in your life that speak of the wonder of Creation and the loving care of God, our Creator. Which gifts from God are you most thankful for? Which gifts do you take for granted? How is God creating in your life now?

Hold in your heart. "Bless the LORD, O my soul" (Ps. 104:35).

Concept A: Stories of the Origins

Review Questions: Stories of the Origins

Question. How did the Book of Genesis lift the hearts of the exiles as they returned to their homeland, Judah?
Answer. The Book of Genesis helped remind the Jews that from the beginning their God had been in charge, bringing forth goodness out of everything. Genesis also helped them understand their origins, who they were, and why they should have hope.

Question. Summarize the difference between the Jewish view of the origins of the world and the Babylonian view.
Answer. In the Jewish view, the one God brings forth goodness—order, beauty, and abundant forms of marvelous life—out of chaos. Human beings are made in God's image and are partners with God in loving all Creation. In

contrast the Babylonians believed that self-serving, violent, and destructive gods had made the earth for their own pleasure, and humankind for their slaves. It was a chaotic world where human beings were caught in the middle of the gods' wars and tried to avoid the gods' wrath.

Question. In the Creation story, why is it said that God rested on the seventh day?

Answer. The Jews' custom of resting on the Sabbath marked them as unique and reminded them during the exile that they were God's people. So the Creation story writer included God's own resting on the seventh day to emphasize the importance of keeping the Sabbath holy as a day to rest, praise God, and be refreshed together.

Question. What is the Catholic understanding of how the biblical Creation account relates to the theory of evolution?

Answer. Catholics believe the biblical story does not contradict the theory of evolution. The Church's affirmation that much scientific evidence supports the evolution theory does not shake the religious truth of the Creation account—that God is the source of all goodness.

Question. What do Adam and Eve desire by eating of the tree of the "knowledge of good and evil" (Gen. 2:17)?

Answer. To be equal to God and to know all things

Question. According to the story of the Fall, who is responsible for suffering and injustice in the world—God or human beings?

Answer. God does not create injustice in the world; human beings do so by their own bad choices.

Question. Which Genesis stories tell about the spread of sin after the first sin?

Answer. Cain and Abel, a story of hatred between brothers that ends in murder; Noah and the Flood, a story about society's depravity; and the Tower of Babel, a tale of arrogance among nations.

Question. To whom does God offer the first covenant? Why is it offered, and what is the sign of that event?

Answer. God offers the first covenant to Noah because he obeyed God. The rainbow is the sign of that covenant, God's promise that the world will never again be destroyed by a flood. It is also a sign of God's love for every earthly creature.

 ## Text Activities: Stories of the Origins

- What difference do a people's beliefs about their origins make to their attitudes about life? Make two columns, one headed "Babylonians' Attitudes" and the other "Ancient Jews' Attitudes." In each column, list the attitudes toward life you might expect to see in each group because of the beliefs its members held about how the world and humans came about.
- "[God] rested on the seventh day" (Gen. 2:2). When was the last time you rested? Create a chart of your typical week, noting how much time is given to schoolwork, school activities, job, family, friends, sleep, and other things you're involved in. Write a paragraph or two about how much time you spend relaxing and unwinding, and how you use that time. If you could say no to one "extra" activity in your life so that you would have more room for relaxing, what would you give up?

- In the Fall, Adam and Eve try to be equal to God. List three situations in the world today where human beings are trying to be equal to God and refuse to acknowledge their dependence on him. Write about one of them that you find interesting or inspiring.
- "Am I my brother's keeper?" What does it mean to be responsible for another person? Perhaps someone in your school, neighborhood, family, or workplace, or some group in your community is at risk or in trouble. Is it your job to help them? Share your thoughts on this in a one-page essay.
- In a paragraph, compare the story of Babel, which illustrates the effect of sin, to the story of Pentecost (Acts 2:1–21), which illustrates the effect of the Holy Spirit. Find a newspaper clipping showing the effect of sin in our society, and another that shows the effect of good.

 ## Additional Activities: Stories of the Origins

Folk Songs

The first eleven chapters of Genesis are like folk songs that capture the spirit of the history of Israel. Tell your students each to bring in the words to a song that centers on an important part of their own country's history and that has been or probably will be sung for many generations. In addition, direct them to write a short explanation of why the song is significant. Invite some students to share their songs and ideas.

Other Creation Stories

Select some students to find the creation stories of other ancient peoples—for example, the Babylonians, the Egyptians, the Japanese, and a Native American tribe. After the students have found and rehearsed their stories, invite them to retell them to the class. Then lead the class in a discussion of how the stories compare with the account in Genesis.

Debate on the Theory of Evolution

Choose two small teams to prepare a debate on how the world came into being. Have one team advocate the theory of creationism and the other the theory of evolution. When the students are ready to debate, you may wish to set up a fishbowl discussion (see the introduction of this teaching manual for a description of this technique).

What Is Dominion?

1. Ask your students these questions:
   - What does the Book of Genesis mean when it says that God gave humankind "dominion" over all living things on the earth [1:26]?
   - We could easily misunderstand dominion in Genesis as the right of human beings to dominate the earth for their own purposes. What could this misunderstanding lead to?

2. Divide the class into two groups. Direct each group to recite alternate verses of Psalm 8. Then ask your students what this psalm tells us about the biblical view of human beings' relationship to the earth.

Sin, Guilt, and Nakedness

Pose these questions for discussion:
- ◆ In the story of the Fall, Adam and Eve try to hide their nakedness after they have sinned. When people sin and feel guilty, how is their experience like that of being naked in a crowd?
- ◆ When people feel guilty, how might they try to cover up, hide, or make excuses for their guilt?
- ◆ Can you think of stories from television, films, or literature that illustrate people hiding their guilt or excusing their sin? [*The Adventures of Tom Sawyer, The Scarlet Letter, The Adventures of Pinocchio, The Simpsons,* etc.]
- ◆ What qualities of God are shown in the story of the Fall? [God knows all things and is more merciful than we might expect.]
- ◆ If we cannot hide from God, why do we even bother trying to hide from other people when we are guilty? Or do we really think that somehow we can hide from God?

Cain and Abel: More Questions

The story of Cain and Abel raises many questions for discussion. If your students did the text activity on page 36, you might wish to explore the concept further with these questions:
- ◆ Considering God's punishment of Cain, what do you think is God's answer to Cain's question, "Am I my brother's keeper?" [Gen. 4:9]?
- ◆ What might be a better word than *keeper* to describe the relationship that God wants us to build with one another?
- ◆ What are some implications of being a "brother" or a "sister" to someone?
- ◆ Is it possible to destroy someone without laying hands on them? Explain.
- ◆ What is it like to be on the receiving end of destructive behaviors like ridicule and gossip?
- ◆ Jealousy is Cain's motivation for killing Abel. Is jealousy one of the chief motives for hate and destruction between persons? between schools? between nations?
- ◆ How can we cope with our jealousy of other people? with their jealousy of us?

Bill Cosby Tells the Story of Noah

Play for the class Bill Cosby's account of Noah and the Lord from *The Best of Bill Cosby* (Warner Brothers Records). As you would imagine, this version of Noah's tale is highly amusing and can serve as a break from serious study. It is not a theological interpretation! However, Cosby's account does have a serious side. Here is one question that could start a discussion of the story as told by Cosby:

◆ Can you think of situations today when doing what God asks can provoke ridicule from classmates, neighbors, or others?

2

Comic Strips of Noah and the Flood

This activity can be a source of review and fun, if carried out with a sense of humor.

1. Before class write the following panel topics on the chalkboard or a transparency:
a. Noah looking about in distress at his sinful neighbors
b. Noah building the ark according to God's specifications
c. Noah moving his family into the ark and herding in the pairs of animals
d. the rain coming down, with Noah and crew waiting for it to stop
e. Noah letting out the dove
f. the dove returning with an olive branch
g. the release of the animals, the family getting off the ark at last
h. Noah offering a sacrifice on an altar, with the rainbow of the covenant appearing

2. Divide the class into groups of six to eight people and give these instructions:
◆ In our next class, your group will be given eight pages of perforated computer paper that are still connected. [Hold up and unfold some continuous-form computer paper as an example.] Each member of your group will be expected to draw one or two panels in a multipanel comic strip that tells the story of Noah and the Flood. You may use markers or crayons; just make sure that the colors are deep enough for the class to see the drawing at a distance. I encourage you to be creative and even humorous if you like. [Either plan to provide markers and crayons for the project or ask the students to bring them from home.]
◆ [Direct the students' attention to the eight panel topics that you wrote on the chalkboard.] Please take about 5 minutes to decide who will draw each of the listed panels. If you have fewer than eight people in your group, decide which panels to eliminate, or assign some people more than one panel. Tonight mull over the panel you will draw. Let your creativity loose.

3. At the next class session, form the small groups once again. Give an eight-page length of continuous-form computer paper to each group at a long table or on the floor. Distribute markers and crayons if the groups do not have their own. Allow about 15 minutes for the groups to draw their comic strip.

4. Provide spaces in your classroom where the groups can hang the comic strips. After the drawings are hung, allow time for the students to admire each of the masterpieces. Then ask this question:
◆ In looking at the comic strips, did you see any differences in how the groups interpreted the story of Noah?

The Rewards of Evil Are, Finally, Evil

The story of Noah relates the destruction of wicked people and the survival of the just man, Noah, and his family. But in real life we do not always see such a neat correspondence between goodness and good fortune, between evil and disastrous lot.

Have the students read Psalm 73 and reflect on the reality that goodness does not necessarily "pay off" in this life. The psalmist cannot see any pay-off for his righteous living; he complains that all the prosperity is enjoyed by wicked people, while he is afflicted with suffering. Yet in the end, he knows that the rewards of a life well lived are far greater than any good fortune the wicked might enjoy. Also, wickedness, it seems, has built-in negative consequences, even though these might not be apparent in the short term.

In the story of the Flood, Noah's rewards for all his troubles are integrity, harmony with God, and finally, God's love. He becomes stronger and wiser because of his obedience to God. These are his long-term rewards.

Starting Over

In the story of the Flood, Noah and his family are saved by God, but after they leave the ark, they must face the task of completely rebuilding their world, which has been destroyed. Here are some questions for discussing the post-ark life of Noah and his family:

- Put yourself in the position of Noah at the end of the Flood. Your whole world has been destroyed, but you and your family have been saved. When you leave the ark and walk onto dry land, how do you feel?
- When people go through a rough period and come out safely, how does the experience change them?
- After the Flood what source of security makes Noah's situation hopeful rather than awful? [the covenant with God]

To end this activity, you may wish to play the rock song "Flood," from the album *Jars of Clay,* by the band Jars of Clay as a meditation on Noah's and our own dependence on God. Invite the students to listen to the song and join in on the chorus.

Concept B: Abraham: The Father of Biblical Faith

Review Questions: Abraham: The Father of Biblical Faith

Question. Who is called the father of biblical faith?
Answer. Abraham

Question. What does God promise to Abram as the covenant? What is the sign of that covenant for Abram's people?
Answer. God promised Abram that he would bring forth a multitude of descendants and that all the land of Canaan would eventually be his people's. The sign of this covenant is circumcision.

Question. Why are Sodom and Gomorrah destroyed?

Answer. Abraham made a bargain with God that the just people in the cities would not be destroyed along with the wicked. But in Sodom the wicked inhabitants proposed the rape of some young men (or angels) to whom Lot had given shelter. Lot offered his own daughters in order to protect his guests —to no avail. So while Lot and his family are rescued by angels, Sodom and Gomorrah are destroyed because of their wickedness.

Question. Who is traditionally known as the father of the Arab peoples?
Answer. Ishmael, son of Abraham and Hagar

Question. What is emphasized as a forbidden act in the story of Abraham's test?
Answer. Human sacrifice

Question. Which of Abraham's sons is destined to become an ancestor of the Israelites? Whom does that son marry?
Answer. Isaac. He marries Rebekah.

Text Activities: Abraham: The Father of Biblical Faith

- Create a story that shows the destructive nature of sin, especially how one act of sin can lead to another and another.
- Identify someone you know of who left behind all that was familiar to him or her in order to follow the call of some good purpose. If possible, ask the person what the experience was like and write it up in one page.
- "Is anything too wonderful for the LORD?" Sarah laughs when she hears she will have a child in her old age. But with God nothing is impossible, nothing is too wonderful! Write about a wonderful event from your life. What were the circumstances? Did you expect it to happen?

  When Abraham said yes to God's call, he received the gift of expectant faith—knowing, with all his heart and soul, that God would take care of him, bless him, amaze him. This journey would be a wonder-filled, God-filled adventure. We, too, can expect that God is with us every moment of our lives.
- Expecting God's goodness to prevail, Abraham does not give up. Abraham pleads with him to protect Lot and his family. Who is someone you care about so much that you would plead with God on his or her behalf? Is it someone who is in trouble? hurting? lost or confused? angry? Write a conversation between you and God about this person dear to your heart.
- How do you define hero? Make a list of your "heroic ancestors," including family heroes as well as national ones. Pick three and write a brief reflection for each about what makes him or her a hero. Be sure to include the hero's imperfections as well as his or her good points. How has he or she made a difference in your life?
- Write your own reactions to the story of Abraham's test. What questions does that story raise for you?

Additional Activities: Abraham: The Father of Biblical Faith

"Spiritually, We Are All Semites"

The term *Semite* is explained on page 39 of the student text. Explain that today the term *Semites* generally refers to Jews and Arabs, particularly Jews. Pope John XXIII offered the insight that "spiritually, we are all Semites." To help your students understand this comment, read aloud Matthew 1:1 and Luke 1:39–55. Then ask your students these questions:
- ◆ What did Pope John XXIII mean when he said that "spiritually, we are all Semites"?
- ◆ Given the passages from Matthew and Luke and the pope's comment, what should the relationship between Christians and Jews be?

Abraham's Sacrifice and the Eucharist

On the occasion of Abraham's covenant with God in Genesis, chapter 15, Abraham makes an offering of several animals. Point out that the roots of the eucharistic celebration—the sharing of the body and blood of Christ—can be seen in Abraham's sacrificial offering. In the sacrifices of the ancients, food was offered because food gave life to those who consumed it; offering food was equivalent to offering one's life to God. In Abraham's time the sacred offering was consumed by the participants if it did not burn completely, and it became a sacred meal. At the Last Supper, Jesus told the disciples that the bread and wine became his body and blood, the perfect sacrifice for the sins of many. Consuming the bread and wine—the food—became a sacred meal, giving eternal life.

The Bedouin Lifestyle

Genesis, chapter 18, opens with Abraham sitting at the entrance of his tent while the day is growing hot. It could be fascinating for the students to learn about present-day nomadic desert peoples, whose lifestyle has not changed much since Abraham's time. Choose a team of students to research the lifestyle of today's bedouins, or nomadic Arabs, including their shelter, food, means of travel, and so on. The team can give a report to the class, including visual aids such as a model of a bedouin tent (complete with sand and rocks), typical attire, and samples of food.

The Continuing Obligation of Hospitality

The New Testament reminds us to be hospitable. Read aloud to your students Hebrews 13:2, which is meant to remind us of Abraham and Sarah's hospitality to the three strangers.
Then ask your students these questions:
- ◆ Why was hospitality vital in the time of Abraham and Sarah?
- ◆ Is there a great need for hospitality in our world today?
- ◆ In what sense might the persons who need our hospitality be like angels, or messengers from God, to us?

♦ How can we be hospitable at school? at home? in our parish? to hungry and homeless people?

♦ Describe the difference between these motives for offering hospitality to someone:

   a. You are kind and welcoming to the person because you think that is what is expected of you.

   b. You are kind and welcoming because you believe that in some mysterious way, you are meeting God in the person.

A Summary of Abraham's Role

Assign the following to your students:

♦ Write a short essay (about one hundred words) sketching Abraham's life and explaining why he is called the father of biblical faith.

Ask several students to read their completed essays to the class.

 ## Concept C: Jacob: A Man Named Israel

 ## Review Questions: Jacob: A Man Named Israel

Question. Why does Rebekah try to maneuver Jacob into the position of principal heir of Isaac?

Answer. Rebekah believes that God wants Jacob, not Esau, to be Isaac's principal heir. She strives to obey what she believes to be God's will at great personal risk.

Question. What strange encounter does Jacob have on the way back to Canaan? What new name is he given then, and what does it mean?

Answer. While staying alone Jacob meets a mysterious being, which Scripture translators have called a stranger, a man, an angel—some even suggest a demon. This "someone" wrestles with Jacob until daybreak, when Jacob, refusing to let go, asks for a blessing. In reply the stranger asks his name, and when he says that it is Jacob, he is told that from now on he will be known as Israel, meaning "one who has contended with divine and human beings."

Question. How does Jacob initiate his family into the worship of the God of Israel?

Answer. He builds an altar on the spot where he heard God's promise at Bethel, and orders his family to rid themselves of their pagan religious trappings in a purification rite.

 ## Text Activities: Jacob: A Man Named Israel

• In the Israelites' understanding, things would work out the way God wanted them to—no matter what or who tried to get in the way. God could bring good out of situations that were weird, puzzling, unfair, or evil. Write a one-page reflection on this idea, including examples from your own life, if possible.

• Imagine a young person "wrestling" with God. What issues might he or she be struggling with? Write a story describing the situation.

 ## Additional Activities: Jacob: A Man Named Israel

The Unusual Ways of God

God's will can come about in unusual ways. An example of this is Rebekah and Jacob's deviousness to ensure that Jacob obtains Esau's birthright. Rebekah and Jacob, however, are not just or blameless in that incident.

1. Direct the students to read Genesis 27:1–45. Then have one student find and read aloud Hosea 12:2–3, and another, Jeremiah 9:4.

2. Ask all the students these questions:
◆ What do the passages from Hosea and Jeremiah say about Jacob's dishonesty?
◆ Why do you think this story was told? [To show God's mysterious ways in salvation history: God sometimes uses weak and sinful people to accomplish his purposes.]
◆ Can you think of an incident, either from history or from your own experience, when some good effect came about in spite of, even because of, someone's weakness or sin?

3. As a summary, refer the students to Mark 8:31–33, which quotes Jesus on how different God's standards and methods are from those of human beings.

World Happenings

The "World Happenings from 2000 to 1700 BC" sidebar in chapter 2 of the student text describes some of the developments going on in the world around the time of the patriarchs. If the students filled in the map on handout 1–D, "World Map," during their work on chapter 1, ask them to refer to that map and perhaps insert a word or a small symbol for each development in its respective area of the world, writing "2000 to 1700 BC" nearby. Ask them if they were surprised to learn that any of these developments happened at the time of the patriarchs.

A Summary of Jacob's Character

When the students have read the story of Jacob's struggle with the mysterious being (p. 49 of the student text), begin this activity.

The character of Jacob is the most skillfully drawn of any in the Old Testament. Although his story is not over until the end of this chapter of the student text, tell your students to write a hundred-word portrait of Jacob, based on their knowledge of him to this point. Tell them that later, when they have completed the story of Jacob, they will write fifty more words, commenting on the development of Jacob's character. After your students finish their initial portraits, encourage volunteers to read aloud their essays. File their papers for safekeeping.

(This writing exercise is continued with the activity "Completing the Portrait of Jacob" on p. 62 of this manual.)

 Pages 51–56

Concept D: Joseph: Treachery, Triumph, and Forgiveness

 ## Review Questions: Joseph: Treachery, Triumph, and Forgiveness

Question. What do Joseph's brothers do to him as a young man, and why?

Answer. They sell Joseph as a slave to traders on their way to Egypt. The brothers stain Joseph's coat with blood so that their father, Jacob, will believe Joseph has been killed. They did this because they resented Joseph for being Jacob's favorite and for being a tattletale.

Question. How does Joseph gain the pharaoh's favor?
Answer. By doing so well at explaining the pharaoh's dreams to him

Question. How does Jacob become a hero?
Answer. By agreeing to part with his beloved son Benjamin, so his other sons can get more grain and rescue the brother they left in Egypt as a pledge that they would return

Question. In what ways do Joseph and his brothers grow through the story?

Answer. Joseph, who in his youth was boastful and proud, gets the heart to forgive his brothers for selling him into slavery. The brothers grow by becoming ready to make sacrifices for the well-being of those they love. The whole family develops from bitterness and hate to tender appreciation of one another.

 ## Text Activities: Joseph: Treachery, Triumph, and Forgiveness

- Do you identify with the feelings of any of the characters in the beginning of this story: the favorite son? the brothers? Reuben? Write a paragraph describing how families can be harmed by jealousy or favoritism.
- In Joseph we find a beautiful example of forgiveness: Joseph forgives his brothers for the extremely hostile and jealous act of selling him into slavery and abandoning him. Write about a person or group in our world who is in need of forgiveness. What was the wrongdoing? Describe any obstacles to forgiving. What could be the outcome of forgiveness in this situation? What might happen if forgiveness is withheld?

2

Additional Activities: Joseph: Treachery, Triumph, and Forgiveness

Joseph and the Amazing Technicolor Dreamcoat

You may wish to play the musical interpretation of the Joseph story entitled *Joseph and the Amazing Technicolor Dreamcoat* (a rock cantata by Andrew Lloyd Webber and Tim Rice, MCA). The musical is quirky and fun but captures the drama of Joseph's story. The words to the songs are generally sold with the recording.

Have the students discuss or write about their favorite character in the musical.

Joseph, Dreams, and God's Help

Joseph says that he can interpret dreams only with the help of God because dreams are revelations from God. Point out to the students that in almost all cultures, dreams have been viewed as one way that God tells us things. Modern spiritually oriented psychology, in fact, sees dreams as God's way of showing us what we may not want to know about ourselves and so block out of our consciousness.

1. Ask the students this question:
◆ How does a superstitious approach to dreams differ from an approach that sees dreams as revealing deeper truths about ourselves? [A superstitious approach interprets dreams rigidly, seeing them as predictors or omens, whereas a spiritual-psychological approach sees dreams as having many possible interpretations, all directed toward discovering some aspect of our personality or our struggle to grow.]

Emphasize that all experiences—perhaps especially dreams—are ways that God speaks to us, if we simply listen with an open mind and heart.

2. Have the students each write down a dream they can remember and what they think God might have tried to reveal to them in the dream.

Famine Today

Assign some students to find the names of countries today where a significant portion of the population suffers from a food shortage or famine. Explain that they should mark each of the countries on a world map. Then they should give an oral report to the class on what happens to the human body when it is malnourished, what happens to families in famine-stricken areas (e.g., migration, the destruction of cultural patterns of living), and what happens to the countryside during a famine.

Select other students to find the names and research the efforts of international relief agencies that aid famine-stricken countries. To tie the reports on famine into the story of Joseph's family going to Egypt, ask the students to imagine the desperation of Jacob and his sons when they faced starvation in Canaan—with no relief agency to help them.

2

Headlines from Egypt

Direct the class in creating an ancient Egyptian tabloid newspaper. Assign the following stories:

1. news items, complete with headlines, on the arrival of Jacob's sons in Egypt and Joseph's accusation that they are spies
2. a people column with the name, background, and parentage of each of the ten sons of Jacob who have come to Egypt; also, a physical description of each brother (from the imaginations of the writers)
3. an editorial praising the governor of Egypt (Joseph) for his wisdom in storing grain during the plentiful years and for his vigilance in watching out for foreigners who might be spies
4. a news summary of the grain shortage in the known world, reporting the kinds and amounts of grain that the Egyptian storehouses sell to visitors from abroad
5. a society item reporting an awards ceremony at which Joseph receives the Egyptian Medal of Honor for his valor and diligence in the service of Egypt and his administration of the national grain supply; also, coverage of the attendance of Joseph's wife and children, how all were dressed, and so on
6. a review of Psalm 105:1–22, a new poem written to praise Joseph

Tell the students that they may include sketches or any other means of bringing the material to life. Photocopy the tabloid and give a copy to everyone in the class.

Completing the Portrait of Jacob

If you used the activity "A Summary of Jacob's Character" on page 59 of this manual, instruct the students to complete the essays they started by adding approximately fifty words about the development of Jacob's character at the end of his life. Then invite the students to share their ideas, particularly their assessment of Jacob's struggle for greatness.

A Family Tree

The students have been exposed to many biblical characters and blood relationships in this chapter. To help them process this information, have them diagram a family tree from Abraham through Joseph and his brothers, indicating all the family members' names and the unions from which they came. Or you might want to simply present the family tree to your class as a way of summarizing the chapter. (Abraham's family tree appears on page 63. You could copy the diagram onto the chalkboard or photocopy it onto an overhead transparency.)

Note: Neither Dinah nor Asenath is mentioned in the student text. In ancient Israelite culture, a woman could not be the head of a tribe. Thus, Dinah, the daughter of Jacob, does not receive the same scriptural coverage that her brothers do. Asenath, the mother of Joseph's children, is simply not a significant figure in the Old Testament.

Abraham's Family

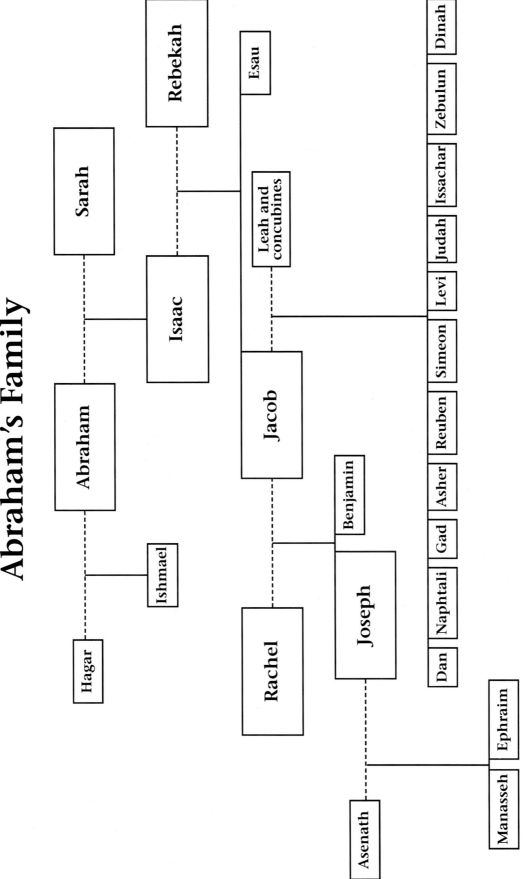

Closing Prayer

1. Remind the students of God's holy presence in the world around us.

2. Pray Psalm 8 aloud with the students. You may want them to alternate verses between the left side and the right side of the room.

3. Read or have a student read Genesis 1:26–31.

4. With words such as the following, invite the students to offer thanks for God's gift of the world:

◆ God said that all Creation is good. Let us each give thanks for one special part of Creation, a part of the world or our life for which we are particularly grateful. You are invited to voice that for which you are thankful. Simply say, "For (fill in the blank with whatever you are thankful for), let us pray." We will answer, "Thank you, God, for your gifts."

5. End by praying together Psalm 98, singing "All the Ends of the Earth," by Robert Dufford (based on Psalm 98, from *Glory and Praise* 3), or playing "All Good Gifts," by Stephen Schwartz, from the musical *Godspell.*

 # Closing Teacher Prayer

Call to prayer. Be still within and without. Be in touch with a remembered moment of God's love. Center yourself in the creative love of God.

Reflect. What have you learned in the process of teaching this chapter? Was it a learning of the head or the heart? Does this reveal God more fully to you? How? What effect could this learning have on your life?

Pray.
God of all creation, we ask your blessing on each of us
as we enter into the mystery
of your ongoing molding and shaping of our life.
May the spirit of God gift us
with the grace of loving receptivity
to your living Word
eager to be born within us. Amen.

(Bergan and Schwan, *Taste and See:
Prayer Services for Gatherings of Faith*)

CHAPTER 3

Freedom:
The Exodus
and the Covenant of Sinai

Major Concepts

A. **The Exodus: Freed from Slavery.** God calls Moses to lead the Israelites out of slavery in Egypt. After the last of ten plagues strikes down Egypt's firstborn but spares the Israelites' children (the Passover), Pharaoh commands Moses and his people to leave. The Israelites safely cross the Sea of Reeds, and the pursuing Egyptians drown. Sustained by God in their wilderness wanderings, the Israelites repeatedly learn to trust in God's care for them. The Jewish exiles in Babylon could identify closely with the Exodus story. *See* the *Catechism,* nos. 62, 287, 697, 707, 1081 (the Exodus—general); 164 (trust in God); 203–209, 2810–2811 (the meaning and importance of YHWH); 218–219 (God's love and faithfulness); 710 (the Babylonian exile); 1150 (signs of the Covenant); 1164, 1334, 1339–1340 (Passover and the Eucharist); 2574–2577 (God's relationship with Moses).

B. **The Covenant of Sinai: An Offering from God.** God promises the Israelites that if they keep the Covenant, they will be the Lord's holy nation. At Mount Sinai, Moses receives the Ten Commandments, which prohibit idolatry, the irreverent use of God's name, killing, adultery, stealing, lying, and covetousness. The Commandments also called on the Israelites to keep the Sabbath holy and to honor their parents. The Israelites saw these and the other laws of the Covenant not as restrictive but as freeing people to live harmoniously with one another. Many of the laws radically advanced justice, while others, like the justification of slavery, were customs later abolished as unjust. *See* the *Catechism,* nos. 709, 1961–1964 (an "old law"); 697, 781, 2052–2082 (the Decalogue—general); 2084–2141 (the First Commandment); 2142–2167 (the Second Commandment); 345–348, 2168–2195 (the Third Commandment); 2197–2257 (the Fourth Commandment); 2259–2330 (the Fifth Commandment); 1646, 2331–2400 (the Sixth Commandment); 2401–2463 (the Seventh Commandment); 2464–2513 (the Eighth Commandment); 2514–2533 (the Ninth Commandment); 2534–2557 (the Tenth Commandment).

C. **Sealing the Covenant.** The Covenant of Sinai, sealed in bulls' blood and surpassing all other covenants, proclaims for all time that the Israelites are the people of God. While waiting for Moses to return from Mount Sinai, the Israelites begin worshiping a golden calf. Moses angrily breaks the tablets of the Law in response. At Moses' pleading, God forgives the Israelites, and the Covenant is renewed. He reveals to Moses the thirteen attributes of God, who is merciful, gracious, and abounding in love and faithfulness. A dwelling place for the ark of the Covenant is completed. *See* the *Catechism,* nos. 203–220 (the attributes of God); 210, 2574–2577 (the love between Moses and God); 401 (Israel's infidelity); 1439 (the prodigal son); 1539 (the priesthood of the Old Covenant); 2056–2063, 2810 (the principal Covenant of the Jewish people); 1996 (grace).

 ## Opening Teacher Prayer

Call to prayer. Be still within and without. Call to mind your need to be forgiven and freed. Center yourself in God, the source of freedom.

Read. Psalm 103

Reflect. What are the words or phrases in Psalm 103 that particularly resonate within you? What are the feelings that stir within you?

Hold in your heart. "The LORD is merciful and gracious" (Ps. 103:8).

 ## Concept A: The Exodus: Freed from Slavery

Pages 58–64

 ## Review Questions: The Exodus: Freed from Slavery

Question. Why were the accounts of the Exodus close to the hearts of Jews during and after the Exile?
Answer. The Jews of the Exile could relate to the experience of being oppressed in a foreign land. The exiled Jews also struggled in a frightening and hostile wilderness as they journeyed to Babylon and back to Judah some fifty years later. And most important for the Jews was God's revelation to their ancestors in the wilderness. Through Moses the people of Israel discovered God's identity, and through the Covenant they found their identity as his people. Similarly, in Babylon, after repenting of their sins, the exiles rediscovered their true identity as God's beloved.

Question. What is the interpretation of the Hebrew name Yahweh given in the scriptural text in Exodus? What is a better expression of the meaning of that name?
Answer. "I am who I am" is a scriptural interpretation that might be better expressed as "I am the One who is always present."

Question. What is the final plague proclaimed by Moses?
Answer. Death for the firstborn of Egypt
Question. What does the Passover seder celebrate?
Answer. It celebrates the Jews' freedom from slavery in Egypt and the longing for freedom everywhere in the world.

Question. What image of God is given in Moses and Miriam's canticle?

Answer. Triumphant, strong, powerful, majestic in holiness, awesome in splendor, capable of doing wonders, steadfast in love, reigning forever

 Text Activities: The Exodus: Freed from Slavery

- Miriam and her mother risk their lives when they defy the pharaoh's orders, but Israel eventually is freed because they had the courage and ingenuity to save Moses' life. Write a one-page essay about someone you know whose courageous act brought about a change for the good. Include a picture of the person, if possible.
- How does it feel to accept someone's help? Is that easy or difficult for you? Perhaps you have a task in front of you that you believe you cannot accomplish on your own. Is there a friend, a family member, a teacher, a neighbor, or someone else who can help you? Imagine a conversation you might have about this with such a person, and write it down.
- Consider the "unutterable mystery of God." Describe in writing one aspect of God that you think you understand. How have you come to know that about him? Find or create a picture or other artwork that represents to you the mystery of God.
- The people of Israel no longer knew their God. But God knew them. No matter how long we stay away from God, even if it is so long that we forget who he is, God never forgets us. Find a song or a poem that speaks of his abiding presence to us and bring it to class.
- Passover and the Last Supper, which is celebrated in the Eucharist, are ways to remember how we have been freed by God. Have you ever had an experience of being liberated or set free? Perhaps you were released from a dangerous situation, a hurtful friendship, a destructive habit that enslaved you, an illness, or suffering of another kind. Write your story and think about the ways God might have been involved in freeing you.
- On their journey the Israelites were protected by God in the pillars of cloud and fire. Reflect on something or someone who has given you a sense of direction in your life. Express your thoughts in writing, or in a drawing or painting.
- "Perhaps the most wonderful miracles are those in which hearts that seem hard and unmovable are turned around by the power of God." Write about an example of this kind of miracle that you have seen in your own life, in the life of someone you know, or in the course of history.

 Additional Activities: The Exodus: Freed from Slavery

Reflections on Equal Rights and Civil Disobedience

Explain to the students that prejudice—like that experienced by the Israelites—brings to mind the history of slavery in the United States and other countries. Although slavery has been virtually outlawed around the world, the struggle to attain equal rights for all people—regardless of race, sex, religion, and so on—continues. In many cases the struggle involves great risk taking by people who dare to confront and disobey unjust laws.

In the account of the baby Moses being taken in and cared for by Pharaoh's daughter, a kind of civil disobedience is implied. Explain to the students that we do not know if Moses' life actually began in this way. The important thing about the story is that the Israelite people who told it must have admired deeply the kind of courage exemplified by Pharaoh's daughter in the story. She defies the law and thus allows Moses to grow to manhood. Explore the significance of her act with questions such as these:

- ◆ What do we know about Pharaoh's daughter from this brief episode?
- ◆ Is she aware of Pharaoh's law?
- ◆ What risk is she taking in breaking the law?
- ◆ Why does she do it?
- ◆ Are people sometimes bound by conscience to disobey civil laws? Can you think of any examples?

After the discussion ask the students to write a short imaginary interview with Pharaoh's daughter, discussing what she did and why. Or ask volunteers to role-play for the class an interview such as this.

The Evils of Slavery

To reinforce your students' understanding of what is at stake in the Exodus story, select some students to prepare brief written and oral reports about slavery in the United States before the Civil War. Some possible topics are the buying and selling of slaves, family separation, punishment, workloads, diet, conditions for children, and general living conditions. Have other students research and prepare reports on slavery in other parts of the world.

Moses' Insecurity and Aaron's Help

Chapter 4 of the Book of Exodus depicts Moses as quite insecure about his ability to do what God is asking of him—that is, lead the Israelites out of Egypt into Canaan. He considers himself neither a leader nor a speaker, and he certainly does not think himself capable of confronting Pharaoh alone. He does not have the faith to believe that God is enough help. So God, in infinite mercy and patience, grants Moses the help of his brother, Aaron. With this scriptural example as a starting point, explain how God understands our desire for the physical presence and help of other people in our times of need. Ask your students to write brief answers to these questions:

- ◆ List three times when you did not think that you could do something alone, times when you needed a companion who would be with you at least for moral support.
- ◆ Who was your companion on each of these occasions? What assistance did that person give you?
- ◆ Did you thank each companion for being there with you?
- ◆ How might God have had something to do with your having a companion in each time of need?

Why Call Moses?

Moses was not overly eager to follow God's marching orders. Five times he resisted God's call. One may wonder why God would call such a reluctant person. Here are some questions to use in exploring this issue:

- ◆ If you had been in Moses' position, would you have hesitated to do what God commanded? Why?

- Do you think that most people—when called on by the circumstances of their lives to do great and courageous deeds—wonder, Why me? Why do I have to do it? Might they be answering a call from God by responding to such opportunities?
- If you had been conducting a talent search for someone to lead the Israelites out of Egypt, do you think that you would have picked Moses? Why or why not?
- Is there a way to determine if someone is destined for greatness? If so, how can we tell?

End the exploration by pointing out that the ways of God are not necessarily the ways of human beings. God frequently picks the outcasts and the weak to confound the strong; after all, Moses was an orphan, a hunted criminal, then a shepherd, and—as seen in his five refusals—not overly brave or ambitious. God picks the weak to show us that it is God, not the chosen person alone, who is accomplishing things.

Reflections on the God Who Is Always Present

Remind your students that *Yahweh,* translated in the scriptural text as "I am who I am," is better translated "I am the One who is always present." The idea of a god who is not only supreme but also a constant presence was revolutionary in Moses' time. Then pose these questions for discussion:

- What do we mean when we say that God is always present? Or, in other words, for the Israelites how was having a god who was always present different from having gods who resided in statues and temples?
- Moses found God in the burning bush. From your perspective how is the presence and power of God revealed today?

Multinational Pharaohs: Same Abuses, Different Times

Pharaoh kept the Israelites' noses to the grindstone because he required their cheap labor for his many building projects. Today many large North American corporations expand into Third World countries because they want to obtain cheap labor. The two phenomena are related in terms of their motivation and their effects. To explore how "pharaohs" still operate today, direct this activity:

1. Ask your students to look at the labels on the clothing they are wearing (they might need to help one another read the labels, such as those attached to the backs of shirts) and to call out the countries where the clothing was made; remind them to check their shoes too. On the chalkboard list all the countries the students name.

2. Divide the countries listed on the chalkboard among the students. Instruct them to research the typical wages of workers in North American–owned factories in their assigned country and the typical wages of workers in U.S. or Canadian factories. More important, stress that the students should try to discover what standard of living those wages support. Have the students prepare reports and present them orally to the class.

3. After the reports have been given, pose these questions to the class:
- What happens to laborers in Third World countries when big North American companies come in, hire them at meager wages, provide no benefits, and operate the factories as cheaply as possible?

3

◆ What happens to workers in North America when North American companies move their operations to Third World countries?

◆ How can companies that exploit cheap labor in other countries be compared to Pharaoh?

◆ Do Christians in this country have a duty to protect the dignity of people in other countries, especially if they use products from those countries? If so, how might they do that?

4. Read aloud this quote from Matthew's Gospel, "In everything do to others as you would have them do to you" (Matt. 7:12). Then ask these questions:

◆ How do these words from Jesus apply to the enslavement of the Israelites under Pharaoh?

◆ Considering the words of Jesus, is it morally acceptable for Christians to exploit workers in Third World countries?

The Plagues: How to Get Someone's Attention

Emphasize to the students that the plagues that beset Egypt in the story of the Exodus are not intended to be punishments from God but, instead, ways of getting Pharaoh's attention. The plagues are supposed to turn Pharaoh's hardheartedness into compassion; they are a way of letting him know that God is on the side of the Israelites. Yet Pharaoh's attention span is short. During some of the plagues, he indicates a willingness to let the people go, but after each plague he reverts to his obstinate, hard-hearted position.

Use questions like the following to relate Pharaoh's short attention span to the students' own experiences with crises or suffering:

◆ Have you, or has anyone you know, ever been plagued with some big problem, crisis, or suffering—like failing grades, a car accident, a devastating illness, or a death in the family?

◆ If so, did the crisis bring about any changes in outlook, behavior, or relationships for you or the person you know? Describe any changes that occurred.

◆ If you or the person you know experienced changes in outlook, behavior, or relationships during the crisis, what happened when the crisis was over? Were the changes permanent?

◆ Some people make lasting changes for the better as a result of hurt or tragedy. Yet others make no change at all, become permanently bitter and angry, or—like Pharaoh—have a temporary change of heart that wears off as soon as the crisis is over. Why do you think people react in these different ways?

Control: Pharaoh's Fatal Flaw

Introduce a discussion of Pharaoh's need to control, saying that essentially Pharaoh thought he was a god. Thus he concluded that he did not have to obey some phony god of the Israelites. Being stubborn about his power, he was convinced that he would be able to control the Israelites. To us today, he appears thickheaded and power-hungry, to say the least. But lest we be too hard on Pharaoh, we should pause to reflect on our own desires to control all of life.

1. Ask your students to list five aspects of their life over which they wish they had complete control. Ask them also to explain in writing why having control in those areas would be important to them. For example, "I wish that I could make person X stop being so nasty to me. This would make my life easier, and I don't deserve such treatment anyway."

2. Afterward pose these questions for discussion:
◆ In general, why do we want to control things in life?
◆ Would your life be better if you could control everything you wanted to control?
◆ How might life be worse if you could control other people, events, and so on?
◆ Why do you think God decided not to give human beings full control over every aspect of their lives and the world around them?
◆ What happens to us when we think that we can absolutely control most aspects of our life or when we try to do so?
◆ What valuable lessons can be learned when we realize that we are not in control of the universe? How can this realization help us live better?

What's So Special About Unleavened Bread?

Give your students the following information, in your own words:
◆ In the years after the Exodus, it became customary for the Israelites to prepare for the celebration of Passover by ridding their households of all leaven and all leavened bread. (Leaven was fermented dough kept from one baking to another, a form of yeast. Leavened bread was any bread made with leaven.) At the beginning of each Passover season, the people would start afresh with new dough to symbolize the start of a new life of freedom. Jewish families still do this today during the Passover season. They serve only unleavened bread called matzo. [If possible, purchase some matzo and give all your students a taste.]
◆ Leaven is an important symbol for Christians too. From the ancient custom of serving unleavened bread during the Jewish Passover came the use of unleavened bread in the celebration of the Eucharist. Saint Paul, referring to the need to get rid of the old leaven at Passover, spoke of the leaven as a symbol of sin. [Read aloud 1 Cor. 5:6–8 so that the students can hear Paul's words.]
◆ In the Gospels, Jesus refers to leaven in a context completely different from that of the Passover. Jesus gives leaven a positive meaning. Yeast is a living organism; it grows and expands the dough. He uses it as a symbol of divine life present in the community of people—the Reign of God. [Read aloud Luke 13:20–21.]

A Seder Meal

If you wish to explore the Jewish ritual of the Passover seder as it is celebrated today, you can find clear and useful helps in a set of resources from Liturgy Training Publications (LTP): *The Passover Celebration* is a participation book for the seder meal; it includes complete texts and music, along with background notes. *Songs for the Seder Meal* is a 30-minute cassette or CD recording of the songs and Hebrew words used in the participation book; some of the songs are in English. See appendix 3 for ordering information.

Another option is to invite someone from the Jewish community to visit your class and share his or her experience of the Passover feast and seder meal.

More on Jesus and the Passover

To build on the previous two activities, you may want to focus additional attention on the connection between the Jewish Passover celebration and Christian tradition. Point out to your students that the lamb that each Israelite family slaughtered on the night before the Exodus to freedom became a figure of Christ for the early Christian community. Jesus was called the Lamb of God; in the Book of Revelation, he is symbolized as the Lamb that was slain, and the holy people of God are described as dressed in robes made white by washing them in the blood of the Lamb (Rev. 7:13–14). Ask the students this question:

◆ Why would the early Christians have identified Jesus with the lamb of the Passover?

One of the most beautiful of all Catholic rituals is the Easter Vigil, with its reading or chanting of the Easter Proclamation, or Exsultet. Through magnificent praises this proclamation describes the relationship between Jesus' death and Resurrection and the Passover and the Exodus. Read aloud this hymn from the liturgy for the Easter Vigil (found in the Church's Sacramentary), play a recording of it, or invite someone from a local parish (the parish coordinator of music or liturgy could recommend a cantor) to sing it for your class and share her or his reflections on it. Ask your students to point out in the proclamation those images that come from the stories of the Passover and the Exodus.

Negro Spirituals and the Exodus

Explain to the class that Negro spirituals, which are great American folk songs, were composed and sung by the slaves in the United States at a time when they could closely identify with the oppression that the Israelites experienced as slaves under Pharaoh. Therefore, many of these spirituals are about freedom and the Exodus, for example: "Go Down, Moses (Let My People Go)," "Sit Down, Sister," "Pharaoh's Army Got Drownded," "Oh Freedom" (sung often during the civil rights movement of the 1960s), and "Free at Last" (referred to by Martin Luther King Jr. in the closing to his famous "I Have a Dream" speech). Find a recording of some Negro spirituals or a book of American folk songs that contains some of these powerful spirituals, and share it with the students. You may even want to sing a few of the songs as a class.

The Use of Manna: Guidelines for Simple Living

Present to the students the following three regulations that the Israelites were given for the use of manna (see Exod. 16:16–26). Then point out that these ideas reappear in the New Testament in a different context: they provide helpful guidelines for leading a simple lifestyle.

First find out more about manna by consulting a resource such as *HarperCollins Bible Dictionary*. Share your findings with the class.

Here are the rules that were given to the Israelites, followed by the parallel ideas from the New Testament:

1. *Gather only as much of the manna as each person requires. There is to be no hoarding and no false security* (Exod. 16:16). This rule parallels what Jesus says in Matthew 6:19–21. Direct your students to the Gospel passage and read it aloud.

Then ask these questions:

- ◆ What are some ways that people today try to find security through false means? [Having an excess of material things often gives a temporary sense of security.]
- ◆ Do you know people who are happy with just enough to care for their needs, people who do not assume that more is better?

2. *Keep none of the manna for the next morning (16:19). Trust God to give you more when you need it.* Jesus tells us in Matthew 6:26 not to "gather into barns." Examine and discuss this passage.

  Then ask this question:

  - ◆ What do you think is the underlying message of this Gospel passage? Is Jesus saying that we should not have a job and support ourselves financially? [The passage is not speaking about whether we ought to work or buy our own clothes and food. Rather, it is pointing to the need for a deep level of trust that God will be with us in all ways. If we are not anxious about material things, we have more space within ourselves for trust in God.]

3. *Gather double the amount on the sixth day so that no work will be done on the Sabbath. The Sabbath is holy to both God and the people (16:22–23).* Jesus observed the Sabbath as a day for rest and worship.

  Discuss the contemporary practice of the Sabbath with these questions:

  - ◆ Why do you think the emphasis on the Sabbath as a day of rest is somewhat lost today?
  - ◆ How are families affected when family members have to work at shopping centers, food stores, and so on, on Sundays?
  - ◆ Would we be better off if we had one day when no one worked except at the most essential employment, like in hospitals? Why or why not?

In addition to the three points above, mention to the students that in John 6:48–51, Jesus compares himself to the manna that the Israelites ate in the desert, calling himself "the living bread that came down from Heaven." Ask the students to explain the comparison.

Concept B: The Covenant of Sinai: An Offering from God

Review Questions: The Covenant of Sinai: An Offering from God

Question. Why did the First Commandment prohibit idolatry?

Answer. Idolatry was prohibited because there is only one God of the Israelites and because human efforts to depict God were bound to fail and should not be attempted.

Question. Why was adultery held in great horror among the Israelites?

Answer. In ancient times the well-being of the family took precedence over the individual's desires because the stability and even the survival of the community depended on it. Adultery often led to vengeance and feuds, and was punishable by death.

Question. Explain the understanding of sin revealed in the Ninth and Tenth Commandments.

Answer. Both Commandments have to do with covetousness, or greediness. They reveal that sin begins in the mind and heart—that is, entertaining the idea of a sin leads to the act. For example, coveting a neighbor's wife can be the first step toward adultery.

Question. In what sense did the Israelites consider the Law as freeing them, not restricting them?

Answer. The Israelites considered the Ten Commandments and other laws to be mutual understandings that enabled people to live in freedom and peace with one another. The rules actually freed people by giving them boundaries that everyone in the community pledged not to cross.

Text Activities: The Covenant of Sinai: An Offering from God

- Throughout their difficult journey, God provided for the Israelites. When it seemed that they would starve, they discovered manna; right before their eyes was nourishment that would sustain them for forty years. Do you recognize the nourishment—the manna—that is sent to you? Reflect in writing on three things you typically take for granted, without which you could not survive. Where do these things come from? Who or what provides them? What do you have to do to get them? Do you know of people who go without these things? Find and copy a psalm that expresses how God takes care of us.
- Consider people who has been forced to flee from their home or country because of war, famine, or persecution. What challenges and fears might they face as they search for a new home? Imagine a teenager in this situation and write a prayer or a poem from his or her perspective about the difficulties of exile, longing for home, and hoping for a better life.
- A relationship is understood as a covenant when both parties promise to be faithful to each other, and genuine love and care is shared between them. Do you know of any relationships that you believe are truly covenants? Find two people who are in such a relationship and interview them to discover what makes their relationship so special and what each of them contributes to it. Write up the results of your interview.
- The first three Commandments pertain to loving and respecting God. Describe in writing how young people can show their respect for God.
- The last seven Commandments are directed toward loving one another. Keep a journal for three days, noting instances when these commandments are upheld and when they are disregarded by you or others. Avoid judging other people; simply observe.
- Which of the Ten Commandments is most challenging for you? for our society? Explain in a one-page essay.

Additional Activities: The Covenant of Sinai: An Offering from God

The Ten Commandments and Other Ancient Codes

Select a few students to research the Code of Hammurabi and other ancient codes of law and to compare them with the Ten Commandments. They should try to determine how the Ten Commandments were unique among ancient codes. Certainly the most distinctive aspect of the Ten Commandments was the insistence on no false gods or images. Explore with the entire class the significance of this feature of the Israelites' ancient code.

This activity might be used in connection with "Reflections on the God Who Is Always Present" on page 69 of this manual.

False Gods

To explore the meaning of the First Commandment, "You shall have no other gods before me" (Exod. 20:3), in more depth, collect plenty of newspapers and magazines that can be used to make a collage of society's false gods. Then lead the group in the following process:

1. Review the First Commandment and the textbook's discussion of the commandment with your class. Talk about the meaning of idolatry. Ask the students to volunteer examples of idolatry they have observed in today's society, such as worship of money, power, or popularity.

2. Distribute to each student a large white sheet of paper or cardboard, a pair of scissors, glue, and magazines and newspapers. Direct the participants each to make a collage of false gods they find in the media. They can use both words and pictures.

3. Post the collages on a bulletin board. Encourage the students to share their observations and their insights into the First Commandment.

Cursing and Obscenities

To focus on some implications of the Second Commandment, which forbids the use of God's name in irreverent ways, give this assignment to your students:
- ◆ The renowned psychologist Rollo May says that cursing and obscenities are a kind of psychic violence that can bring on physical violence. Write about an instance when cursing or obscenities were used as a weapon of psychic violence. The instance need not be a personal experience; you may simply retell an account you have heard. Please leave out any names or other identifying information. Include your thoughts on the following questions:
  - • What effect did this use of language have on the persons and on the situation?
  - • What is your opinion about cursing and obscenities?

Keeping the Sabbath

To discuss the Third Commandment, "Remember the Sabbath day" (20:8), pose these questions for discussion:
- ◆ Do most people you know observe Sunday with the same reverence that the Israelites had for their Sabbath? Explain.
- ◆ Other faiths besides Christianity and Judaism—Islam, for example—take one day each week for rest and worship. Physically, psychologically, and spiritually, why is it important to set aside a day such as this?

◆ What good things can you do for yourself on Sundays so that you can experience the true spirit of the Sabbath? [Emphasize that rest can also mean enjoyment.]

3

Honoring Parents

1. Regarding the Fourth Commandment, "Honor your father and your mother" (20:12), use these questions for discussion:
◆ Is it possible to be unhappy, even angry, with parental rules and decisions and still retain respect for your parents? Explain.
◆ At what point in a disagreement with parents does a son or a daughter cease to honor them, thus sinning?
◆ In an ancient nomadic society, where everyone was sorely needed just for survival of the community, family harmony was essential. Is it as essential today for children to honor their parents and for family harmony to reign?
◆ What would a society look like if its children did not honor or respect their elders?
◆ On page 67 of your textbook, the author says that any society must be judged by how it treats its youngest and oldest citizens. What reasoning would support this statement? Do you agree with the statement?

2. Ask the students to write a paragraph or two in response to this question:
◆ What are one or two things you can do (that you are not already doing) that would show your parents that you honor them?

You Shall Not Kill

Murder, in the physical sense, is illegal and immoral for obvious reasons. However, murder of another's character can be committed through lies, slander, and vicious gossip. Murder can also be an act of omission—for example, when the rich do not feed the poor or when the powerful do not protect the powerless.

1. To further examine this Commandment, "You shall not murder" (20:13), offer these questions for discussion:
◆ How can rage turn into murder? What are some of the factors that lead to murder?
◆ Is it possible that without even being aware of it, we can build up anger until it becomes murderous hatred? How is this possible?
◆ Are the factors that lead to murder the same factors that lead to the mini-murders of slander and vicious gossip?
◆ How can the spreading of lies about someone be a type of murder?
◆ Can one person kill another person's spirit? How?

2. Tell the class members each to bring in a newspaper or magazine clipping that describes some form of "death dealing" perpetrated by one human being or group on another, whether the death be physical or emotional. Examples might be cases of starvation, child abuse, spousal abuse, libel or slander, people being driven off their farm, pollution with hazardous wastes, or inhumane working conditions. Also assign a brief written explanation of why the death happened, that is, what factors in the individual or the societal perpetrator caused the murder?

3. Divide the class into groups so that the students can share their findings. Then ask some students to explain their articles and reactions to the entire class.

Valuing Life

Another approach to the Fifth Commandment, "You shall not murder" (20:13), would be to emphasize that the Commandment is about affirming the value of life. Explain to the students that Catholics are encouraged to hold a "consistent life ethic"—that is, they should be opposed to all actions that violate the sanctity of life (Joseph Cardinal Bernardin referred to this concept as the seamless garment). Some issues that need to be examined in accordance with a consistent life ethic are these: abortion; euthanasia; war; defense spending that takes resources away from programs that support life; nuclear weapons; capital punishment; poverty; and discrimination of any kind, which devalues persons. The bishops of the United States have urged Catholics to maintain a consistent life ethic toward all issues of human life, from the womb to the tomb.

Engage the students in a discussion of how violence also violates the Fifth Commandment because violence does not uphold the sanctity of life. Note for the students how violence saturates the media—films, television shows, the news, video games, music. Pose these questions:

◆ Is violence always wrong? Explain.

◆ Why do you think violence is depicted so prevalently in today's society? What is the appeal? Do you think seeing violence on an everyday basis desensitizes you to it?

◆ What effect, if any, would making an effort not to view the violence have on people?

◆ Should violence be censored?

◆ To follow the Fifth Commandment, do you need to avoid watching violence, doing violence, or both?

Adultery

1. Use these questions for a class discussion of the Sixth Commandment, "You shall not commit adultery" (20:14):

◆ How does adultery harm the people involved? their children? their friends? the larger society?

◆ What attitudes about sexuality foster adultery?

◆ How is adultery depicted on television and in movies? Can you name some specific examples?

◆ Does our culture glamorize the notion of having an occasional extramarital affair?

2. You might bring in one of the scandal sheets that can commonly be bought in supermarkets. Point out the numerous stories of infidelity; then ask your students why stories like these are so popular (if they were not popular, the tabloids would not publish them).

3. Point out to the students that the Sixth Commandment is really about faithfulness and integrity in all relationships. Adultery is one way—perhaps the most obvious way—that faith and honesty between persons is broken. Ask the students:

◆ Can you think of other ways that people break trust with each other, whether they are married, same-sex friends, or other-sex friends? How are these ways of breaking trust like adultery?

3

Stealing

Here are some questions to use in a discussion on the Seventh Commandment, "You shall not steal" (20:15):
- ◆ What happens to a group of people or to a society when its members steal from one another? For example, what would be the effect on the student body and others in the school if someone started stealing things out of lockers? if many students cheated on exams?
- ◆ How can the hoarding of riches while others starve be a type of stealing? Can we steal from the future, or from future generations? How might this be done? [By failing to care for our natural resources, accumulating a huge national deficit that future generations will have to pay off, destroying the ozone layer, etc.]
- ◆ If we refuse to give due credit or praise to another person, we steal his or her right to affirmation, which is necessary for self-esteem. How do you feel when you do something well and know that you deserve commendation or praise, but it is withheld?
- ◆ How do some people steal from their employers without actually breaking the law? [By withholding part of a day's work but receiving a full day's pay]
- ◆ How does this commandment apply to cheating and plagiarism?
- ◆ Is it possible to steal from ourselves? How? [By robbing ourselves of the development of our own potential!]

False Witness

1. To explore the Eighth Commandment, which forbids giving false testimony, pose these questions to your students:
- ◆ Does the Eighth Commandment apply to lying? Explain.
- ◆ Have you ever been falsely accused? How did you feel? What did you do?
- ◆ What is so damaging about lying about another person?
- ◆ What is perjury? What does it do to a legal system that is supposed to promote justice?

2. Read aloud Matthew 26:59–66, which describes Jesus before the Sanhedrin, and Matthew 26:69–75, the account of Peter's denying Jesus. Ask your students these questions:
- ◆ Which of these incidents of false witness strikes you as most horrible? Why?
- ◆ How does Jesus serve as a model for anyone who is hurt by false witness?

Covetousness

Both the Ninth and the Tenth Commandments address covetousness. Coveting is the first step toward taking. People covet because they feel that possession of a person or object will fill some vacuum for them. In other words, coveting begins with a feeling of powerlessness, a kind of hopelessness, the belief that God will not provide what we need and that only the objects we want to possess—whether persons or things—will bring contentment.

1. Offer these questions for discussion:
- Is anyone allowed to possess another person? In ancient Israel it was customary for a woman to be literally the property of her husband, but we have long since left that custom behind. How do people today try, or at least wish, to possess another person?
- Why do we covet the property of other people if that property is not necessary to our survival?
- If we believe that owning a particular something is crucial to who we are, what does that say about our self-image?
- Does advertising push us to covet other people's goods? How?

2. Ask the students to bring in advertisements that seem to foster covetousness, or bring magazines to class yourself and distribute them. These can be shared in small groups. From their ads each group could select the one that most clearly encourages covetousness, and all the selected ads could be shown and explained to the entire class.

Rewriting the Ten Commandments

Direct the students each to write their own version of the Ten Commandments. Or let them work in small groups. Urge them to keep the idea of each Commandment but to put it in words that young people today could identify with. Post these new versions of the Commandments in the classroom.

Concept C: Sealing the Covenant

Review Questions: Sealing the Covenant

Question. What did blood symbolize for the ancient Israelites?
Answer. Blood was the sign of life itself. In the ancient world, blood rituals were practiced as a way to seal covenants between kings.

Question. Why did the Covenant of Sinai surpass all other covenants in the minds of the biblical editors?
Answer. Because at Sinai God proclaimed for all time that the people of Israel were the people of God, a never-to-be-repeated event in Judaism

Question. Explain what the last attribute of God means and the intention behind it: "Yet by no means clearing the guilty, / but visiting the iniquity of the parents / upon the children / and the children's children, / to the third and fourth generation" (Exod. 34:7).
Answer. God forgives those who want forgiveness. The greatest sin is a belief that we have no need to be forgiven. The intention of the thirteenth attribute is to suggest that God does not let wrongs go unpunished. Belief in

personal punishment in an afterlife developed later in Jewish history. So if an individual died without being punished for injustices, it was believed that the punishment must then have fallen on his or her children.

3

Text Activity: Sealing the Covenant

- When you try to live out a pledge that you have made to someone, what difficulties can arise? Think of a commitment or pledge that you have struggled with. Why was it a struggle? Write a letter to that person (you decide if you want to mail it) expressing how you feel about it.
- Moses knew that God was closer to him than his most treasured friend. And God is just that close to each of us as well. List some of the kinds of heartfelt things that most people would share only with their best friend.

Additional Activities: Sealing the Covenant

Bullish Idols

Aaron's golden calf idol would not have been at all unusual to the neighbors of the Israelites—or, indeed, to many groups around the Near East during that period. Choose one or two students to research the worship of calves and bulls in world religions. Request answers to questions such as these:
- ◆ Where was, or is, bull worship practiced?
- ◆ Why did people select the bull?
- ◆ Describe some rituals of bull worship. Tell the researchers to prepare an oral report, complete with visuals, to present to the class.

Making God Real: A Role-Play

Sometimes people seek physical idols because God seems too abstract. Ask for four volunteers to do a role-play. Give them these directions:
- ◆ Kim and Kelly say that they do not believe in God anymore. They believe only in what they can see, touch, or sense in some other way. Two of their friends, Dan and Candace, who do believe in God, try to respond to Kim and Kelly's need for a concrete, tangible God. How can the two believing friends try to make God real for Kim and Kelly?

When the role-play is done (5 to 10 minutes should be enough time), ask the class for its reactions. Highlight any noteworthy aspects of the role-play that the class missed, and elaborate on the points brought up in discussion.

Poor Old Moses, Who Tried His Best

Poor Moses—he tried to do God's will, but the people simply would not cooperate. Imagine going through everything he did and then finding that the people had made an idol! Assign this reflection-writing activity:
- ◆ Have you ever felt like Moses must have felt? Think about a time when you wanted to do something positive, worked hard at it, and

then experienced nothing but misunderstanding. In writing, describe that time. Who was there? What were you trying to do? How hard did you have to work? How and why were people ungrateful? What was your reaction?

Encourage the students to share their stories within small groups.

Moses the Mediator

Moses the Maligned turns back into Moses the Mediator in Exodus 32:7–20; 33:1–11. He begs God to forgive the Israelites, and God relents. The student text's coverage of these passages provides a good opportunity to discuss peace-making, forgiveness for wrongdoers, and prayer.

1. Read aloud Exodus 32:31–33 and 33:12–17, with the students following along in their Bibles. Moses is clearly shown as a mediator, arguing and pleading with God for the people he loves.

2. Conduct a discussion about Moses the Mediator and forgiveness of neighbors, using these questions:
- Why is it hard to pray for people who have wronged us?
- Name some public figures—national or international—you believe guilty of some great wrong. Would it be hard to pray honestly for these people? Why or why not?
- What would you ask for if you were to pray for these people?
- How can we act as mediators between God and persons who we feel have done wrong?
- What do the passages we have just read tell us about God—or at least about the writer's view of God?

3. Ask the students to write a prayer for someone they know who has done something wrong and is in need of forgiveness. Encourage them to keep this person in their prayers, no matter how difficult that may be.

Interviews About God's Images

1. Tell your students each to interview two adults. They are to ask the following questions:
- When you think of the God of the Old Testament, what two images immediately come to mind? Explain.
- When you think about your relationship with God, what two images immediately come to mind? Explain.

2. Have the students prepare and bring to class a written report of their interviews. Then ask volunteers to share what they found out. Specifically, were the adults' perceptions of God close to the attributes of God described on page 75 of the student text?

Extra! Extra! The Exodus Project

Wrap up your discussion of the Exodus by having your students put together a tabloid newspaper from the time of Moses. A small group can complete the project, or you may choose to have all the class members participate.

Here are the parts of the paper that students will need to write or design:

1. a masthead
2. news stories on the plagues, the Passover, the crossing of the Sea of Reeds, Moses' journey up Mount Sinai, the Law, the incident of the golden calf, and the Covenant
3. two Dear Moses letters and his responses
4. an obituary
5. a food column on how to cook quail, including a recipe
6. two cartoons
7. want ads
8. a weather report, including a map and forecasts
9. letters to the editor
10. commercial advertisements

Appoint one or two people to serve as editors and one or two other people to do the layout. Publish the paper by making enough copies to provide one for each student and one for display.

Closing Prayer

Before the time for prayer, assign a reader for each of the Ten Commandments (found in Exod. 20:1–17).

To begin the prayer, remind the students that Yahweh, "I am the One who is always present," is indeed present in their midst. Invite the ten previously assigned students to read the Commandments in order, pausing after each for quiet reflection. Then invite the class to offer prayers of petition. End with the students reading aloud together Exodus 34:6–7, the passage on the attributes of God.

 ## Closing Teacher Prayer

Call to prayer. Be still within and without. Center yourself in the God of mercy.

Reflect. What have you learned in the process of teaching this chapter? Was it a learning of the head or the heart? Does this reveal God more fully to you? How? What effect could this learning have on your life?

Pray.
Merciful God,
heal us of our brokenness,
purify us of our sinfulness.
As in the time of Passover,
you spared the lives of your people;
spare us now, O God.
You released your people from death;
release us from that which holds us captive,
and renew your covenant of life in us. Amen.

(Bergan and Schwan, *Taste and See:*
Prayer Services for Gatherings of Faith)

CHAPTER 4

The Law:
Living Out the Covenant

Major Concepts

A. **Leviticus: Holiness and Ritual.** The whole collection of laws from Exodus through Deuteronomy, known as the Law of Moses, spells out more precisely how Israel is to keep the Covenant. The Book of Leviticus provides instructions for Israel's worship. Besides regulations for rituals, Leviticus, in its Holiness Code, teaches how to live out the holiness of worship in just and compassionate relationships. It also describes sacrificial rituals of atonement that provide much of the language Christians use to characterize Jesus Christ's redemption of the world. *See* the *Catechism,* nos. 433, 578 (Yom Kippur); 457, 580, 601, 613–615, 654 (the atonement of Jesus); 1539 (the priesthood); 1544, 2747 (Christ as the High Priest); 1804 (virtues); 1807, 1889, 2055, 2062, 2658 (the love of God and neighbor); 1961–1964 (the Old Law); 2096–2100 (worship and sacrifice); 2129 (idolatry); 2449 (love for the poor); 2811 (holiness, idolatry).

B. **Numbers: Priestly Regulations and Inspiring Stories.** This book consists of priestly regulations, a census report, and more tales of Israel's wilderness wanderings. The Israelites grumble about their plight and challenge Moses' authority. They continue to falter in their trust in God's care for them. In the generation that came from Egypt, only Caleb and Joshua will reach the Promised Land. Even Moses and Aaron will not enter Canaan because God punishes them for treating the Israelites irreverently. Soothsayer Balaam predicts that Israel will overcome other nations and refers to a star coming from Jacob, which early Christians interpreted as a prophecy of Christ's coming. *See* the *Catechism,* nos. 121–123 (the importance of the Old Testament for Christians); 222–227 (faith); 303 (divine providence); 431 (God's forgiveness); 436–437, 711–712 (the Messiah); 525 (a star); 672 (sin and the Church); 751, 759–762, 1093 (the Church's origin); 1539, 1541 (the Levites); 2576–2577 (Moses' relationship with God, Miriam's healings).

C. **Deuteronomy: The Law and Love.** This book repeats the story of Israel's liberation and Covenant with God by way of three sermons attributed to Moses, addressed to the Israelites at the brink of the Promised Land. Deuteronomy stresses the importance of keeping the Law, and reminds readers of how God never ceased to care for the Israelites during their long journey from Egypt to Canaan. Based on a code of laws discovered in the Temple about thirty years before the exile, Deuteronomy was composed by the Deuteronomists, who were probably part of a Jewish reform movement calling for strict adherence to an extensive legal code. The Shema is at the heart of all Deuteronomy's laws, recalling the Covenant's essence—God loves us and we must love God above all. Deuteronomy closes with Moses dying and Joshua leading Israel. *See* the *Catechism,* nos. 201, 2083, 2096–2097 (the Shema); 214, 218–219, 303 (God's love for Israel); 538–539 (the temptation of Jesus); 709, 1961–1962 (the Law); 710 (the exile); 2055, 2083, 2196 (the Great Commandment); 2056–2063 (the Decalogue); 2061 (the love of God and the Law); 2449 (love for the poor).

4

Opening Teacher Prayer

Call to prayer. Be still within and without. Center yourself in God, who calls us to trust.

Read. Psalm 131

Reflect. In what particular area of your life are you most reluctant to surrender your fears and concerns to God in trust? What makes you worry and feel anxious?

Keep in your heart. "I have calmed and quieted my soul" (Ps. 131:2).

Concept A: Leviticus: Holiness and Ritual

Pages 78–81

Review Questions: Leviticus: Holiness and Ritual

Question. List three names given to the whole collection of laws that spell out the terms and specifics of the Covenant.
Answer. The Law of Moses, the Mosaic Law, or simply the Law.

Question. What kind of handbook is the Book of Leviticus?
Answer. A handbook of instructions for Israel's worship.

Question. Why did the Israelites offer animal sacrifices?
Answer. They sacrificed animals as an atonement for sins, to repair the damaged relationship between themselves and God. The animal's blood, poured out on the altar, signified life itself given to express the offerer's sorrow; the altar signified the presence of God.

Question. What is Yom Kippur today?
Answer. It is the Day of Atonement, the holiest day of the year, when Jews atone for their sins of the past year. The ritual no longer includes animal sacrifice.

Question. What are three moral teachings found in the Holiness Code in the Book of Leviticus? Why does Leviticus include moral teachings along with instructions for worship?

Answer. [Any three of the following teachings are correct.]
- leaving some of the harvest for the poor to glean
- not withholding a laborer's wages until the next day
- not cursing the deaf or putting a stumbling block before the blind
- not taking vengeance or bearing a grudge ("loving your neighbor as yourself")
- not oppressing foreigners, but treating them as you would your own people
- not fashioning dishonest weights and measures
- calling a jubilee every fifty years in which debts are canceled and people have an opportunity to redeem lost property

The moral teachings are included because they show how true worship is expressed in a person's everyday life, in just and compassionate relationships. Holiness is not simply observing the right rituals but also loving God, which is shown through loving one's neighbor.

 ## Text Activities: Leviticus: Holiness and Ritual

- Write a brief reflection on this question: *If someone goes to church each Sunday and keeps the rules of his or her religion but shows little or no concern for justice and peace—as reflected in the virtues listed here—can that person be considered a good Christian?*
- In writing, describe a time when you felt the need to be forgiven by someone.
  - Were you conscious of being sorry for your wrongdoing?
  - Were you aware of the need to admit your fault and take responsibility for it?
  - Did you have a desire to make up for the offense?
  Catholic Tradition includes these concerns as part of the elements of a good confession in the Sacrament of Penance and Reconciliation: contrition, confession, and satisfaction.
- Create and write down a holiness code for your school, family, workplace, or community. Name at least six "musts" for expressing love of neighbor. How might you apply the concept of jubilee to your holiness code?

 ## Additional Activities: Leviticus: Holiness and Ritual

A Sense of God's Presence: Spiritual Guides

The Book of Leviticus calls Israel to worship the all-holy God depicted in Exodus 34:5–9. In this passage Moses meets God face-to-face. We, however, acquire our sense of who God is from other people. Ask your students to explore their personal history of learning about God:
- We learn about God from other people. List the five people who have most shaped your notion of what God is like.
- Now describe how each of these people has contributed to your sense of what God is like. Give examples of talks you have had with them, events you have experienced with them, behaviors or attitudes you have observed in them, and so on.
- Finally, next to each person's name, write down the predominant image of God that that person gave you (God as liberator, creator, or law enforcer, for example).

Invite your students to share in small groups their reflections on the people who have shaped their image of God.

Why We Need Regulations for Worship

Perhaps the reason we need regulations for worship rituals is not clear to your students. Here are some questions to use in discussing our need for certain set patterns of worship:

- ◆ One way to think about the Levitical regulations for worship is to compare worship to a basketball game. Imagine that you go to a Friday night game here at school. What patterns, rituals, or regulations are followed at every game? [The teams' pregame warmup, the crowds' sitting on home and visitor sides, the playing of the national anthem, the introduction of the teams, the tip-off, and so on. On the chalkboard, list all the patterns, rituals, or regulations that the students call out.]
- ◆ Why do we have all these rituals and regulations at basketball games?
- ◆ If basketball games had no rituals and regulations, would we know a basketball game if we saw it?
- ◆ What patterns, rituals, and regulations have you experienced at Mass or other worship services? [List the students' answers on the chalkboard.]
- ◆ What purpose do you think rituals and regulations serve in worship?

Summarize by explaining that regulations for worship are necessary so that the worship is identifiable and purposeful for a group. In ancient times regulations for worship took on greater importance for Israel than for other peoples because Israel's God was different from pagan gods. The Israelites' worship demonstrated that they had one God who loved and chose them, and their worship gave them a sense of their identity as a loved and Chosen People. Thus, all the regulations for worship found in Leviticus were experienced by the Israelites not as oppressive but as essential to their identity.

Leviticus: Laws to Live By Today

Handout **4–A**

1. To discuss the relevance of the Holiness Code today, divide your class into ten small groups and distribute handout 4–A, "Laws to Live By Today." Assign each group a passage and tell students to discuss it and its related question from the handout. You may want to assign to the students who do Leviticus 19:16 the task of finding out about the Kitty Genovese case of 1964. In this case a woman was stabbed to death in New York City as thirty-seven people witnessed the attack but failed to call the police. Tell them to prepare a response to be shared with the whole class.

2. After you have discussed these laws as a class, point out that the inscription on the U.S. Liberty Bell, "Proclaim liberty throughout the land," comes from Leviticus 25:10. Ask the students to read that scriptural excerpt in the context of Leviticus 25:8–22, which describes the jubilee year, and to comment on why the passage inscribed on the Liberty Bell is particularly appropriate for a country founded on the principle of equality.

3. End this activity by posing these questions for class discussion:
◆ Do you see a difference between laws that are concerned with cultural customs or experiences and those that state unchangeable moral principles? Can you give some examples?

The Jubilee Year

The jubilee year sounds like a wonderful idea, especially to people who are in debt or who have lost their property. It supports the ideal of God as the true owner of the land and the Israelites as tenants, with the point being that land monopolized by a few is contrary to the will of God.

1. Discuss the following questions with the class:
◆ If we were to experience a jubilee year in our age, what might that look like?
◆ What would be the happy effects of having a jubilee year as described in Leviticus [25:8–22]?
◆ If such a thing as a jubilee year were in effect today, who would complain about it, and why?
◆ Would our society be better off if it had a jubilee year?
◆ Would anyone really suffer in a jubilee year?

2. Ask your students each to write down ten ways that a jubilee year would affect their family and to compose a paragraph either agreeing or disagreeing with this statement:
◆ I wish that we had a jubilee year in our time.

Concept B: Numbers: Priestly Regulations and Inspiring Stories

Review Questions: Numbers: Priestly Regulations and Inspiring Stories

Question. What is the lesson for the Israelites and us in the story of the quail in the desert?
Answer. That God will provide, especially when things look bleak. He will give us far more than we ever dreamed of.

Question. Name two instances of rebellion against Moses' authority in the desert.
Answer. First Moses' own sister and brother, Miriam and Aaron, claim they have authority equal to Moses'. God rebukes them, saying that only Moses sees the Lord face-to-face or intimately. Miriam's skin becomes diseased, and she holds up her people's journey while she spends a week outside the camp for purification. In another story someone challenges Moses and Aaron's authority, and others incite a political rebellion, accusing Moses of leading Israel out of Egypt on a wild-goose chase. The rebels and their families are de-

stroyed, and God gives a sign—almond blossoms growing from Aaron's staff—to confirm that Aaron's tribe has been chosen for the priesthood and is not to be challenged.

Question. According to Numbers, why will Caleb and Joshua be allowed to enter the Promised Land, but Moses and Aaron will not?

Answer. Because Caleb and Joshua trusted in God's power to protect them in Canaan. God is angry about Moses and Aaron's sarcastic outburst at the Israelites at Kadesh, which changed the people's experience from one of renewed faith to one of fear, so God punishes the brothers. God tells them they will die without entering Canaan because they have not shown forth his holiness in how they treated the people.

Question. How did the early Christians understand the oracle of Balaam about a star from Jacob?

Answer. They saw it as a prophecy of Christ's coming. The nativity story in Matthew's Gospel with its reference to a star also helped the first Jewish Christians understand that Jesus was the Promised One.

 ## Text Activities: Numbers: Priestly Regulations and Inspiring Stories

- *Providence* means that God provides us with what we need, when we need it—sometimes through an event or a person. What are the things you need in your life that are provided for you? Where do they come from? Write a poem or a prayer reflecting an experience of providence and your feelings about it.
- Find a psalm in which the writer describes how God is with us (or pleads for God to be with us) when we are frightened or in trouble. Identify the number of the psalm and write a few paragraphs reflecting what that psalm means to you. Apply it, if possible, to a risk you have taken in your life or a dangerous situation you found yourself in.
- Explain in writing what this story tells us about the ways God wants us to treat one another. Think of a situation in your school, city, country, or the world where people are not being treated in a way that reflects God's holiness. Describe the causes of the mistreatment and what needs to happen for change to come about.

 ## Additional Activities: Numbers: Priestly Regulations and Inspiring Stories

The Forbidding Sinai Desert

Refer the students to the map titled "Out of Egypt to the Wilderness and Promised Land" on page 87 of their text, which shows the traditional, though disputed, route of the Israelites in the Exodus. Encourage the students to imagine what it must have been like to wander in the desert for so many years. No doubt it was at times terrifying for the Israelites.

4

Assign a group of students to find out what a day in the Sinai desert might be like now:
- the average temperature of both day and night
- the availability of water
- distances between major towns or oases
- the terrain
- the flora and fauna
- health hazards

Grumbling Versus Being Grateful

In Numbers 11:1–15 the Israelites complain bitterly, once again, about their food. Like students who grow tired of cafeteria food, the Israelites want tastier things to eat. Moses is upset and despairs, asking God to do him the favor of killing him. First (in the Book of Exodus) the Israelites demanded food, and God sent manna. Now they are tired of the manna and want meat. Are they never satisfied? Satisfaction, of course, depends on one's perspective.

Ask the students each to list three times when they have been dissatisfied with or have grumbled about something that was adequate but not all they had hoped for. (Their lists might include cafeteria food, their own appearance, their means of transportation, their clothes, their vacation opportunities.) Tell the students to choose one of their examples and write a brief essay that compares their situation with that of the Israelites in Numbers 11:1–15. Their essay should answer this question:

◆ How could I turn disappointment and grumbling into a spirit of gratitude for all that God has given me?

Moses' Heavy Burden

In Numbers 11:14–15 Moses is in terrible distress about the constant complaining of the Israelites. His burden seems just too heavy. Read the passage from Numbers aloud to your students. Then tell them to write their reflections on these questions:

◆ Have you ever had an experience like that of Moses, a time when you felt that the burden on your shoulders was far too heavy? Describe the experience.
◆ How did you cope with the pressure?
◆ What part, if any, did you ask God to play in dealing with your problem?

Building Community: Overcoming the Effects of Sin

Numbers, chapter 12, describes the destructiveness caused by Miriam and Aaron's jealousy of Moses and their attempt to gain power. Conduct a class discussion about overcoming such destructive attitudes and behaviors as they exist in a community or a group of friends. These questions could help the discussion:

◆ Can you cite some similar examples of destructiveness from around school, in families, at work, or in your parish—examples of times when pettiness or jealousy, competitiveness or backbiting hurt the efforts of a group?

- ◆ Can one person in an organization successfully block that organization's efforts?
- ◆ What nourishes solidarity in families, among friends, or in school?
- ◆ Give an example of an activity that this class could undertake in order to build solidarity in a community that is trying to work together.

The Risks of Faith

The Israelites do not want to cross into territory where they might run into trouble—a land supposedly peopled by giants. Despite God's rescuing them time and again, they do not have enough faith to follow God's lead into the Promised Land. Faith demands some sort of leap into the unknown. Nothing is ever accomplished without faith.

1. To illustrate this point, ask your students to respond to these questions:
- ◆ Is faith required when a person wants to go out on a date with someone? If so, describe the aspects of faith that are required.
- ◆ When a person tries out for a team, a band, or a club, is faith involved? How?
- ◆ When two people decide to get married, is faith required? Why?
- ◆ Is anything ever really accomplished without faith—that is, without taking a leap into the unknown?
- ◆ Is there a difference between faith as we have described it and a simple lack of appropriate caution? Explain.

2. Then give these instructions to your students:
- ◆ In writing, describe one of your own leaps of faith—a time when you put your trust in someone or something or even in yourself and took a leap into the unknown. What did you learn from the experience? How were you better off after taking the leap?

World Happenings

Ask the students to read the sidebar "World Happenings from 1700 to 1250 BC" on page 83 of the student text, which describes events and developments that occurred near the time when the Israelites wandered in the desert outside of Canaan. Then pose these questions for discussion:
- ◆ How were the Israelites primitive in comparison with some other cultures of the time? [They had no nation as such; they were nomads. They had not settled into a stable life of agriculture, nor had they begun the production of implements. They were certainly not powerful enough to build an empire, although they could fend off enemies. They had no leadership comparable to a king or a pharaoh.]
- ◆ In what way were the Israelites advanced? [Give the students a hint: Point out the sidebar paragraph called "India," which mentions a Hindu hymn praising "the unknown god," who is lord of all that exists. Explain that the monotheistic belief expressed in the hymn was not typical of the ancient Hindu culture; the Hindus believed in thousands of deities. Polytheism was the dominant form of belief in ancient times. Allow the students to conclude that the relatively "uncultured" Israelites were onto an insight that would change the world—belief in the one God.]

God Always Loves Us

Review with the students the dynamics of God's relationship with the Israelites in the Book of Numbers.

According to the account in Numbers, God periodically becomes angry with individuals or with the whole people of Israel, but God is constantly extending another chance to them, is always ready to forgive and forget and start all over again with them.

The following discussion is intended to reinforce the point that God always loves us. Begin by asking your students these questions:

◆ How many of you have heard someone say, "God doesn't love you when you do this or that"? Is that statement ever true?
◆ Why do people say things like that?
◆ Do most people act as if they believe that God loves them?
◆ What actions tell you that a person believes in God's unconditional love?

Make the following statement to your class:

◆ God loves us always, unconditionally, and never stops loving us, even when we sin. This is not to say that sin does not alter our relationship with God, but any change is our doing, not God's. We, not God, are altered by sin. Sin can harden our heart and close our mind so that in time we love less and less, but it never changes God's love for us. Despite their somewhat primitive notion of God, the Israelites who wandered in the desert believed deeply in the constancy of God's love for them.

Concept C: Deuteronomy: The Law and Love

Review Questions: Deuteronomy: The Law and Love

Question. What device or style of writing was used as a framework for the Book of Deuteronomy?
Answer. The story is set into the framework of three sermons by Moses to the Israelites as they stand on the plains of Moab poised to cross the Jordan River and enter the Promised Land.

Question. Give three examples of laws in Deuteronomy.
Answer. [Any three of the following laws are correct.]
• Every seven years debts must be forgiven, although the approach of a "release year" must not deter one from lending money to a poor neighbor.
• Slaves who have served six years must be released in the seventh.
• Interest on a loan may be demanded of a foreigner but not of an Israelite.
• Selling an Israelite into slavery is punishable by death.
• Millstones owned by the poor may not be taken in pledge for a loan because people cannot grind flour without millstones.
• Parents and children may not be punished for each other's crimes.

Pages 86–91

Question. What is the Shema? Explain its importance in Judaism.

Answer. At the heart of all the laws in Deuteronomy is the great prayer called the Shema (from the Hebrew word that begins the prayer, meaning "hear"). Called the essence of Judaism, this prayer has been repeated daily by Jews from biblical times up to the present and reminds them that God is one, and the one whom they are to love with their entire being—heart, soul, and strength.

Question. Which Gospel stories show that Jesus was inspired by God's Word in the Book of Deuteronomy?

Answer. Jesus quoted Deuteronomy 6:5, about love of God, to the Pharisees who tried to trip him up with their question about which commandment of the Law was the greatest. In another Gospel passage, the story of Christ's temptation in the desert, Jesus likewise used verses from Deuteronomy three times to respond to the devil's temptations.

 ## Text Activities: Deuteronomy: The Law and Love

- In writing, share a story that is told and retold in your family. What special meaning or message does the story hold?
- Find a newspaper or magazine article that depicts a situation in which sensitivity and care are being shown to a person or group who is oppressed or poor. Write your reactions to the article.
- In the Shema the Jews attempt to express and pass on their burning love for God. Has someone in your life passed on a sense of God's love to you? If so, write about this person and the ways she or he has taught you about God's love. Also reflect on any opportunities you have taken to pass on a sense of God's love to another.
- Compose an essay, a cartoon, a poem, or a song that retells one of the stories about ancient Israel's journey through the wilderness. Use a modern setting and modern characters.

 ## Additional Activities: Deuteronomy: The Law and Love

Is God Too Loving?

Some people claim that there is a danger in making God seem too understanding, too compassionate, too forgiving. They declare that "a little fear doesn't do anyone any harm." Pose these questions to your students:

- ◆ Do people find a loving God harder to believe in than a tough, demanding God? Why or why not?
- ◆ Does too much emphasis on God's love lead to an attitude of "anything goes"?
- ◆ Is it possible to believe in a perfectly loving and forgiving God but not have an attitude of "anything goes"? How do we reconcile God's love for us with God's expectations of us?
- ◆ How would you explain that God is perfectly loving?

The Law and Showing Off How Good We Are

One of the problems with having many religious rules to follow is that some people begin making their observance of the rules a source of boastful pride. Following the rules of a religion is not, in itself, particularly virtuous. Moses knew this, and so did the long line of Israelite prophets who came after him. Unfortunately, by the time of Jesus, the Pharisees and many scribes had forgotten the greatest commandment—to love God above all else—and the commandment to love one's neighbor. However, they scrupulously followed the letter of the other laws. To examine Jesus' perception of the Law, use the following activity:

1. Read Matthew 23:1–6 aloud to your class. Then ask the students what they think the passage implies. After this, remind them that Jesus came to fulfill the Law and that the heart of the Law is loving God and loving our neighbor as we love ourselves.

2. Read aloud Numbers 15:37–41. This passage explains the reference to tassels that the students heard in Matthew 23:5. It indicates that the tassels' purpose is to remind the people of the Commandments—not to show off their rigid adherence to the Law, as if they, not God, were responsible for their salvation.

3. Finally, pose these questions to your students:
◆ Orthodox Jews today use the tassels and other symbols, such as phylacteries (see the sidebar "The Prayer of Israel: The Shema" on p. 92 of the student text), as reminders to keep the Commandments and be holy. What symbols do Christians have as reminders to keep the Commandments?
◆ Nothing is stopping any of us from creating our own symbolic reminder about keeping the Commandments. If you were to make such a symbol, what would it be? [To take this exercise a step further, instruct the students each to design and make some symbol they can wear to remind themselves of the Commandments. It should be unobtrusive but have religious significance.]

The Shema: The "Creed" of Judaism

Explain to the students that Judaism has no official creed, such as the Christian Nicene Creed. However, the Shema—the scriptural verses in the sidebar on page 92—contains the essence of the Jewish faith. Recited daily by Jews, morning and night, the Shema is what Judaism is all about.

Ask the students to read the Shema. The Shema expresses the reality that love for the one God is at the heart of the Jewish faith; for Jews, this love is the most important value in life. In fact the Shema is so crucial to the faith of Jews that besides being a daily prayer, it is taught to Jewish children as soon as they can speak, as one of their first learnings. Also, the last words uttered by religious Jews when they are dying, or prayed for them if they are too weak to speak, are those of the Shema. Thus the proclamation of Israel's love for the one God is among the Jewish person's earliest conscious memories and last life experiences.

Explain to the students that some uninformed people assume that Jews are law-bound and unlike Christians, who are love-bound. People with this perspective do not understand the essence of Judaism, which is love of God. Suggest this exercise to the students:

◆ The point can be made that whatever a culture teaches first to its children and expresses at the time of a person's death must certainly reflect the central values of that culture. Think about the culture of which you are a part: North American, Christian, and so on. If you had to think of one thing that is most typically taught first to children in your culture, and one thing that usually happens as a person in your culture is dying, what would those things be? How do they express the values of your culture? How are they different from or similar to the values of Jewish culture?

No Promised Land for Moses: Unfair?

Some students might raise strong objections to Moses' being forbidden to enter the Promised Land. After his heroic struggles with a recalcitrant mob, he is allowed to look at Canaan from atop a mountain, but this is like a starving person looking from afar at a rich banquet. Little explanation for Moses' punishment is given in the Bible. All it says is that Moses doubted God's power and relied instead on his own tongue-lashing to get the people to stop grumbling and that this made him unworthy to enter the Promised Land.

Urge the students to consider whether God is unjust in the story. The answer, of course, is no. Moses has been granted a privilege no one has ever had before: he has met and communicated with God face-to-face. Moses' face has glowed radiantly after these meetings with God. In all of Moses' trials, God has never failed him. Yet, nearing the final leg of the journey, Moses thinks that his efforts can shape up the Israelites, and in so doing he denies that all along God has been guiding him and Israel. God is just in denying Moses the last reward because if Moses were allowed to enter the Promised Land, the people would forget that God is in charge of all their affairs—and that not one of them, not even Moses, is exempt from having to trust entirely in God. If Moses were to enter the Promised Land, the people might give him, not God, the credit for getting them there.

The story of Moses, the greatest of the prophets, reminds us that no matter how great a human being is, that person is still utterly in the hands of God. When we forget that fact, we can begin to think that we human beings are gods.

The Route of the Exodus

Direct the students to the map titled "Out of Egypt to the Wilderness and Promised Land" on page 87 of the student text, which shows the route traditionally hypothesized as the one taken by the Israelites from Egypt to Canaan. Using the scale of miles on the map, tell the students to calculate approximately the number of miles that the Israelites would have traveled on this route, which according to the Scriptures took them forty years.

Then ask the students to imagine that the Israelites traveled the straightest and shortest possible land route from Egypt to Canaan; have them calculate approximately what that distance would have been. Ask them how many miles longer the traditionally hypothesized journey is. (The trip shown on the map is about 880 miles, and the shortest possible trip is about 330 miles.) Point out to the students that the Israelites wandered, stopping for a while at various places rather than traveling nonstop. Then make comments such as these:

◆ We can view the Israelites' journey from Egypt to Canaan as symbolic of a person's inner journey—for example, from the slavery of a bitter attitude or a bad habit to the freedom of a hopeful, caring attitude or a better way of acting. The Israelites certainly wanted to get to the Promised Land and at times were impatient when they had not yet arrived.

Pose these questions for discussion:

◆ How is the slowness and roundabout nature of the Israelites' journey like a person's inner journey?

◆ In a personal journey as well as in the Israelites' journey, why is the shortest, fastest possible route not necessarily the best one?

◆ By taking the longer, slower route, what lessons did the Israelites learn that they might not have learned if they had arrived at the Promised Land quickly?

◆ Give an example of how a person on an inner journey might benefit from taking the longer, slower route, even though that route seems full of troubles.

Handout **4–B**

Closing Prayer

Handout 4–B, "My Help Comes from God," can be used by your students as a closing prayer. In advance select one student to read the passage from Numbers and one to lead the litany, which is adapted from Leviticus.

Closing Teacher Prayer

Call to prayer. Be still within and without. Center yourself in God's goodness.

Reflect. What have you learned in the process of teaching this chapter? Was it a learning of the head or the heart? Does this reveal God more fully to you? How? What effect could this learning have on your life?

Pray.
Dear God, at the center of life
is the mystery of trust and surrender.
It is the heart of love,
the spring of new life and all creative effort,
and the touchstone of true freedom.
Help us to trust in your promises. Amen.

(Bergan and Schwan, *Taste and See:
Prayer Services for Gatherings of Faith*)

Laws to Live By Today

- *Leviticus 19:9–10.* How could the spirit of this law be followed today?

- *Leviticus 19:11.* How does this law relate to modern attitudes toward income taxes, testimony in court, the setting of prices, and the destruction of reputations through gossip, published articles, or books?

- *Leviticus 19:13.* What does this law tell us about the situation of the working poor and our duties, in justice, to them?

- *Leviticus 19:14.* Do we put stumbling blocks in front of people with disabilities today, for instance, in parking lots? in buildings? in employment? anywhere else?

- *Leviticus 19:15.* Does our society treat weak or poor people differently than it does rich or powerful people? Cite some examples.

- *Leviticus 19:16.* Can you recall any news stories about people standing by idly while a neighbor was killed or assaulted?

- *Leviticus 19:17.* Give an example of how we might incur sin because of our hatred for someone. Can the law apply to nations as well as to individuals?

- *Leviticus 19:18.* List four practical examples of how this law could be followed in your own life.

- *Leviticus 19:33.* How does this law relate to our treatment of migrant workers, undocumented aliens, refugees, and immigrants?

- *Leviticus 19:35.* Give an example of how this law could be applied in a business today. Be specific about the kind of business.

My Help Comes from God

A Reading from the Book of Numbers

Reader. The LORD spoke to Moses, saying: Speak to Aaron and his sons, saying, Thus you shall bless the Israelites: You shall say to them,
> The LORD bless you and keep you;
> the LORD make his face to shine upon you, and be gracious to you;
> the LORD lift up his countenance upon you, and give you peace.

So they shall put my name on the Israelites, and I will bless them.

(6:22–27)

A Litany in the Spirit of Leviticus, Chapter 19

Leader. May we always remember the poor, the needy, the victims of oppression. They are God's children just as we are. God, grant us the strength to aid your poor. For this grace we pray.

All. God, hear your people.

Leader. Trustworthy God, may we deal with one another truthfully. Just as we owe you truth, so we owe it to one another. And because we hate to be deceived, may we never deceive our neighbor. For this grace we pray.

All. God, hear your people.

Leader. God of the poor, protect all workers who are being exploited. May we struggle for justice and the dignity of all people who work, especially migrants and those who work in sweatshops in developing countries. Encourage and watch over those who want to find employment but cannot. For this we pray.

All. God, hear your people.

Leader. Loving God, may we be advocates for the rights of persons with disabilities. Help us learn from them and appreciate their unique contributions to humankind. For them we pray.

All. God, hear your people.

Leader. God, our liberator, stop us from stooping to slander and lies, gossip and half-truths. May we speak kindly, justly, carefully, and honestly. For this grace we pray.

All. God, hear your people.

Leader. Most essentially, loving God, give us the courage to love our neighbors as ourselves and to love you with our whole being. For this grace we pray.

All. God, hear your people.

[Other petitions may be offered.]

Psalm 121: A Prayer of Total Trust in God

All. I lift my eyes to the mountains.
Where is help to come from?
My help comes from Yahweh,
who made Heaven and earth.
Yahweh does not let our footsteps slip!
Our guard does not sleep!
The guardian of Israel
does not slumber or sleep.
Yahweh guards you, shades you.
With Yahweh at your right hand
the sun cannot harm you by day
nor the moon at night.
Yahweh guards you from harm,
protects your lives;
Yahweh watches over your coming and going,
now and for always.

Amen.

CHAPTER 5

The Land:
Finding Hope for the Future
in God's Gift

Major Concepts

A. **Making Sense of the Past.** During the Babylonian Exile, the Deuteronomists composed a history of the Israelites from the time they entered the Promised Land. This history served as a self-examination for the Israelites, which helped them turn the despair of the exile into a time to build new hope for the future in their homeland. *See* the *Catechism,* nos. 401 (Israel's infidelity); 710, 2811 (the exile).

B. **Joshua: Sweeping into the Promised Land.** The Book of Joshua offers miraculous accounts of Joshua and the Israelites entering the Promised Land and settling there. These accounts show that the Israelites' taking of the land was a gift from God, not something they achieved on their own. Joshua represents everything Israel was supposed to be—completely faithful to God. The overriding message of the accounts of the Jericho conquest and other battles is that victory comes when people place their trust entirely in God. Joshua divides the land among the twelve tribes of Israel and sets aside cities of refuge. *See* the *Catechism,* nos. 62, 218–219, 227, 301, 303, 2097 (trust in God); 142–144 (the obedience of faith); 309–314 (God brings good out of evil); 401 (Israel's infidelity); 707 (Joshua); 1911 (refugees); 2112–2114 (idolatry).

C. **Judges: Saving Israel from Itself.** The Book of Judges tells stories of God raising up tribal leaders called judges to deliver Israel from destruction. In each story the Israelites follow a cycle of unfaithfulness to God, disaster, repentance, and deliverance. Twelve judges are mentioned in the Book of Judges, six of them major. They are not always faithful to God either, which proves to be the undoing of both Gideon and Samson. Some of the stories are gruesome, like that of Deborah and Jael. The purpose of the stories is to recount the many ways that God helped free Israel from its enemies. *See* the *Catechism,* nos. 64 (Deborah); 401, 710 (Israel's infidelity); 431, 2084 (God delivers); 2112–2114 (idolatry).

D. **Ruth: An Israelite Foreigner with a Great Destiny.** The Book of Ruth teaches how God brings good out of difficulty and tells how King David came to have a Gentile as his great-grandmother. Ruth, a Moabite, pledges to remain with her mother-in-law, Naomi, despite the anticipated destitution they will face in Israel. Ruth's pledge binds her not only to Naomi but to the God of Israel and the Israelites. Ruth's loyalty and selflessness impress Boaz, who later marries her. Although Ruth's nationality by law excluded her from membership in the Israelite community, she becomes the Lord's choice as forebear to the greatest king in Israel's history. The Books of Joshua, Judges, and Ruth all portray a God of surprises who brings good out of the darkest times and characters, leaving us with a powerful message of hope. *See* the *Catechism,* nos. 312–314 (providence and evil); 1611 (Ruth); 2579 (David).

5

Opening Teacher Prayer

Call to prayer. Be still within and without. Remember that it is God who accompanies us in our victories and our losses; God wants the best for us. Center yourself in the peace of knowing God's ever abiding presence.

Read. Psalm 20

Reflect. Recall a time you were in trouble—either as a victim or because of your own mistakes or choices. Were you aware of God's presence at that time? Looking back, how did God help you?

Hold in your heart. "May he grant you your heart's desire, / and fulfill all your plans" (Ps. 20:4).

Concept A: Making Sense of the Past

Review Questions: Making Sense of the Past

Question. Which biblical books are considered part of the Deuteronomic history?
Answer. Joshua, Judges, the First and Second Books of Samuel, and the First and Second Books of Kings.

Question. What purpose did this history serve for the Jews in exile?
Answer. The history served as a self-examination for the people of Israel. It helped turn the disaster of the exile into a time of reflection and transformation, filling the exiles' hearts with hope and readying them for their return to their homeland.

Text Activity: Making Sense of the Past

• Over and over in the Old Testament, we hear about the mistakes of the Israelites and the people and events that helped them get back on track. God offers us *unlimited* chances to turn from our mistakes—no matter what we have done—and to start over. It's always *our* choice, however, to make a fresh start. Have you ever had the opportunity to pause and examine your past? What did you discover? As a result of your reflecting, did you choose to make any changes? Describe in writing what it feels like to be given another chance, and the transformation and hope that can accompany that moment.

 ## Additional Activities: Making Sense of the Past

Exile and Transformation

A time of exile like the ancient Israelites experienced can plant and nurture the seeds of transformation. Either the direct experience of exile or the empathetic understanding of it can effect profound change in people.

1. Show a movie that deals with the theme of exile and transformation. Ask the students to keep in mind the theme, which can help us understand the experience of the ancient Israelites in exile.

2. After the film is shown, pose the following questions for class discussion:
- ◆ Describe the experience of exile in the movie—who experienced it? what was it like? and so on. How did the person cope?
- ◆ How was the person in exile changed? Do you think the person would have changed had the exile not been experienced?
- ◆ Why was the exile so painful for the ancient Israelites, and how did they cope? Who was to blame for it?
- ◆ How did God help the exiles?
- ◆ Is exile always deserved, or can it be the result of ignorance or hatred?
- ◆ What are some experiences of exile, or rejection, that people today experience?
- ◆ What makes the difference between a person's exile being a change for the better or a crushing experience?

3. For homework have the students write a short fictional piece that shows how experiencing exile helps to transform a person's character.

Self-Examination

This activity can help the students to reflect on how their past behavior affects the present and to seek awareness of and forgiveness for the times they have been unfaithful.

1. Tell the students:
- ◆ The Exile served as a time for the ancient Israelites to examine their collective conscience and understand how their past had led them to the painful place in which they found themselves. Once they understood their mistakes, they could begin to make changes that would bring them closer to God again.
- ◆ Although nothing as momentous as the Exile usually occurs in our life, sin by its very nature exiles us from God and from one another. Today in class we will examine our own conscience by asking how faithful and loving we have been to God, to others, and to ourselves.

5

Handout **5–A**

2. Distribute handout 5–A, "'O LORD, You Have Searched Me and Known Me,'" an examination of conscience. Begin with a few moments of quiet to recall God's holy presence and to allow the students to enter into the reflection. You may wish to play meditative music in the background.

3. End the reflection time by praying Psalm 139:1–18. Keep the reflective music on and invite the students to close their eyes while you read the psalm slowly. When you are done, ask the students to write a brief prayer at the bottom of their handout (or on the other side), asking God for whatever strength or healing they need in their life—especially that which will help them to be more faithful, more the person God has called them to be.

5

Option. You may wish to design a reconciliation service around this activity and invite a priest to celebrate the sacrament of Penance and Reconciliation with your class.

Pages
96–
103

Concept B: Joshua: Sweeping into the Promised Land

Review Questions: Joshua: Sweeping into the Promised Land

Question. What was the practice known as the ban? Explain a lesson that the scriptural accounts of the ban contained for the Jews.
Answer. The ban was essentially an order to destroy everything in a conquered town and to take nothing for one's own. The scriptural accounts of the ban taught the Jews how totally and exclusively they were to devote themselves to God. The accounts of the ban also served partly as a warning to Jews against having anything to do with other religions and their terrible practices, such as child sacrifice and fertility rites involving temple prostitutes.

Question. What characteristics of Joshua made him a model for the exiled Jews to follow?
Answer. Joshua was strong, courageous, careful, honest, unshaken by failure, a keeper of treaties, and an upholder of the Law. Also, his heart was on fire with love for God, and by obeying him, he brought Israel into the Promised Land.

Text Activities: Joshua: Sweeping into the Promised Land

- Reminders to keep God's Law can sound like "how to keep God happy." But morality, far from being something we must do to *please God,* is meant to *protect us.* Write a brief essay about a law that irks you. Argue both its pros and its cons, in separate paragraphs.
- *Read Psalm 114.* This psalm was written long after the events described in Joshua. Write your reactions to the language used by the writer.

- Even though Joshua was a great leader, he was humble before God. Taking off his sandals—as Moses did when he encountered God in the burning bush—was a sign of his awe and respect. List five things that cause you to feel awe and explain why.
- In writing or in art, create something that reflects what shalom means to you.
- In our culture, worshiping idols takes on various forms, such as spending excessive time and energy to accumulate wealth. Think of four other kinds of idol worship around us that could interfere with a person's devotion to God.
- Interview three people about the meaning of obedience: a parent or a grandparent, a priest or a religious sister or brother, and a peer. Explore with them the meanings that go deeper than our typical understanding of "doing what someone else tells you to do." Report your findings in an essay and include your own thoughts on the topic. How does this relate to the Israelites' understanding of obedience?
- Sanctuary was originally given to accidental murderers to protect them from the vengeance of the victim's survivors. Ironically, today sanctuary is often denied to innocent people from war-torn countries who are trying to escape being murdered. Find and read a newspaper or magazine article about refugees seeking sanctuary. Write your thoughts on the story and include your reaction to this question: *Do we have a moral obligation to offer sanctuary?*
- Joshua was a born leader—and Hitler was also. Write a paragraph about how to choose leaders who are worth following and how to avoid those who are not.

 ## Additional Activities: Joshua: Sweeping into the Promised Land

Relying on God's Power

This activity is meant to help the students understand the importance of humility: knowing how much we rely on God's grace for our accomplishments and needs.

1. Remind the students that the overriding message in the stories of Joshua is that when the people put their trust entirely in God, they are victorious.

2. Divide the class into groups of three or four to discuss the miraculous ways Joshua and his people. Then have the groups describe times in their own life when they placed all their trust in God and God helped them.

3. When the class reconvenes as a whole, call for volunteers to share stories from their group. Then ask these questions:
   - What happens when people begin to believe that they can accomplish good things without God's help?
   - How can we increase our trust that God will help us in times of need?

The Fall of Jericho: Notes on a Scholarly Controversy

The importance of the story of Jericho lies in the biblical writers' belief that God had helped the Israelites take the city. For your own information, however, and possibly for your students', it is interesting to learn that scholarly controversy surrounds the question of whether the Israelites actually took Jericho as described in the Book of Joshua. Because no evidence of walls or a major settlement from the period of Joshua remains, some archaeologists propose that Jericho was already in ruins when the Israelites arrived in Canaan around 1200 BC. The famous walls of the ancient city of Jericho may have been of a much earlier period.

Even before this archaeological explanation was proposed, biblical scholars had long thought that the account of the conquest of Jericho, developed by a late priestly source centuries after the supposed event, was actually a theoretical reconstruction of the capture of Jericho, rather than a living memory of it. In that light the capture of Jericho, whose legendary walls were supposedly impenetrable, represents the miraculous conquest of all Canaan with God's help; the theological importance of taking over the Promised Land is emphasized by the story of the fall of Jericho.

Whether the students would benefit from knowing of these scholarly hypotheses is a matter for your own judgment. The student text takes the stance that some kind of Israelite victory happened at Jericho—whether over a heavily fortified city or a small settlement—which formed the core of the biblical account. This is quite likely. However, the important point to emphasize with students is that the meaning of the scriptural account lies in its message that God was with the Israelites, enabling them to take the land that had been promised to them.

The Ban Lives On

1. Joshua's complete destruction of Jericho reflected a common military practice of his time. We now think of that practice as barbaric, but it is still going on. Help the students understand that practice of the ban is not dead, by discussing these questions:

- How does modern warfare still include the ban, even if we do not call it that anymore?
- How could nuclear warfare be considered the ultimate ban?
- Why did Joshua put the ban on Jericho? Were his reasons really any different from those that motivated the United States to drop the atomic bomb on Hiroshima and Nagasaki?
- The Israelites believed that God was on their side when they wiped out Jericho. Did the United States believe that God was on its side when it wiped out two Japanese cities with the atomic bomb?
- The ancient Israelites' image of God permitted the ban. Given the developments in Judaism's and Christianity's image of God, is there any room in the Judeo-Christian tradition today for the image of God that is exemplified by the ban, nuclear weapons, and chemical weapons?

2. Assign some students to prepare brief oral reports on the destructive capabilities of nuclear and chemical weapons, the use of defoliants in the Vietnam war, the scorched earth policy of the Germans in World War II, and General Sherman's march to the sea in the U.S. Civil War. The point to reinforce is

that if we are shocked by Joshua's putting the ban on Jericho, we should be just as horrified at these more recent practices, which are essentially equivalent to the ban.

A Star for Joshua: The Epic

Divide your class into groups of four or five students each and give them this task:
- Your group is casting a new movie about the life of Joshua. You must pick someone to play the part of Joshua. Of all the actors presently starring in films or TV shows, whom do you choose? After you have decided, prepare a list of reasons for your selection.

Allow the groups 10 minutes or so to come to their decision. Each group should select one spokesperson. Form the spokespersons into a group in the center of the classroom. They are to pick the star for the movie called *Joshua: The Epic,* while the rest of the class listens to their discussion.

When the group in the center has made its final choice, ask the class how well the star matches the biblical Joshua.

Concept C: Judges: Saving Israel from Itself

Pages 104–110

Review Questions: Judges: Saving Israel from Itself

Question. Describe the fourfold pattern that occurs repeatedly in the Book of Judges.
Answer. The Israelites fall into sin, experience disaster, repent of their sin, and are delivered by a judge, triumphing over their enemies. They then live in faithfulness and peace for a time before the cycle begins again.

Question. In the Bible what was the role of the judges? List the six major judges.
Answer. The judges were tribal leaders through whom God delivered the people from destruction. The six major judges were Othniel, Ehud, Deborah, Gideon, Jephthah, and Samson.

Question. How would the story of Deborah and Jael have given the exiled Jews a sense of hope?
Answer. It nurtured their hope that they too, with God fighting for them, would one day overcome their oppressors.

Question. Why does God tell Gideon to reduce the size of his forces?
Answer. God points out that with a large army, the Israelites would probably credit any victory to their own might, not to God's power.

Question. Describe Samson's character. Why was such a character included among the judges?
Answer. Samson is a violent man with an uncontrolled passion for women. He is physically strong but morally weak. Samson was included among the

judges for several possible reasons. Perhaps the Deuteronomists' purpose was to marvel at the kind of people God can make use of. Perhaps Samson also reminded the exiles of how their blessed nation had also become deluded and morally weak, bringing ruin upon itself.

Text Activities: Judges: Saving Israel from Itself

- Write a short story about a young person that illustrates the cycle of sin, disaster, repentance, and deliverance.
- Gideon destroyed the altar of Baal because it symbolized the worst offenses of the surrounding culture. If you could destroy something that represented evil in our society—and it would cause people to be outraged at you— what would it be?
- Research and write about a person or group from history whose weakness ultimately led to destruction.
- In writing, compare and contrast the characters of Joshua and Samson. What can you learn about leadership from them?

Additional Activities: Judges: Saving Israel from Itself

When Leaders Pass Away

When Joshua died, Israel found it easy to start slipping away from the Covenant. Clubs, teams, and organizations find the resignation or passing on of leaders difficult too, particularly when the leaders were inspiring types who were able to mobilize the members to do great things.

1. In small groups have the students think of a group or organization— they may or may not be a member—that has a visible and active leader. Direct them to evaluate the effectiveness of the leadership by discussing these questions:
   ◆ Does the leader handle all responsibilities for leading the group, or do others in the group share the work?
   ◆ How are decisions made? Who makes them? Do members of the group have a voice in decision making?
   ◆ What would happen to the group if the leader suddenly left? How would the group continue to function?
   ◆ In what ways could the leadership be more effectively shared, thus ensuring a smooth transition between leaders?

2. Gather the students and ask them if they know of any instances when the passing on of a leader caused a group to fall apart. Then ask the following questions:
   ◆ What can leaders do to ensure that when they leave an organization, club, parish, or team, it continues to work effectively and be true to its ideals?
   ◆ Should leaders share power and train others to take leadership?
   ◆ Why do some people refuse to share leadership?

3. Invite the students to talk about the discussions they held in the small groups, encouraging comments and questions.

5

Promises Broken: People Forget

Joshua 24:1–28 tells of the Israelites' renewal of the Covenant at Shechem. Of course, the people renege later on, and the stories of their infidelities and their rescues appear in the Book of Judges.

1. For purposes of review and to make the point that people sometimes have to relearn old lessons, ask the class these questions:
   ◆ Where in our earlier study of the Old Testament have we seen the Israelites making promises to God and then breaking them?
   ◆ Why do people make promises that they will soon back away from? What makes us want to pledge ourselves to something? What accounts for our weakness in holding to pledges?

2. Read Judges, chapter 2, aloud to your class. This passage explains both the Israelites' constant lapsing into idol worship and the role of the judges in delivering them from the consequent messes they get into. Relate the Israelites' behavior to people's behavior today, using these questions:
   ◆ In our time what activities are equivalent to forgetting God and worshiping false gods or idols?
   ◆ What are the consequences when people worship false gods today?

Resisting the Lure of the Canaanites

Explain that the Israelites found it difficult to resist the lure of the Canaanite culture. Tell the students that the tension between resisting foreign cultures and giving in to them would be a continuing problem for the Israelites in the coming centuries. In Joshua's time the people generally resisted Canaanism, but in later generations the lure of the Canaanite culture would lead them astray many times.

The Book of Joshua's accounts of slaying the Canaanites and sacking their cities were revised and edited by the Deuteronomists probably more than six hundred years after the events described. The Deuteronomists knew in hindsight what disasters lay in store for their predecessors because of their failures at resisting Canaanism. So the passages that commanded the Israelites to have nothing to do with, and even to destroy, the Canaanites may have been exaggerated. The imposition of the ban on Jericho (Josh. 6:16–21) is an example of behavior that may have been exaggerated by later editors to emphasize the loathsomeness of all things Canaanite.

Handout **5–B**

To give the students a sense of what it meant to live in tension with the Canaanite culture, use handout 5–B, "Life in Canaan: Caught in the Middle," which is a fictionalized account of one Israelite family's struggle to be true to God. After the students have read the handout, discuss these questions with them:
   ◆ What pressures to conform to the Canaanite culture did the Israelites experience?
   ◆ To us today it seems obvious that the Canaanites' practices of idolatry, temple prostitution, and child sacrifice were wrong, and that the Israelites' beliefs were right. But it was not always so clear to the ancient Israelites. Why may it have been less clear to them in their situation than it is to us today?
   ◆ The Israelites who gave in to Canaanite ways probably did not think that they were giving up on God but, rather, simply accommodating their faith to the pressures of the world around them. They likely saw

5

themselves as just trying to survive in a difficult world. How is this similar to the way that many of today's Christians approach their faith?

◆ Can you think of any times when you have felt caught in the middle—that is, when you have felt the tension between the values you have been raised to have and a set of values or practices that are at odds with those beliefs?

◆ How did you resolve this tension, if you did resolve it? What were the consequences of your decisions?

Option. You may wish to assign the students to write a contemporary account of an individual's or family's struggle to be true to their religious values, as was done in the handout.

5

God's Call to Gideon, the Youngest and Weakest

From the Scriptures it is evident that God prefers to call the youngest or the weakest to do great things. Of course, young or weak persons have to depend more completely and obviously on God's help, thus showing that it is God who accomplishes the great deeds through the persons who are God's instruments.

1. To discuss God's calling the youngest or the weakest, pose these questions to your students:

◆ How might young people see the story of Gideon in relation to their own experience?

◆ Does anyone ever accomplish great things without the help of God? What if the person does not believe in God?

2. If your students are keeping a journal, they could respond to these questions with brief essay answers:

◆ Describe a difficult thing that you have been called to do, something that shook your confidence.

◆ What was the outcome?

◆ Did you ask for God's help? Did you feel that God was helping you?

An Imaginary Talk with Gideon

Assign the students to write an imaginary conversation with Gideon concerning his call from God and his subsequent reaction. The students should format the conversation like dialog in a play, taking about 15 minutes to do so.

When time is up, ask for volunteers to read their dialog. Invite comments and questions on each dialog from the rest of the class.

Drinking, Smoking, Pregnancy, and Biblical Wisdom

Samson's mother is told not to drink wine or strong drink nor to eat anything unclean during her pregnancy. This wisdom from the Bible has been supported by scientific evidence (although the definition of what is unclean has changed). Select some students to research why doctors advise expectant mothers to avoid drinking alcohol and smoking, even in moderation. Your researchers should present their findings in a brief report to the class.

Point out that many of the dietary laws of the Israelites were wise, too. For example, their prohibitions against eating pork indicate experience with pork that carried disease-causing parasites such as trichinae. These dietary laws were said to have come from God because, after all, God wished for the Chosen People to be healthy and strong.

It would be interesting to invite a Jewish person who practices these dietary laws to speak with your class about how these laws are carried out today and why they are important to the Jewish faith.

5

More on Samson's Character

The last sidebar activity in the "Judges" section begins an exploration of Samson's character that can be taken to greater depth in this exercise. Samson's uncontrolled passion for women, violent temper, and lack of self-discipline lead to his downfall. He betrays his consecration to God. To explore the scriptural portrayal of Samson, pose the following questions to your class:

- Why is Samson considered a deliverer of the Israelites?
- Is Samson's final act, the tearing down of the Philistines' temple, the act of a man converted to true faith in God? Or is it merely an act of vengeance?
- The story of Samson has been made into films. What makes his life a good subject for movies?
- Can you think of any similar characters (they need not be historical) who have been the subject of movies?
- In the years that followed Samson's life, stories about him increased the Israelites' hatred for the Philistines, their chief enemy for a long time. Can you give examples of stories, songs, movies, plays, or symbols in this country that are used to fan the flames of nationalist feeling against another country?

Flawed Folk Heroes

1. Assign the reading of folktales about Johnny Appleseed, Paul Bunyan, Daniel Boone, Davy Crockett, and Wild Bill Hickok. Tell the students each to prepare a brief oral report that answers these questions:

- Are these folktales history, legend, or a mixture of both?
- Are the heroes completely admirable? flawed? some of each?
- What makes folktales like these and stories like that of Samson popular?

2. Follow with a discussion about contemporary heroes. You may wish to pursue this line of questioning:

- Who are some contemporary heroes of almost Samsonian proportions? [List these on the chalkboard.] What makes these people heroes? Do we expect impeccable moral behavior from these people? If so, is it realistic to expect these people to be perfect models of morality? If these people are not completely virtuous, should we admire them?
- Do people need heroes? Why or why not?
- Who are some of your heroes? What attributes make them heroes to you?

Samson: A Subject of Art and Music

Ask some of your students to find paintings, poems, plays, movies, and operas inspired by the story of Samson. Paintings could be shown to the class, and synopses of the other works of art could be given orally.

Concept D: Ruth: An Israelite Foreigner with a Great Destiny

Pages 111–115

5

Review Questions: Ruth: An Israelite Foreigner with a Great Destiny

Question. What were the two purposes of the Book of Ruth?
Answer. (1) To teach how God could create a blessed ending out of a difficult situation, and (2) to tell how it came about that King David had a Gentile as his great-grandmother.

Question. What does Ruth pledge in her famous speech to Naomi?
Answer. Ruth pledges to stay with Naomi. Her pledge binds her not only to Naomi but to the God of Israel.

Text Activities: Ruth: An Israelite Foreigner with a Great Destiny

- Have you ever had a friend who stuck by you in difficult times? Write an essay about friendship, including those qualities of a friend you believe are most important.
- Think about someone you know who is truly kind. Write a speech about that person that you might give if a party was held in his or her honor.
- What lessons does the Book of Ruth teach about foreigners? Find a newspaper or magazine article that describes the experiences of a person or group who has immigrated to our country. Read the article, summarize it in writing, and, if possible, connect it to the lessons presented in Ruth.

Additional Activities: Ruth: An Israelite Foreigner with a Great Destiny

Widowhood Among the Israelites

Tell the students to reread Ruth 1:1–14. The beginning of the story is somber. A family determined to survive a famine emigrates to Moab, only to have the father die, leaving his widow to raise their two sons alone. The sons grow up and marry, but then they too die, leaving their young widows childless.

Read aloud (or have your students read) Isaiah 1:23; 10:1–2; Deuteronomy 14:28–29; 24:17,19–21. After these passages have been read, pose these questions for discussion:

- Why was childless widowhood looked upon by the Israelites as particularly tragic?
- How is the status of widowhood today both different from and similar to the status of widowhood in the time of Ruth and Naomi? Today who in our society would be comparable to widows in ancient Israel?
- It has been said that the humaneness of a society can be ascertained by how it treats its weakest, most vulnerable members. By that standard was ancient Israel a humane society? What about the United States today?

5

The Wonderful Relationship Between Naomi and Ruth

Unfortunately, mothers-in-law are often the butt of jokes and stereotypes. Ruth, however, models a beautiful relationship with her mother-in-law, Naomi. To examine the qualities of Ruth and Naomi's relationship, offer these questions for discussion:

- What characteristics of Naomi and Ruth's relationship made it wonderful? Why did they have a relationship such as this?
- What virtues do you find personified in these two women?

The song "Wherever You Go," by Gregory Norbert, is based on Ruth 1:16–17. Hearing it is a lovely way to catch the spirit of gentle fidelity and commitment to another person that is present in the Book of Ruth. The song is available on the album or in the songbook *Glory and Praise 3*.

The Modern Right to Glean: Hunger in Our World

Begin a discussion about Ruth's right to glean the fields of Boaz and about the story's relationship to modern times. Invite your students to respond to these questions:

- Does the biblical law allowing poor people, aliens, widows, and orphans to glean still apply today?
- How might urban Christians fulfill their obligations to poor people, aliens, widows, and orphans, given that they do not have fields to glean?
- What efforts are being made to help hungry people around the world today? How is our country involved? our community? your parish?
- Beyond charity as a motivator to feed the hungry, why should we be concerned about the plight of hungry people?

In addition to the discussion above, you might ask your students to keep track of the food that is wasted or that spoils in their household during one week. Tell them to turn in a brief summary of their findings.

Option. Have several students work with the food service director to arrange a day to raise awareness of food waste in the school. The goal is to have food that is normally unfinished and thrown away gathered into a pile in a visible place in the cafeteria. Several students rotating throughout the day could intercept food being thrown into trash cans and collect it on a table near the exit of the cafeteria for all to see. It could sit there for the entire next day, with a sign posted above addressing the issue of hunger and waste.

An Important Inclusion

Read Matthew 1:2–6 aloud, with your students following along in their Bible. Point out that the passage is tracing the genealogy of Jesus. Ask the students these questions:

◆ What is the significance of a Gentile [Ruth, a Moabite] and a prostitute [Rahab, a Canaanite from Jericho] in the lineage of Jesus? What does mention of these women indicate about the Gospel writers' view of God's ways?

◆ Why would it have been especially significant for Jewish believers of the postexilic period (the time when the Book of Ruth was completed) to know that David had descended from both a Gentile and a Gentile prostitute? [Their understanding of God as the God of all the nations was developing; they were moving from an exclusive, nationalistic notion of God to an inclusive, universal notion.]

A Letter to Orpah

One way to help your students summarize the story of Ruth and formulate their own response to it is to have them do the following exercise.

1. Read these instructions to the class:

◆ Imagine that you are Ruth. You want to tell Orpah, who decided to stay on in Moab, about all the things that have happened to you since you arrived in Judah. A messenger is going to Orpah's town and will take a letter to her if it is written on one sheet of paper.

◆ Write a letter to Orpah, highlighting the main events of your life since the two of you parted.

2. When the students have finished writing, ask them to sit in groups of three or four and read their letters to one another. Each group should compare notes to see what its members included and what they omitted in the letters. Then ask the class which events were most frequently forgotten and which event was almost always emphasized. Finally, ask your students if God was mentioned. Would Ruth have mentioned God?

Closing Prayer

This closing prayer combines written reflection by the students and a guided meditation. The focus is on trusting in God's help as a response to one's fears, a theme that is relevant to the era of the judges.

1. Remind the students that God is truly present in and among them, at all times, in all places. Pause for a moment's reflection.

2. Introduce this time of prayer with the following explanation. You might also play some meditative instrumental music during this part of the activity.

◆ We have been reading about how Gideon and Ruth trusted in God's help. In each case God helped the person overcome fears and concerns.

Most of us are weighed down with fears and worries. This time of prayer is an invitation to share those fears and worries with God.

3. Read these directions to your class:

◆ Take out a piece of paper. You will need to do some writing, but you will not have to turn it in. In this first part of our prayer, I would like you to list your fears and worries—as many as you can think of, or maybe admit to. Sit quietly for 2 or 3 minutes and write down all the things that cause you some anxiety. They can be things from the past, the present, or the future, but they must be real to you. Keep your list private; no one else should see it. [You may want to assign a definite number of worries—fifteen or twenty—if your class needs specific limits.]

5

4. Give the students time to write down their fears and concerns. The next step in the closing prayer is a guided meditation. If you have not played soft music so far, you might wish to do so now. Slowly and clearly read aloud the following meditation, pausing where indicated by ellipses (. . .):

◆ First, I want you to get into a relaxed position. Sit up straight, both feet on the floor, with your hands resting comfortably in your lap. Close your eyes now, and keep them closed until I tell you to open them. . . .

Breathe deeply, and as you exhale, let your body become more relaxed. . . . Breathe in slowly . . . and out slowly . . . in . . . and out. . . . Let your whole body relax: . . . your feet, . . . your legs, . . . your torso, . . . your arms, . . . your neck and face. . . . Let all tensions cease. . . . Breathe deeply. . . .

Visualize a place where you feel secure and comfortable, someplace where you could talk with someone in privacy. It might be a room, a place in a forest or on a beach. . . . Put yourself in the scene and continue to breathe calmly. . . .

Now imagine that you are joined by a man who greets you by saying: "Peace be with you. Do not be afraid." . . . Suddenly you realize that this person is Jesus. . . . He sits next to you. . . .

Jesus looks at you with care and concern. . . . Then he says, "My friend, I want to ask you to give me a priceless gift. Share your fears with me. Unburden yourself for a while. Tell me what you're afraid of." . . . You know that you can trust Jesus, so you tell him all your fears. . . .

You look into his eyes. . . . Jesus says: "Be not afraid. I hold you in the palm of my hand always. I will be with you until the end of time." . . . A rush of emotion fills you. . . . He stands to leave, saying, "Peace be with you, my friend." . . .

When you are ready to come back into the here and now, open your eyes.

(As an alternative to the guided meditation, lead your class in reciting together Psalm 23.)

5. Give the students these instructions:

◆ To close this time of prayer, write a message from your heart to Jesus in response to our meditation. It can be a prayer of thanks, praise, petition, contrition, or all of these. End your message with "Amen. Alleluia!"

Closing Teacher Prayer

Call to prayer. Be still within and without. Center yourself in God's graciousness.

Reflect. What have you learned in the process of teaching this chapter? Was it a learning of the head or the heart? Does this reveal God more fully to you? How? What effect could this learning have on your life?

What gift did you receive from your students? Which students do you feel are especially in need of God's tender care today?

Pray.
Loving and gracious God,
you have placed in our heart
a marvelous capacity for remembering.
You are a God of history—
a history filled with light and darkness.
Help us to remember your story and our own,
and in the remembering,
fill us with gratitude and joy. Amen.

(Bergan and Schwan, *Taste and See: Prayer Services for Gatherings of Faith*)

"O Lord, You Have Searched Me and Known Me"

(Ps. 139:1)

Spend a few moments quietly asking God to help you see clearly and honestly into your heart and mind as you begin this examination of conscience.

Write your responses to the questions below. No one will collect this handout.

1. Bring to mind the areas in your life in which you feel you have failed to measure up to what God has called you to.

   _____

   _____

2. Think about your relationship with your parent(s) or guardian(s). Have you hurt that relationship or failed to act in ways that could strengthen your family?

   _____

   _____

3. Consider your relationships with your friends. Have you been a source of growth for your friends, or have you sometimes caused them to be less than they could be as persons?

   _____

   _____

4. What about your relationship with yourself? Have you expected the most of yourself? Have you been kind and forgiving to yourself when you have failed? Or have you put yourself down or been filled with self-pity?

   _____

   _____

5. Can you identify a common thread or common problem that is at the root of your difficulties? Is it pride? self-centeredness? impatience? a judgmental attitude? a bad temper? Try to sum up or crystallize in a brief statement how this weakness or difficulty is manifested in your life.

   _____

   _____

   _____

Life in Canaan: Caught in the Middle

Read the following excerpt in order to better understand the Israelites' struggles to resist the Canaanite culture. Be prepared to discuss your reactions with the class.

"O Baal, lord of the seasons, protector of the harvest, nourish these crops with your sacred gift of rain! O great Ashtarte, receive now the embrace of your heavenly consort, Baal most high. Give life to these vines and these shoots. Bring forth abundant treasures of grapes and wheat for our nourishment. Let Baal be king! Baal is our god!"

This prayer to the Canaanite god of fertility and his divine mistress, Ashtarte, was perhaps typical of prayers actually offered by devout Canaanites at the start of their spring planting. Imagine for a moment that you are an Israelite youth living in a fertile valley in Palestine. Your grandfather was a nomad, a desert wanderer who had followed Moses from Mt. Sinai to the banks of the Jordan. Your father had fought under Joshua and had received a rich piece of land from his tribal chieftain when the Promised Land was divided. But your father had never learned the art of farming.

"My son," your father says to you on your 13th birthday, "it is time for us to learn the ways of the land. We must put behind us the ways of the desert. No more will we tend flocks, as I and my father did in the days of Moses and Joshua. If we are to succeed in this new land which Yahweh our God has given us, we must take on the ways of the people who have always lived here. We must learn to live from the soil, my son, so that we can bring prosperity and honor to our household."

"But father," you respond, "where am I to learn the ways of the farmer? How shall I begin?"

"Ah, let us be clever, my son. We will study the ways of our neighbors. We will learn from them what it is that causes the vine and the shoot to blossom. I have watched the Canaanites. I am learning the secrets of the land."

Together you and your father travel around the valley. You observe the Canaanites at work in the field. You start to talk to some of them. You visit their homes. You share a meal. You begin to learn the mysterious secrets of agriculture. One day a Canaanite neighbor tells you that the suc-

cess of the crops depends upon the favor of the local gods—Baal and his mistress, Ashtarte. If Baal is pleased with your sacrifice to him in the spring, he will have sexual intercourse with Ashtarte and the fruit of their union will be rich crops of grapes and olives, figs and wheat. If Baal is not pleased with your sacrifice, the crops will fail.

Sometimes—your neighbor continues—to urge Baal into action, it is necessary to go to the local Baal temple. There priests and their consecrated mistresses engage in sexual intercourse themselves. This stimulates Baal to act. It reminds him of his sacred duty to humankind. It is a great privilege to give your maiden daughter as mistress to the priest; Baal is pleased by this consecration of your virgin daughter to him. Sometimes, when Baal is angry with people, he may remain silent. Then a greater sacrifice is called for to stir him into action—a daughter, or even a son, must be burnt in offering. Baal will listen then. He will embrace Ashtarte, and the crops will grow and multiply.

You and your father leave the house of your Canaanite neighbor and walk in silence for some time. Finally, you begin to speak:

"Father, are we to do as this man said?"

"I do not know, my son."

You can see that your father is very troubled, uncertain as to what to think.

"Father," you begin again, "what about all those stories you and Grandfather taught me about Yahweh our God? Does Yahweh know about the Baal god? Is Yahweh stronger than he is? Must we worship Baal too, Father?"

"I do not know, my son. We must think about this. We must talk to our brothers. Such a strange story this man has told us! So unlike our ways! And yet, if this is what one must do to become a farmer . . . I do not know. We will think about it. We will talk to our brothers." (*The People of the Book,* by Anthony E. Gilles [Cincinnati: Saint Anthony Messenger Press, 1981], pages 37–38. Copyright ©1983 by Anthony E. Gilles. Used with permission of the author.)

CHAPTER 6

The Kings: Becoming a Nation

Major Concepts

A. **Stories of Transition to Nationhood.** Israel's lack of a central leader by the end of the era of the judges threatens its security and does not meet the ideal of a people united in keeping God's Covenant. The Books of Samuel and the beginning of the First Book of Kings describe Israel's first three kings—Saul, David, and Solomon. The Deuteronomists, writing about four hundred years after Israel was united, had mixed feelings about Israel's nationhood because they understood that some of its features had led to the nation's downfall. *See* the *Catechism,* nos. 439, 695, 711–716 (the Messiah); 709–710 (Israel's downfall).

B. **Samuel: Anointer of Kings.** The prophet Samuel leads the Israelites as priest and judge, and Israel lives in peace under his leadership. The people want a king to succeed him so they can be powerful like other nations. Samuel warns that a king will bring trouble because God alone is the king of Israel. But Samuel obeys God's command to fulfill the people's wishes. He anoints as king an ordinary, shy man named Saul. *See* the *Catechism,* nos. 64 (Hannah); 2578 (Samuel).

C. **Saul and David in Conflict.** The major theme of the First Book of Samuel is Saul's reign. Saul breaks faith with God, who leads Samuel to secretly anoint David as king. Saul becomes jealous of David and tries to kill him. Saul's son Jonathan and David develop a deep friendship. David, though imperfect, remains loyal to his people and even to Saul. *See* the *Catechism,* nos. 437 (Joseph); 695 (the anointing of David).

D. **King David: Nation Builder.** At Saul's death David is publicly anointed king of the southern tribes of Judah and eventually of all Israel. A series of betrayals and murders accompanies his rise to power, but he is unwavering in his loyalty to Saul and those close to Saul. David ends the Philistine threat and unifies the Israelite tribes. He makes Jerusalem the capital and brings the ark of the Covenant there. In the Davidic Covenant, God promises that the line of David's royal descendants will endure forever. Jews expected their Messiah to be from David's line, a promise Christians believe is fulfilled in Jesus. David commits many grievous sins to cover up his adultery with Bathsheba. With Nathan's help he repents, but he and his family suffer a series of tragedies and treacheries. David is a prime example of God working through flawed humans. His devotion to God made him a model king and a figure of hope for the exiles. *See* the *Catechism,* nos. 143–144 (faith); 306–308 (God acts through humans); 436, 439, 559, 695, 711–716, 840 (the Messiah); 1431 (repentance); 2072 (the Commandments); 2258 (murder); 2380–2381 (adultery); 2464 (lying); 2579–2580 (David).

E. **King Solomon: Temple Builder.** The First Book of Kings shows Israel's unfaithfulness despite the prophets' warnings. It was written to remind the exiles that they, not God, broke the Covenant and that they could be restored through repentance. Solomon succeeds his father, David. God grants Solomon's request for wisdom, best illustrated by his clever way of determining which of two women was the real mother of a child. Yet Solomon turns out to be unwise in the ways of God as his reign is marked by oppression, royal extravagance, and idolatry. Solomon directs the building of Israel's first Temple in Jerusalem. God warns him that the Temple will fall if Solomon and his descendants forsake the Covenant. When they do so, God says Solomon's line will lose the throne and all the tribes but Judah. In forty years Solomon leads Israel from a union of tribes loyal to God's Covenant to idolatry and near slavery. *See* the *Catechism,* nos. 401 (infidelity to the Covenant); 709–710 (Israel's downfall); 1849 (sin); 2112–2114 (idolatry); 2580 (the Temple).

Opening Teacher Prayer

Call to prayer. Be still within and without. Call to mind your own need for healing and forgiveness. Center yourself in the God of mercy.

Read. Psalm 51

Reflect. What words or phrases in Psalm 51 speak to your heart? When have you experienced God's healing and merciful love in your life?

Hold in your heart. "Have mercy on me, O God" (Ps. 51:1).

Pages 118–119

Concept A: Stories of Transition to Nationhood

Review Questions: Stories of Transition to Nationhood

Question. Why did the tribes of Israel need to become a nation?
Answer. Temporary leadership could not build unity across the tribes or keep people from deciding for themselves what to do. Morally and spiritually, things were going downhill. And the lack of unity also threatened the existence of Israel, which did not stand a chance against the mighty Philistines.

Question. Who were the first three kings of Israel?
Answer. Saul, David, and Solomon

Question. Why did the Deuteronomists have mixed feelings about Israel's becoming a nation with a king?

Answer. The Deuteronomists saw the whole process of becoming a nation from the perspective of about four hundred years later. They understood that some features of being "like other nations" (1 Sam. 8:20), though attractive, were the seeds of destruction that had led to the nation's downfall.

 ## Text Activities: Stories of Transition to Nationhood

- Imagine living in a society where everyone "did what was right in their own eyes." What would that be like? Write a short story describing this kind of society.
- You have probably heard this: The grass is always greener on the other side of the fence. Sometimes we look at what other people have—their families, houses, possessions, bodies, and so on—and we believe our lives would be better if we had what they have. But have you ever considered what challenges those other people face with what they have? Write a paragraph giving an example of one such challenge. In a second paragraph, write how this relates to the Israelites' desire for a king.

 ## Additional Activity: Stories of Transition to Nationhood

United We Stand

By having the students reflect critically on the effects of unity, they can understand better how a lack of unity affected the ancient Israelites.

1. Direct the students to think of a historical or contemporary situation either where unity is lacking or where a group is strongly united. The situation can concern a nation, a city, a neighborhood, a school, a church, a family, and so on. Ask them to give examples.

2. Then ask questions like these:
- What are the benefits of unity? What are the detriments of disunity?
- Is unity always good? What if a group of people were united around something that is not good for them, such as idolatry?
- Do you think that the phrase "United we stand, divided we fall" was true in the Israelites' case? Is it true in every case?
- Do you think your school is a good example of unity? If so, in what ways? If not, how could the school's unity be improved?

6

Concept B: Samuel: Anointer of Kings

Review Questions: Samuel: Anointer of Kings

Question. What does Samuel warn will happen if the people have a king?

Answer. A king will draft their sons to make arms, build chariots, and reap harvests, and their daughters to make perfumes, cook, and bake. A king will also take their fields, vineyards, olive groves, servants, donkeys, sheep, and a tithe of their grain. A king will also make the Israelites into slaves.

Question. Whom does Samuel anoint as the first king?
Answer. Saul

Text Activities: Samuel: Anointer of Kings

- Read 1 Samuel 2:1–10 and Luke 1:46–55. Mary's Magnificat is said to have been modeled after Hannah's hymn of praise when she gives Samuel to the Lord. List the similarities. Then write a brief essay on the meaning of these songs for our times.
- Samuel is described as both a judge and a priest, implying that in Israel, politics and religion were inseparable. Why was that? Do you see issues of poverty, injustice, and corruption as being primarily political or religious? Write a paragraph explaining your stance.
- Is it possible for God to rule over us today even though we have elected officials in our local and national governments? Share your reflections on how that might or might not be possible.
- What does it mean for a nation to be a "light to all the others"? Do you think our country is like this? Find a newspaper or magazine article that reflects your opinion and write a paragraph about it that answers these questions.

Additional Activities: Samuel: Anointer of Kings

Listening to God

This activity attempts to cultivate in the participants Samuel's attitude of humility and openness in prayer.

1. Remind the students that Eli, who at least in this case functioned as Samuel's spiritual director, was the first to realize that God was calling Samuel. Eli then made a suggestion that is a wonderful opening for any prayer. He told Samuel to say to God, "Speak, for your servant is listening."

2. Then ask the students these questions:
- ◆ Have you ever had an experience in friendship where one person did all the talking and never listened to the other person? Were you the one who never had a chance to be heard? If so, how did that feel?

6

- When you pray do you mostly talk or mostly listen? Which is easier to do? Why?
- Do you think listening is important in prayer? Why or why not?

3. Teach the students what they need to enter a meditative state in which they can listen to God: a quiet place, a prayerful posture, deep breathing for relaxation.

Lead the participants through an experience of meditation or centering prayer. If they experienced the guided meditation suggested at the end of chapter 5 of this manual, let them know that this kind of meditation is different in that no words will be read in the background; rather, they will sit in quiet (except perhaps for music, if you choose to play quiet instrumental background music) for about 15 minutes. Explain that you will lead them through the first few minutes, and then they will be on their own.

Begin by inviting the students to sit comfortably—feet flat on the floor, hands folded or palms open on their lap (or desk), eyes closed—and to pay attention to their breathing for a minute or two. Start the meditation by saying, "Speak, Lord, for your servant is listening." Invite the students to repeat this several times to themselves in silence and then to release this thought and simply rest in God's presence.

Tell the students that sometimes a word or phrase—such as "Lord," "Jesus, friend," or "Love"—may be repeated quietly to keep focused on simply being present to God. Assure the students that many distractions will enter their minds as they try to open their hearts to God through meditation; they are to just let these distractions go and not let them become a major source of disturbance. It might be helpful to give them an image for letting go of distracting thoughts, such as releasing them like balloons or allowing them to float away on a feather. When a distracting thought enters their minds, they are to gently release it and return to their focusing word.

After 15 or so minutes, bring the students back gently (you could use a chime or, if you are playing music, gradually increase the volume). Invite the students to return to the present and, when they are ready, to open their eyes, still in silence. Then close the meditation time by praying the Lord's Prayer together or leading the class in a brief, spontaneous prayer.

Invite the students to journal about their experience, or initiate a discussion about it. Ask them what it was like to listen for God.

If this has been a positive experience for them, you may wish to make it a regular form of prayer for the class; if time allows, once a week would be an effective practice. (For more detailed instructions on meditation, you may wish to refer to *PrayerWays*, by Carl Koch [Winona, MN: Saint Mary's Press, 1995], pp. 105–115. A helpful resource on centering prayer is *Open Mind, Open Heart: The Contemplative Dimension of the Gospel*, by Thomas Keating [New York: HarperCollins, 1994].)

Barren Women: God's Choices

To focus on the mysterious ways that God calls forth leaders and servants, ask the students to name barren women other than Hannah, Samuel's mother, who were chosen by God to bear a special child. (Sarah, the mother of Isaac, and Elizabeth, the mother of John the Baptist, are the most famous examples; students may also recall that Samson's mother had been barren.) Just as God chose weak, young, obscure people to be prophets, leaders, and kings, God selected barren women to bear extraordinary children. Ask your students why this might be so.

The answer is that by choosing barren women for a special purpose, God has proven in another way that only God is powerful and wise. By raising up the lowly (which barren women were considered to be in ancient societies), God has reminded humankind to depend on God and follow the laws of God.

Why Have a King?

The transition from a tribal confederacy to a monarchy was a major development for Israel, and it brought mixed results for the nation. The historical record and the testimony of the prophets indicate that the long-term results were more bad than good. Ultimately, however—and this is the story of God's ways in the Old Testament—God brought good out of even the worst situations and behavior of the people of Israel.

Discuss these questions with the students:

◆ Why did the idea of having a king appeal to the Israelite people? [They wanted to be like other nations, which had kings, but something else was also at work. The loose confederacy of the twelve tribes of Israel could not present a united front against their enemies; the tribes had no central government and had previously worked together only in emergencies. The tribal confederacy was somewhat like the weak, ineffectual union provided by the Articles of Confederation for the thirteen independent American states after the Revolution. The Israelites felt that with the central government and stable form of succession that a monarchy would bring, they would be more secure, particularly against the constant threat of the powerful Philistines. They would be able to raise and equip an army that would have at least a fighting chance against the Philistines' iron weapons, which were a new development in warfare.]

◆ What disadvantages of having a king were not apparent to the people when they demanded that Samuel appoint one? [The tendency to rely on the king rather than God for help, the move toward building a royal empire and all the wealth and corruption that go along with that, the exploitation of subjects, etc.]

◆ What does the First Book of Samuel say about Samuel's reaction to the idea of having a king?

◆ According to the First Book of Samuel, what was God's reaction to the idea of a king for Israel?

Point out to the students that in 1 Samuel, the idea of a monarchy is at times treated favorably and at times treated negatively. In places, Samuel and God seem distressed at the prospect of a king (see 1 Sam. 8, 10:17–19), but in other passages, the idea of a monarchy is presented in a highly favorable way (see 1 Sam. 9, 10:1–16). In 1 Samuel 8:7, God says that the people's request for a king is their way of rejecting God, whereas in 1 Samuel 9:15–17, God seems to be the one who comes up with the kingship notion. The First Book of Samuel, then, is ambivalent on whether there should be a monarchy.

Ask the students:

◆ Could God really have been ambivalent about whether Israel should have a king? Does God waver on difficult questions?

A plausible explanation for the inconsistencies in 1 Samuel has been proposed by biblical scholars. Share this explanation with your students:

◆ As we know, the individual books of the Scriptures generally were not written from beginning to end by a single author. Many hands and perspectives were involved in the final product. Biblical scholars tell us that a couple of traditions were at work in creating the First Book of Samuel.

One writer's tradition saw the monarchy as a wonderful gift from God for Israel. Most likely, this pro-monarchy person wrote before the disastrous effects of the monarchy had hit Israel.

Another writer was antimonarchy. That writer inserted passages such as chapter 8, verses 10–22, predicting the exploitation and subjugation of the people by a future king. Why? He most likely wrote after the kings, especially Solomon, had proven their corruption and injustice. (The deeds described in the passage just mentioned are amazingly similar to the deeds of Solomon during his reign.) Hindsight, as we know, is always more accurate than foresight.

The meaningful question, then, is not, Did God waver on the difficult issue of the monarchy? but rather, What different experiences of the people are represented in the First Book of Samuel?

Pages
122–
127

Concept C: Saul and David in Conflict

Review Questions: Saul and David in Conflict

Question. Why does God reject Saul after he becomes king?
Answer. God rejects Saul because Saul shows himself to be unfaithful, swayed by his own anxieties, and subject to the pressures of those around him. He does not truly trust in God and follow God's commands.

Question. How does the story of David repeat the theme of God's choosing the weakest and lowest?
Answer. God instructs Samuel to overlook Jesse's older, taller sons, who seem to have obvious regal potential, and to secretly anoint the youngest son, David, as king.

Question. What two biblical incidents tell of Saul meeting David?
Answer. In one incident David is brought to play the harp for Saul to lighten his dark moods. The other is the story of young David who, armed only with a slingshot, prevails against the Philistine giant, Goliath.

Question. Why does Saul want to murder David?
Answer. David's popularity, attractiveness, and skill begin to arouse jealousy in the insecure and emotionally unstable Saul.

Question. With whom does David have a deep friendship?
Answer. Jonathan, Saul's son

Question. How does David show loyalty to Saul even though Saul wants to destroy him?
Answer. David doesn't kill Saul, even when he has a chance to, and David also swears he will never harm Saul's descendants.

Question. How does Saul's life end?
Answer. Battling the Philistines, Saul kills himself rather than be captured, and the Philistines fasten his body to the walls of one of their cities.

6

Question. What is the theme of each of the two Books of Samuel?

Answer. The First Book of Samuel completes the theme of the reign of Saul. The theme of the Second Book of Samuel is the rise of David to his kingship.

Text Activities: Saul and David in Conflict

- "The key to their success will be fidelity to God." Comment on this notion as it applies to your life, to someone you know, or to a group of people.
- Do you know of someone who possesses far more inner beauty and strength than he or she might show on the outside? How did you come to know what he or she is really like? Write an essay about this person, including your thoughts on 1 Samuel 16:7.
- Have you ever had an experience where being loyal to a friend meant being disloyal to someone else? Write a story featuring young people that illustrates this challenge of loyalty.
- Who is someone you consider powerful? Write a paragraph about what he or she has taught you about the meaning of power and how it should be used.

Additional Activities: Saul and David in Conflict

Polytheism Around the Ancient World

Direct the students to the sidebar "World Happenings from 1250 to 900 BC" on page 125 of the student text. Point out that many of the civilizations of that time were far more advanced in culture, knowledge, and technology than Israel. Some, such as Egypt, had peaked and were going into decline. Others, such as civilizations in America, Europe, India, and the Near East, were just coming into their own as sophisticated cultures. Israel, on the other hand, with its nomadic history, was not and had not been a sophisticated culture. (Perhaps the desire to be more sophisticated, like the other nations, was part of what prompted the Israelites to ask for a king.)

Call the students' attention to the fact that although the sophisticated societies were advanced in many respects, they still believed in more than one god—a belief that we today consider a primitive notion. Assign some students to research ancient polytheism in some of its various forms and then report to the class on why the sophisticated cultures believed in many gods. Provide these questions as guidelines for the research:

◆ How did polytheism originate?
◆ What was polytheism's appeal as a way of explaining reality? as a way of managing life?
◆ Why didn't the ancient peoples come earlier to a belief in the one God?

Note for the class that even the Israelites, who were among the earliest peoples to believe in the one God (along with the Zoroastrians of Persia), flirted with polytheism throughout their early history. Even some of Israel's kings, including Solomon, offered sacrifice to various deities as a matter of expediency.

Telling the Story of David and Goliath

This activity is intended to capture some of the dynamism of the storytelling that went on among the ancient Israelites.

1. Request a volunteer to tell the story of David and Goliath (1 Sam., chap. 17) as if she or he were telling the story to small children. Give your volunteer storyteller time to prepare and then tell the story to the class. Beforehand, remind the class that the storyteller is imagining that they are children.

2. After the storyteller has finished, ask the rest of the students this question, then rephrase it and ask the storyteller the same:
- What elements of the story did the teller stress because it was being told to young children?

3. Finally, discuss these questions with the students:
- Why has this story been a popular tale for children over the ages? What is its universal and timeless appeal? What lesson does the story teach?
- If you were making a children's movie of David's life, whom would you cast as young David? as Goliath? as Jonathan? as Saul? as King David? Why?

Did God Cause Saul's Evildoings?

Here are some questions for starting a discussion of God's possible role in the evil done by Saul:
- According to the First Book of Samuel, Saul's moods were caused by "an evil spirit from God" [18:10]. Is God ever the source of evil? If you took every word of the Bible literally, wouldn't you have to conclude that yes, God can be the source of evil?
- What is a different explanation of why chapter 18, verse 10, was included in the story of Saul? [Ancient people assumed that the mental states we would now call mental illnesses were sent by God. Now we know that these mental disturbances have complex causes and are not God-sent. Scholars have speculated that Saul suffered from a severe form of depression.]
- Some news stories tell of people who do violence because, as they say, "God told me to." What would you say to such people?
- Did Jesus ever speak of "evil spirits" as being sent by God?

Turning to a discussion of Saul's jealousy in particular, ask the students these questions:
- Why was Saul, a king, jealous of David?
- Is jealousy common? Why or why not?
- By looking at Saul, what can we conclude about the causes and effects of jealousy?
- How could honesty, generosity, and humility help to dispel jealous feelings?
- In modern times is the attitude of keeping up with the Joneses the most common form of jealousy?

Jesus Refers to the Story of David and the Holy Bread

Have your students read Mark 2:23–28. In this passage Jesus refers to David's accepting the holy bread from the priest Abiathar in order to feed his men. Note that Jesus rooted his teaching in the Hebrew Scriptures, a point that cannot be emphasized too often.

Next discuss the slaughter of Ahimelech and the people of Nob.
- ◆ Why did Saul order the killings?
- ◆ Is this what usually happens when anger and jealousy get out of hand?
- ◆ Can you recall any news stories that have reported acts of violence based on emotions similar to those of Saul?

6

David's Gifts and Our Own

In examining Saul's sad career, we see that good qualities can be overshadowed by evil. Neither was David the sweetheart of the Israelites by the end of his career as king. But the remarkable qualities of David in his youth had enabled him to become a highly successful leader.

1. Ask your students this question:
- ◆ What qualities of the young David indicated that he would be a good king?

Handout **6–A**

2. Just as God gave David certain qualities that would enable him to be a great king, so God gives each young person special skills and traits that suit him or her for some mission that is as yet unknown. To help the students identify their own gifts, use handout 6–A, "What You Offer the World." The handout asks the students to look over a list of skills and traits, circle those that apply to themselves, and then write a description of how they use five of those gifts on an everyday basis.

3. After the students have completed the self-examination, pose these questions for class discussion:
- ◆ Why does God give people different skills or traits—that is, gifts?
- ◆ Is the world better because we are all different?
- ◆ What would the world be like if we all had all the skills and traits on this list?
- ◆ Write down one definite limitation or deficiency that you have in either the skill area or the trait area.
- ◆ Is it possible that your limitation could actually be a good thing? How? What has this limitation taught you about yourself and other people? [The students may write answers to the preceding questions, or they may share responses in class.]
- ◆ We all have gifts of diverse skills and traits. What responsibilities do these gifts bring with them?

4. You might finish the exercise by asking your students each to write a short prayer of thanksgiving for all the skills and traits that God has given them.

Concept D: King David: Nation Builder

Review Questions: King David: Nation Builder

Question. How does David continue to show loyalty to Saul and those close to Saul?
Answer. David's response to the deaths of Saul, Abner, and Ishbaal is not even relief; it is deep anger at their murderers and profound mourning at the losses.

Question. Why is Jerusalem an ideal choice as capital?
Answer. Because Jerusalem had never belonged to any one of the twelve tribes, David could not be accused of playing favorites by bringing his court there. Also, Jerusalem was ideally located in the territory between the northern and the southern tribes.

Question. What does David do as he brings the ark of the Covenant into Jerusalem, and what is Michal's reaction?
Answer. He dances joyfully before the ark, praising God, and Michal berates him for acting like a fool.

Question. What is the Davidic Covenant? What is its connection with the later Jewish expectation of a messiah?
Answer. Scripture scholars call God's promise that David's line of descendants will endure forever the Davidic Covenant. Devout Jews remembered God's promise and waited for the reappearance of a leader from the royal line to be Israel's Messiah.

Question. How does David sin grievously, and how does Nathan help him to repent?
Answer. He commits adultery with Bathsheba, then lies and manipulates others, finally arranging for Bathsheba's husband to be killed, to cover up his sin. Nathan helps him recognize his sin by telling him a parable, and Nathan assures David that God forgives him and will not ask for his life, but prophesies much trouble in his family.

Question. Why did the Deuteronomists leave the account of David's sins in their history? What message can it give us?
Answer. They make it clear that David is not above God's Law; he must repent for his sins, and he will suffer greatly for them. The message for us is that God works through limited and sinful persons, giving us all hope that God somehow brings about divine purposes even through our flaws.

Question. Give three examples of how the sons of David cause him tragedy and grief. In general, what is David's response to their terrible deeds?
Answer. Amnon rapes his half sister Tamar, Absalom kills Amnon, and Absalom plots to take over David's kingship. David does not punish Amnon, and he trusts Absalom to come back into his court after killing Amnon, failing to recognize Absalom's treacherous intentions. David seems to be a permissive parent whose devotion to his sons makes him abandon good sense.

Question. What characteristic of David made him a model of what the kings, and all Israel, should have been?
Answer. His devotion to God

6

Text Activities: King David: Nation Builder

- The plot in this story is illustrated in our times by the controversy over assisted suicide. Although physician-assisted suicide is practiced mostly with the terminally ill, the implications go much further. Is it wrong for someone to choose suicide as a means of avoiding suffering? Should one who assists in a suicide be held responsible? Find an article about this topic and write a few paragraphs explaining your point of view. Research what the Catholic Church teaches and include it in your essay.
- Is it possible to be intensely loyal to someone who has acted like an enemy to you? Think of someone you care about who has treated you badly. How could you still be loyal to him or her? Write your thoughts in a paragraph.
- Politics, at its worst, can involve using or oppressing people. What does it look like at its best? Write about several examples.
- Read 1 Corinthians 13:4–7. Write a brief essay explaining the difference between love and lust and between love and infatuation.
- List three virtues and three flaws of David, giving an example of how he demonstrated each. Do the same for a leader of our time. Are you aware of your own flaws and weaknesses? Do you believe it is possible that God can work through you in spite of these? Have you ever experienced that? If so, write a description of what happened.
- In a paragraph describe a character on television or in a movie who reminds you of Amnon or Absalom.
- Etched on U.S. currency are the words "In God we trust." Do you think this is true of U.S. citizens, or does our national security depend on trust in weapons, the military, wealth, prisons, and so on? Write an essay on your thoughts and observations.
- Are you familiar with the story of King Arthur of Britain? Look up the legend of the Round Table. In writing, compare Arthur's story with David's.

 ## Additional Activities: King David: Nation Builder

Praying for Guidance

David is portrayed in the Scriptures as, above all, devoted to God. Despite some terrible mistakes for which he is later repentant, David listens to God in making decisions.

1. Here are some questions for discussion regarding the role of prayer in making decisions:
- David repeatedly consulted God before making decisions. What does this say about how we should approach important decisions?
- Did Saul always consult God before making decisions? What were the consequences for him?
- Do you think that any of our political leaders turn to God in prayer when making decisions?
- How do we receive God's guidance if we do pray? [Remind your students that God's guidance usually comes from the Scriptures, Church Tradition, wise counselors, and our reading of the signs of the times. It takes two to pray—God and ourselves. God will "speak," but we must know how to listen and be willing to listen.]

2. Perhaps the students are struggling with decisions of their own. You might emphasize "listening" to God by taking them through the meditation exercise explained on page 121 of this manual. Or they could write a dialog between God and themselves about the decision to be made. They might first spend time looking through the Scriptures or some of the resources listed above to see what guidance is offered. Your assistance, as well as your encouragement that God's wisdom does come to us if we seek it, will be vital.

O Jerusalem!

The holy city of Jerusalem has been fought over, occupied, and ruled by many different nations since the time of David. Select one or two students to prepare a time line showing all the groups who have ruled Jerusalem from the time of David to the present.

Another student could report on why the Muslims consider Jerusalem a holy city.

6

The Davidic Covenant

The Covenant between God and David, described as Nathan's prophecy in 2 Samuel 7:1–17, was a promise that God would bring forth a royal dynasty from David's family and that this royal line would endure forever. Ask the students to consider (1) what such a promise meant to the Israelites and (2) how it was misinterpreted.

1. *Meaning.* The promise meant that God's unfailing love and faithfulness would be with the people forever. This assurance of unconditional love and help from God was surely the best news imaginable for devout Israelites.
2. *Misinterpretation.* The promise was misinterpreted by many Israelites and their kings. Throughout the centuries after David's reign, the northern kingdom of Israel and the southern kingdom of Judah had some terribly unfaithful moments—the reigns of oppressive kings and corrupt officials, times of idolatry, periods when their national policy was on an arrogant, disobedient course. The Judahites in particular, whose kings were of the house of David, assumed that because Israel was under God's protection, their immoral, defiant behavior would not result in the loss of their kingdom. They assumed that somehow God would rescue them from the inevitable consequences of their arrogance. When the kingdom of Judah finally did fall, crushed by the Babylonians in 587 BC, many Judahites could not believe what was happening to their nation, because they remembered the Davidic Covenant.

   Explore this issue further with the students, using these questions:
   - When we say that God loves us unconditionally—without limits and even when we sin grievously—what do we really mean? Do we mean that God will prevent us from ever suffering the consequences of our own choices? Or even from suffering when we are not at fault?
   - Is love—such as that of parents for their children or married persons for each other—compatible with being angry with the one loved or with disapproving of what that person does?
   - After committing adultery with Bathsheba and arranging for the murder of her husband, Uriah, David's fortune begins to turn bad. Even though he is sincerely contrite, from then on his life is full of grief and tragedy. Does this mean that God did not forgive David or that God was abandoning the Davidic Covenant?

Psalm 51: A Lament for Grievous Sin

Direct the students to Psalm 51, the most famous of the penitential psalms:

> Have mercy on me, O God,
>   according to your steadfast love;
> according to your abundant mercy
>   blot out my transgressions. . . .

Traditionally, the psalm has been attributed to David; it is supposedly David's outpouring after the prophet Nathan makes him recognize the seriousness of his sins of adultery and murder.

Note that the last two verses of the psalm were added during the Babylonian exile, after Jerusalem had been destroyed. Thus the Judahites in exile must have seen a parallel between David's great sin and their own wickedness, which had brought about the loss of their homeland and the Temple. In exile they became truly remorseful, just as David was after Nathan confronted him.

Have the students pray aloud Psalm 51, with different parts of the class or small groups taking different verses. Then have the students write a brief paragraph for their own reflection purposes, on this theme:

◆ Have you ever felt like the ancient people who prayed this psalm? Have you ever wanted to start over again after making a big mistake? Did you experience forgiveness in that incident?

When Leaders Sin

All of us have heard of political, church, athletic, business, and military leaders who have been exposed as anything but noble or admirable. Each case eats away at the public's sense of trust in institutions and in people in general. In the context of the story about David and Bathsheba, discuss the issue of leaders' sins.

◆ What are some recent examples of people in leadership positions—in government or in business, for instance—who have been exposed as doing wrong?

◆ What are some of the effects on society when these leaders commit great wrongs?

◆ What can we reasonably expect about the moral behavior of leaders or public persons?

◆ Does it make sense for people to become cynical about public officials in general because of those who do wrong?

David the Parent

Amnon rapes his half sister Tamar, but David's punishment for his son is hardly typical of what the Israelites did to the rapist of a virgin. (David gets angry but apparently takes no action against Amnon; under the Mosaic Law, a man who rapes a virgin is to be executed.) After Absalom has Amnon murdered, David takes Absalom back without ever mentioning the murder. Then Absalom turns against his father in a plot to overthrow him.

It might be instructive to talk about parental permissiveness and the problems it can cause. You can use these discussion starters:

- What do you think David should have done when he learned that Amnon had raped Tamar?
- If Tamar had been raped by a common man, would the treatment of the man have been as light as that of Amnon?
- What happens in a society when double standards for punishment exist? Does our society have double standards for punishment?
- Was Absalom justified in having Amnon slain?
- If David had punished Amnon (short of executing him), do you think Absalom would have killed Amnon?
- What happens when parents let their children get away with wrongdoing?

David and Saul: Unique Characters

Assign this task to your students:
- First, list the ways David and Saul were different in character and deed; then list the ways they were similar.
- Then write a brief summary of the most significant thing you have learned from the careers of these two figures.

When the students have finished writing, invite them to share their responses.

6

Concept E: King Solomon: Temple Builder

Review Questions: King Solomon: Temple Builder

Question. Give three examples of Solomon's wisdom.

Answer. (1) Solomon settles a dispute over a child by calling for a sword to divide it in half, knowing that the real mother would never allow that. (2) He utters three thousand proverbs and writes one thousand and five songs. (3) He discusses plants, beasts, birds, reptiles, and fishes.

Question. How does Solomon oppress and exploit the people?

Answer. He forms an elite group of administrators and introduces forced labor and taxation to provide supplies for the palace and government officials.

Question. What is God's warning at the time the Temple is dedicated?

Answer. If Solomon and his descendants forsake the Covenant, the Temple will become a heap of ruins.

Question. What burdens does Israel inherit from Solomon?

Answer. Idolatry is the worst burden Israel inherits. Also, the people are oppressed by taxes and forced labor, and the kingdom faces an impending breakup.

Pages 136–141

Text Activities: King Solomon: Temple Builder

- Who or what do you look to for wisdom? Write a paragraph about this source of wisdom in your life.
- Find an article about a corrupt or oppressive government of a country in the world today. How do you think world leaders and citizens outside that country can approach this problem? Write an essay about this issue and possible responses or resolutions.
- Being portable, the ark held the Covenant of a people on a journey. The Temple, on the other hand, was set in stone, representing security and stability. Write a reflection on how both the ark and the Temple can remind us of God's presence with us.
- In writing, compare and contrast the characters of Saul, David, and Solomon. What did each, despite his flaws, contribute to the salvation of Israel?

6

Additional Activities: King Solomon: Temple Builder

Killing One's Enemies

David counsels Solomon to murder David's enemies as soon as he takes power. Solomon takes David's advice. Lest your students get the idea that this is the way to behave toward enemies, read Matthew 5:38–48 aloud to them. Then, using these questions, lead a study of the Christian treatment of enemies:

- Would Jesus have approved of David's counsel and Solomon's actions?
- Are there places in the world where political figures murder their rivals to keep control? Are any of these countries ruled by supposed Christians?
- Do people find David and Solomon's approach to enemies easier or harder to follow than that of Jesus? Explain.
- Can you give any examples of people who treat their enemies as Jesus taught us to?

Being Fair

The story of Solomon's judgment in the case of the two prostitutes (see pp. 137–139 of the student text) can be a starting point for a consideration of how to be fair in difficult cases. Tell the students that in this activity they will have a chance to be wise like Solomon.

1. Divide your class into groups of about four or five students. You must end up with an even number of groups. For identification purposes, assign a different number to each group (group 1, group 2, etc.). Then give these instructions:

- Within your group, come up with two situations that would be difficult to resolve fairly. These may be either real-life or fictional cases. If they are real-life cases, please do not disclose the names of the people involved; just make up names. A reporter from each group must write down all the circumstances of the two situations. If you are a reporter, be sure to neatly and clearly write each case on a separate sheet of paper, because the cases will be read by another group. Also, put the number of your group in the upper right-hand corner of each sheet so that later we can identify where the situations came from.

2. When the groups have finished developing and recording their cases, direct them to exchange their two cases with those of another group. Then give the groups time to discuss the cases they have received and to come up with fair or just solutions to those situations (somewhat like Solomon rendering his wise judgments).

3. Have the groups that exchanged cases with each other meet and discuss the solutions that each group has found for the other's cases.

4. Bring the class back together to discuss these questions:
◆ Is being fair an easy thing most of the time?
◆ Should we expect life to be fair, or should we only hope that life will be fair?
◆ What makes a situation difficult to resolve?

6

Why Build a Temple?

Explain to the students that the decision to build a Temple was highly significant for Israel, somewhat like the decision to have a king (see the activity "Why Have a King?" on pp. 122–123 of this manual).

1. To highlight the significance of the Temple's construction, go over the following information with the students:
◆ Previous to Solomon's building of the Temple, the Israelites housed the ark of the Covenant—the symbol of God's presence—in a tent, or tabernacle. It was portable; thus, wherever the people moved, God went with them. This tent of the meeting was where God and Israel met through Moses. It was the place of revelation. In their nomadic period, God always journeyed with the Israelites and was present among them. Later, in Canaan, the ark of the Covenant was carried at the head of the Israelite forces during battle. God was not a stationary god who could be pinned down to one place but, rather, a god who lived with the people wherever they were.
◆ Chapter 6 of the Second Book of Samuel reports that David had the ark of the Covenant brought to the new capital, Jerusalem, and placed in a tent—still a temporary dwelling. In the next chapter [2 Sam. 7:1–7], David wonders whether he ought to build a suitable, permanent home for God, and God replies with a seeming preference for tent life over the stable life of a house of cedar! Nevertheless, God promises [7:8–13] that David's heir (who will be Solomon) will build a suitable place for God, a dwelling to correspond with the newfound stability of the Israelites.

2. Ask the students to consider what the building of the Temple signified for the Israelites of Solomon's time. Here are some possible answers:
• God, like the Chosen People, would have a permanent, stable place. At last the Israelites and God would have a home.
• Israel would be more like the major nations of the time, which had monarchs, land securely their own, and temples for their gods.
• God could be worshiped in dignity.
• The people would have a center for their religion and their religious identity.

For the Deuteronomists, who wrote most of the history of Israel after Solomon's time, the Temple meant a centralized location for worship. It eliminated the need for the Israelites to worship in other places, where they were constantly tempted to idolatry. The Temple stood for worship of the one God. In exile they focused on the importance of the Temple (which by then had been destroyed) because a return to and rebuilding of the Temple would mean a purification of the people's corrupted religious practices.

3. Ask the students to consider what, for the Israelites, might have been the disadvantages of building the Temple. List these on the chalkboard as students call them out. If they need help, here are some possibilities:
- People could begin to associate God with a certain place instead of thinking of God as being wherever they were, accompanying them in their journeys and struggles.
- Elitism, power games, and corruption could develop among those who served in the Temple.
- God could be associated not merely with dignified surroundings but with enormous wealth and power. God might not be thought of as a poor nomad in a tent, available to the people, but as a monarch reigning from a palace.
- Solomon would have to nearly enslave his people in order to support this building project.
- If the Israelites prided themselves on being more like other nations (which had temples for their gods), they might start acting like them—that is, idolatrous and unjust.
- The association of worship and religion with a particular building and strict set of religious practices could lead to a ritualistic emphasis. In that case religion would be seen not so much as a matter of how faithfully one lived (the emphasis of the Deuteronomists and the Law) but as a matter of how meticulously one fulfilled the rituals of the Temple.

4. Invite the students to consider these questions:
- What is your predominant image of a church? Is it (*a*) a building where people come to worship according to prescribed rituals or (*b*) a community of people who are enlivened by God's presence among them?
- What is your predominant image of religion? Is it (*a*) devotion to a set of religious practices, attendance at church services, and keeping all the rules or (*b*) living everyday life in a way that is faithful to God's love and justice?

5. In summary, note that the *a* response to each question represents a "Temple" orientation and the *b* response represents a "tent" orientation. Both orientations have their place, but remind the students of this: It has been said that one meaning of the Incarnation is that "God pitched his tent among us." The Gospel of John says, "And the Word became flesh and lived among us" (1:14). Biblical scholars tell us that the Hebrew word for "to make a dwelling" means literally "to pitch a tent." This is a very intimate, personal understanding of God's relationship with us. Christianity and the Incarnation suggest more of a "tent" orientation than a "Temple" orientation to church and religion.

Acts of Oppression

Ideally, governments are servants of their people's welfare. Obviously, most governments are far from ideal. If you wish to talk about the ways that some governments, like Solomon's, oppress their people, use any of the following activities:

Small-group discussion. Ask your students each to bring to class one magazine or newspaper article that illustrates the oppression of a population by its government—even while government officials live in luxury. Divide the students into small groups, where each member can explain her or his article.

Consciousness-raising posters. Have your students make posters about the plight of oppressed people in some countries. Hang the posters throughout the school in order to raise the students' consciousness.

Supportive letters. *National Catholic Reporter* and *Sojourners* frequently publish articles about political prisoners, and the Nobel prize–winning organization Amnesty International regularly publishes bulletins worldwide about prisoners of conscience. The object is to rally letters, on prisoners' behalf, to officials in the oppressive governments. Your class might duplicate these articles or bulletins and post them in prominent places, or even write letters on the prisoners' behalf. This could be done each week or so.

Wealth and Goodness

The queen of Sheba was impressed with Solomon's wisdom and wealth. The story of Solomon could leave students with the impression that wealth is connected to goodness. This is clearly not the perspective of the Old Testament nor that of the New Testament.

Read 1 Timothy 6:10 to your students. Then pose these questions:
- What does Saint Paul mean by his comment?
- Notice that Paul says that the love of money, not money itself, is the root of all evil. What is the implication of this phrasing?
- Which is more prized in our society today: money or virtue?
- Is a high standard of living the ideal goal for a nation? a family? an individual? What are some worthy goals for nations? families? individuals?
- Is greed a common vice in our day? Can you think of some examples?
- Do people have to hurt others, like Solomon did, to be wealthy?

Israel's Empire: How Huge Was It?

Direct the students to the map entitled "The Empire of David and Solomon" on page 138 of the student text. Point out that the map shows the nation of Israel at its greatest extent—that is, during Solomon's reign, before the division into the kingdoms Israel and Judah.

1. To give the students an idea of how much territory the empire covered, ask them to do the following:
- First, calculate the approximate number of square miles in the empire outlined on the map, using the scale of miles provided there. This can be a very rough calculation. [The students may treat the parts of the kingdom as squares or rectangles. They can measure the length and width of each part in inches and then convert the length and width to miles. Next, they can multiply length by width (in miles) for each part. When they add the square miles of the parts together, they will arrive at the approximate total number of square miles in the empire. The total is about 16,700 square miles.]

◆ Next, look up your own country in a world atlas. Find the pages that indicate the number of square miles for each state or province. Locate your own state or province and write down the number of its square miles.

◆ Last, compare the size of Israel's empire with the size of your state or province by using this formula:

$$\frac{\textbf{Square miles in Israel's empire}}{\textbf{Square miles in my state or province}} = \textbf{Ratio of areas}$$

Examples:
• Students in California would conclude that the empire was about one-tenth the size of California.
• Students in New Jersey would conclude that the empire was about twice the size of New Jersey.
• Students in Ontario would find that the empire was about one-twenty-fifth the size of Ontario.

2. Summarize the point of the activity by asking the students these questions:

◆ The Israelites under Solomon thought that they had a vast empire. Does it seem vast to you?

◆ Mighty kings and generals throughout history have often thought that they "ruled the world." What does this activity tell us about their perspective?

Would Solomon Have Listened to Paul?

With your students following along in their Bibles, read aloud the words of Saint Paul to his disciple Timothy in 1 Timothy 6:17–19. Then ask:

◆ Would Solomon have heeded these words of Paul if he had heard them? Why or why not?

Solomon and Constantine

In the context of studying Solomon's reign, point out to the students that religion inevitably seems to be corrupted when it becomes too entangled with government. Israel's religion was certainly the poorer for Solomon's influence; he used religion to glorify his own name. One might wonder if the Israelites built the Temple out of devotion to God or because Solomon ordered it to be built, imposing horrendous taxes and levying human labor.

In the fourth century AD, Constantine began a trend of "Christian" kings and emperors dominating the Church, using it for their own ends. Constantine understood that people of the same religion are more unified than people with diverse beliefs. So he used his considerable power to push people to convert to Christianity. By giving Church officials authority and positions in government offices, he made them useful to the state. Thus the Church reinforced the power of the state.

Emphasize the point that when religion becomes a servant of the state instead of an independent voice, trouble is not far off.

Closing Prayer

Give the students a sense of the love that the Israelites had for the Temple and for their capital, Jerusalem, by creating a prayer service around Psalm 84 ("How lovely is your dwelling place . . .") and Psalm 122 ("I was glad when they said to me, / 'Let us go to the house of the LORD . . .'"). Both of these psalms have been beautifully set to music: "I Rejoiced," by John Foley, is from the album *Wood Hath Hope* (Saint Louis Jesuits, 1978). "How Lovely Is Your Dwelling Place," by Michael Joncas is from the album *A Voice Cries Out* (New Dawn Music, 1979).

For a reflection during the prayer service, ask the students to silently consider these questions:

- ◆ Is there a Jerusalem in my life—a place that makes me want to rejoice because I feel whole and welcome there, because I feel that it's a special place for me to be who I really am?
- ◆ What is a temple in my life—a situation or relationship or place where I somehow feel in touch with God or become aware of deep goodness?

Closing Teacher Prayer

Call to prayer. Be still within and without. Center yourself in God's steadfast love.

Reflect. What have you learned in the process of teaching this chapter? Was it a learning of the head or the heart? Does this reveal God more fully to you? How? What effect could this learning have on your life?

What gift did you receive from your students? Which students do you feel are especially in need of God's tender care today?

Pray.
Generous God,
you are the giver of all things.
Through every single thing,
we are touched with your loving presence.
Your love is everlasting,
healing and restoring us.
Your love is ever faithful,
giving courage and strength.
Your gracious love carries us,
lightening the burdens of our life.
You are our life,
the breath of our being. Amen.

(Bergan and Schwan, *Taste and See:
Prayer Services for Gatherings of Faith*)

What You Offer the World

Look over the following lists of skills and traits. Circle the skills and traits that you have been gifted with.

Skills

developing new ideas	initiating projects	learning from others	assembling information
observing	comparing	budgeting	deciding
communicating	persuading	inspiring	leading
studying	memorizing	speech making	visualizing
using tools	interviewing	supervising	designing
listening	computing	negotiating	planning
analyzing	training others	researching	sensing needs

Traits

determined	friendly	serious	thoughtful
cooperative	logical	realistic	open-minded
joyful	loyal	insightful	practical
perceptive	enthusiastic	sympathetic	artistic
honest	attentive	encouraging	energetic
imaginative	responsible	farsighted	strong
reliable	warmhearted	outgoing	humorous

On the back of this handout, describe how you use five of your skills or traits on an everyday basis.

CHAPTER 7

The Prophets:
Crying Out the Word of God

Major Concepts

A. The Kingdom Breaks Up. Despite the prophets' call to remain faithful to God's Covenant, most of the people of Israel and their wicked kings continue on a self-serving path that eventually leads to exile. Following Solomon's death, the people of the north do not accept Rehoboam, the southern king, and the kingdom is divided—Israel in the north and Judah in the south. The north's King Jeroboam enshrines golden calves to keep his people from going south to worship in Jerusalem. Ahab marries Jezebel, gaining for Israel the military strength of Phoenicia at the cost of putting Baal in God's place. *See* the *Catechism,* nos. 61, 64, 218 (prophecy); 401 (Israel's sin); 709–710 (the Exile); 2112–2114 (idolatry); 2584 (prophetic prayer).

B. Elijah and Elisha in the North. Elijah and Elisha, nonwriting prophets of the northern kingdom, warn the Israelites of idolatry's consequences. Elijah speaks out against the wicked powers of his day—King Ahab, Jezebel, and the prophets of Baal. Elijah, who discovers God's strength in the ordinariness of life, demonstrates God's power over the impotent Baal. Elijah went to Heaven in a fiery chariot. Elisha carries on Elijah's mission and is known for performing many miracles, particularly healings. *See* the *Catechism,* nos. 35, 2085 (God's revelation); 61, 64, 218 (prophecy); 164 (trust in God); 269 (God's omnipotence); 307 (divine providence); 523, 696, 718–719 (Elijah); 548 (miracles); 2581–2584 (Elijah and prayer).

C. Amos and Hosea in the North. Amos, a shepherd from Judah, condemns Israel's disregard for God's Law, calls for true worship backed up with justice for all, and pleads with God to spare Israel's destruction by its own sin. Gomer's infidelity to Hosea gives him the words and images to describe Israel's unfaithfulness to God. Though Israel will be punished for its betrayal, it is forever beloved by God. The northern kingdom of Israel falls to the Assyrians around 721 BC, and the people scatter. *See* the *Catechism,* nos. 218–219, 1611 (the relationship between God and Israel is like a marriage); 1807, 2426, 2445–2446, 2449 (social justice); 2097 (worship); 2100 (Hosea).

D. Isaiah in the South: The Greatest Writing Prophet. Although all Judah's kings descended from King David, they mostly lead the people to idolatry and greed. The Book of Isaiah is the work of three principal authors who spoke to the people before, during, and after the Babylonian Exile. Named after Isaiah of Jerusalem, or First Isaiah, the Book of Isaiah begins by warning Judah to turn from injustice and idolatry and also describes Isaiah's vision of God in the Temple. Isaiah prophesies that the Messiah (whom Christians believe to be Jesus) will be born to rule forever in peace. The faith of King Hezekiah helps save Jerusalem from the Assyrians' conquest. Isaiah predicts disaster for Judah but also offers hope that Israel will again become a light to the nations. *See* the *Catechism,* nos. 64, 218 (prophecy); 439, 461–463, 522 (the Incarnation); 497, 711–712 (Jesus as Immanuel); 709–710 (the Exile); 1063 (Isaiah).

E. **Micah in the South: Sympathy from the Bottom of Society.** Micah, a poor man himself, condemns those who oppress the poor. He calls the nations to beat their swords into plowshares and tells them God requires justice, kindness, and humility. He prophesies that someone from David's line will lead Israel to peace and justice. Although it appeared that few listened to the prophets, the exiles learned from them, and people continue to be challenged by their messages. *See* the *Catechism,* nos. 437 (Jesus in the line of David); 709–710 (the Exile); 1807, 2304 (peace); 2307–2317 (avoiding war); 2445, 2449 (the poor); 2573 (Jacob).

Opening Teacher Prayer

Call to prayer. Be still within and without. Center yourself in the God who leads and guides us.

Read. Psalm 25

Reflect. What words or phrases in Psalm 25 fill you with a sense of hope?

Hold in your heart. "Lead me in your truth, and teach me" (Ps. 25:5).

Concept A: The Kingdom Breaks Up

Pages 145–148

Review Questions: The Kingdom Breaks Up

Question. In what ways were the prophets the conscience of Israel and Judah?
Answer. They warned the people that they had strayed from true worship and forgotten their role as witness to the Lord before the nations.

Question. Why do the northern tribes form their own kingdom?
Answer. They do not wish to be oppressed by Rehoboam in the same way his father had oppressed them. When Rehoboam calls for more brutality, not less, the northern tribes reject him.

Question. How does Israel's King Jeroboam break the Law of God? Why does he do so?

Answer. He enshrines two golden calves, one at Dan and the other at Bethel. He hopes to keep his people from going south to Jerusalem to worship, where they might rekindle their loyalty to the house of David.

Text Activities: The Kingdom Breaks Up

- Name a type of leader (such as a bishop, a president, a general, or a principal) and list five ways she or he can be a servant in that role.
- In previous chapters you identified the kinds of false gods people worship today. Write your opinion in response to this question: *Why do people turn to these kinds of false gods?*

Additional Activities: The Kingdom Breaks Up

Research on Divided Countries

Select some students to find out about countries that have split up either because of conflicts from within or because of outside influences, for example, the former Yugoslavia, the former Soviet Union, Ireland, Vietnam, Korea, Germany, Cyprus, and Palestine and Israel. Suggest that they pay particular attention to possible religious dimensions of the conflicts.

The American Civil War and its devastating effect on the Union would probably be of great interest to your students. Assign other students to research the American Civil War.

Give all the students an opportunity to speak briefly to your class about their findings.

After the presentations, shift the focus to the division of the ancient nation Israel. Begin by having the students reread 1 Kings 12:16. Then discuss these questions:

◆ Solomon's son Rehoboam refused to listen when the northern tribes of Israel pleaded for justice and mercy. What was the people's reaction to not being heard? [They felt cut off from the heritage of David and thus under no obligation to David's descendant. They rejected Rehoboam and made Jeroboam king.]

◆ How does their reaction correspond to the way that people today react when their leaders do not listen to their needs?

Point out that although Rehoboam's brutal oppression was one cause of the breakup of the nation, the rebel Jeroboam, declared king in the north, was motivated more by power than by genuine concern for the oppressed Israelites. His desire for power added fuel to the fires of division. In fact Solomon himself had been motivated by political purposes more so than religious ones when he made Jerusalem the sole place of worship in the nation.

Ask the students,

◆ What are some other ways that religion has been used throughout history to justify political, military, or economic ends?

Golden Calves Again

To illustrate how history repeats itself when a society ignores the lessons of its own experience, ask your class these questions:

- When Jeroboam is declared king in the north, he immediately breaks the Law and enshrines two golden calves. Where have we heard about a golden calf before?
- What happened when the Chosen People made the earlier golden calf?
- Why was it a grave offense for Jeroboam to raise up non-Levite priests?

Concept B: Elijah and Elisha in the North

Pages 148–154

7

Review Questions: Elijah and Elisha in the North

Question. How does the story of Elijah and the starving widow demonstrate trust in God?

Answer. Although the woman has only enough flour and oil for a barley cake for herself and her son, she believes Elijah when he promises God's help if she shares the cake. Having trusted that God will provide whatever is needed, the woman never goes hungry again.

Question. In what way does Elijah experience the presence of God at the cave?

Answer. In a gentle breeze ("the sound of sheer silence" or "a tiny whispering sound")

Question. How did the biblical storytellers describe Elijah's leaving the earth? What belief arose later about Elijah?

Answer. The storytellers describe Elisha alone witnessing a flaming chariot with fiery horses coming between him and Elijah, and Elijah disappearing in a whirlwind. This tale eventually gave rise to the belief that Elijah would return to announce the coming of the Messiah.

Question. Give four examples of Elisha's miracles.

Answer. [Any four of the following examples are correct.] Elisha purifies Jericho's water supply, which has been causing deaths and miscarriages. He helps a widow avoid selling her children to pay her debts. He blesses a childless couple, and they beget a son. Later he raises this child from the dead. He purifies poisoned stew and multiplies loaves of bread to make enough for a hundred people. He cures Naaman of leprosy.

Text Activities: Elijah and Elisha in the North

- Write a modern-day story that tells the lesson of this story about the widow.

- What are your dreams for the future? Think about ways of helping to heal the world. Then respond in writing to this question: *If anything were possible, what would you do to heal the world?*
- "We may not find God's power in big, obvious successes or triumphs but in his quiet movement in our everyday life." Read this sentence to three adults you know. Ask them if they believe it is true. If they say yes, ask if they can think of an example of his quiet movement in their life. If they disagree with the statement, ask them to explain their viewpoint. Write the results of your interviews.
- Write about an experience from your life that shows either the destructive effects of evil or the nature of good, which is fruitful and multiplies.
- In a paragraph, respond to the following questions:
  - Have you ever used the word *miracle* for an event you witnessed or for a solution to a situation you thought was unsolvable?
  - Was the event or the solution a suspending of the natural order? Or did you use the word *miracle* simply to say that it was wonderful beyond expectations? or spooky?
  - Did the event have anything to do with faith?

 ## Additional Activities: Elijah and Elisha in the North

An Unexpected Source of Food

Point out to the students that Elijah is certainly called to receive his nourishment from some unlikely sources. During the great drought in Israel, God tells him to go hide by a stream, where ravens will feed him—not your typical source of a good meal! Likewise, when the stream goes dry, Elijah is sent to be fed at the home of a poor widow who herself is starving.

It seems that the scriptural writers were trying to convey a message that has timeless relevance: We are not always "fed" (sustained in more than just a physical way) by the most likely source of nourishment. Sometimes an apparently unlikely source of sustenance and support has the greatest power to sustain us, if we have faith that God is at work in the process.

Discuss these questions with the students:
- How can a person be fed in more than a physical sense?
- Can you think of some unlikely places or situations that might end up being nurturing or supportive for a person?

If your students do not come up with any examples for the last question, be ready with your own. For instance, offer the situation of a gruff coach who shows up at a wake held for a student's deceased mother. He is not a likely source of nourishment. Paint a scenario in which the coach ends up "feeding" the grieving student. Here is another example of an unlikely source of support:

- Mary, one of the "brainy" kids in her school, flunks a course for having plagiarized in her term paper. Her friends and a lot of other kids tease her about it, with now-you-know-how-it-feels jokes. Only Therese, the girl whose locker is next to Mary's, offers sympathy. Therese gets low grades, and Mary hasn't associated with her much before this. Therese does not seem like someone who could give Mary emotional support, but Mary finds that she does just that.

Elijah's Companion

The story of Elijah's fleeing Jezebel (1 Kings 19:1–18) is worth further discussion. In this story God is a companion to Elijah as the prophet journeys. Studying the passage can help your students understand both how God helps us and how we can be companions to one another.

1. Begin this activity by asking your students to quickly review the passage from 1 Kings. Then invite them to discuss these questions:
◆ When Elijah sits under the broom tree, how does he feel? Why does he feel so desperate?
◆ For what reasons do your peers get desperate and say, "I have had enough"?
◆ What does the angel do for Elijah?
◆ Why does God send bread and water and not other food and drink? [Bread and water are the most basic needs for sustenance of life.]
◆ Have you ever known of anyone who seemed supported or sustained throughout a terrible or desperate situation, such as the terminal illness of someone close to him or her? How did the person seem to be supported?

2. Tell your students the following:
◆ The story of Elijah's desperation is interesting because it not only shows God's faithfulness to Elijah but tells us something about how we can be companions to people who are desperate and see no reason for living.
◆ The word *companion* comes from two Latin words: *com,* meaning "with," and *panis,* meaning "bread." Our companions are the people who share bread with us, who give us life, who help us when we are low. Companions feed us physically, emotionally, and intellectually so that we can get on with our journey. Bread and water were chosen for Elijah's food because they fill the basic physical needs that humans have, but they also symbolized for Elijah that God did care about him.

3. In the second part of the story, God comes to Elijah in a gentle breeze, reversing Elijah's and our expectation that God would come dramatically. God is a god of surprises, and God acts in all of life—not only in the big events. To reinforce this point and to extend the activity on page 151 of the student text, pose these questions for discussion:
◆ Do people expect God to come to them in some dramatic way? Why?
◆ Why do you think God came to Elijah in the gentle breeze rather than in the powerful wind, the earthquake, or the fire?
◆ Name some of the "gentle breezes" in life where we might find God if we are looking.
Remind the students that sometimes God does come quite dramatically. For instance, in the Exodus account of God's theophany (19:16–19), God comes in the thunder and lightning. The point is not to expect that God will come to us in any one way—gentle or dramatic.

Faith Equals Commitment

1. Discuss the following with your class:
◆ The student text, in reflecting on Elijah's message to his people, says, "Biblical faith calls for commitment, not standing on the sidelines be-

ing careful." Luke echoes this when he quotes Jesus as saying, "Whoever is not with me is against me, and whoever does not gather with me scatters" (Luke 11:23).

◆ We often prefer our faith to be comforting, not challenging. Yet our faith often calls us to do things we are not comfortable doing and that may even end up making us suffer.

2. Ask the students to write a response to the following situation:

◆ Your teacher's gradebook has disappeared. You do not know at first who took it, but later you discover it is a girl who is very popular and someone you are just beginning to be better friends with. You value her friendship. She took the gradebook because her grade in just this one course will make the difference between her getting into a top college or not. The teacher is furious and has said that if the gradebook is not returned the next day, the entire class will be punished. As a person of biblical faith, what do you do?

3. After everyone has completed their writing, allow students to share their responses. Then ask:

◆ Is it easier to do nothing in a sticky situation?
◆ Should people of biblical faith bury their heads in the sand? On the other hand, are they always required to stick their noses into every situation? How does one judge when it is appropriate to take action?
◆ Does one's commitment to faith usually involve risk?

7

Is It Really a Miracle?

How is a miracle defined? Who is to judge whether a certain occurrence fits the criteria? In this activity students will research the definition of miracle and find out what criteria the Catholic Church uses to determine whether something is miraculous.

1. Remind the students:

◆ Elisha—like Jesus—performed many miraclesas as signs of God's love. Miracles have occurred throughout history and still occur today. However, the Catholic Church is skeptical when it comes to classifying a miracle. It uses strict criteria in its thorough investigations of reported miracles.

2. Then ask the students:

◆ How would you define a miracle? Is it a miracle when an emergency room team revives a heart attack patient?
◆ Do you know or have you heard of any miracles taking place recently? Describe them.

3. Instruct some students to find out how the Catholic Church determines that certain occurrences are miracles: What are the criteria, and who are the judges? Tell them to find two examples in the last millennium of officially declared miracles. Direct the students to write a report on their research and to include a bibliography.

4. After the students have turned in their reports and they have been evaluated, conduct a class discussion reviewing the information in the reports.

An Early Prophet's Cry for Social Justice

Review with your students the story of Naboth's vineyard. Afterward, explain that Elijah's confronting Ahab about the means for taking Naboth's vineyard illustrates how prophecy in that period was beginning to take a strong stance for social justice.

Naboth could not see selling the vineyard, because in his mind, it was really God's land, given to the patriarchs and their descendants to care for forever; Naboth saw himself as a trustee of God's land. In protesting the murder of Naboth and the taking of his vineyard, Elijah was asserting the primacy of the Covenant (which held everyone, king and commoner, as equal before the Law) over Baalism (which tended to favor people of status and wealth). Thus the confrontation over Naboth's vineyard represents a shift toward a type of prophecy that increasingly called not only for faithfulness to the one God but also for faithfulness to the social justice inherent in the Covenant.

7

Evil Is Self-Destructive

This activity can be used in conjunction with the activity on page 152 of the student text to explore further the consequences of good and evil. On that same page, the author states that "evil is often self-destructive, while good is usually fruitful and multiplies." Ask your students to find examples of this idea in newspapers or in history books. Instruct the students to bring to class one article or passage from a book that demonstrates the self-destructive power of evil or the fruitfulness of good. They should be prepared to explain their choice to the class.

Some students may, in fact, want to argue against the statement in the text; its validity may not be at all apparent to them. If so, encourage these students to debate the point.

In summarizing this activity, note for the students that the fruitfulness of good is not always apparent in the short term, and sometimes not even in the long term. We might not see good multiplying; it may be hidden for a long time, like a seed in the ground. Eventually, though, that seed will grow and multiply. This reality is at the heart of our faith in a good God: we believe that eventually—in the long, long run—goodness will triumph over evil, that evil will never conquer the power of goodness. That is what is meant by "Love is stronger than death." Ask the students to offer some examples of instances where the triumph of good over evil did not become apparent for a very long time.

Leprosy: The Ancient Scourge

Assign one or two students to do a written and oral report on leprosy. In ancient times this disease was most dreaded, and it reappears throughout the Bible. Knowing some facts about leprosy will enhance your students' understanding of Naaman's situation.

After the oral report has been given, ask the class to think of groups of people today who might be the equivalent of the lepers of ancient times.

A Map Exercise: Prophets to Israel and Judah

Direct the students to the map entitled "Prophets to Israel and Judah" on page 146 of the student text. Most of the prophets' names will be unfamiliar to the students because they have studied only Elijah and Elisha. However, the students can begin to refer to the map even before studying all the prophets. For one thing, looking over the map and the names of the prophets early on can acquaint them with the many names they will hear later. In addition, the map can be used throughout this chapter and chapters 8 and 9, as follows: Tell the students that as they study the prophets in chapters 7, 8, and 9, they should use a colored pencil to draw a line under the name of each prophet mentioned on the map. (The colored pencil marks can later be erased if the textbooks are to be passed on to other students.) Also, on a separate piece of paper, they should keep a running list of the prophets as they are studied, with a one-sentence summary of each prophet's message. Later, in chapter 9 of this manual, a chart in handout form will be offered to the students (see handout 9–A, "The Prophetic Tradition"). The chart summarizes the eras, locales, and messages of the prophets.

7

Concept C: Amos and Hosea in the North

Review Questions: Amos and Hosea in the North

Question. What does Amos condemn in Bethel and Samaria?
Answer. He condemns the people's unjust, exploitative actions toward the poor and weak at Bethel. In Samaria he condemns the rich women whose greed is indulged at the expense of poor people. In general he criticizes Israel's disregard for God's Law.

Question. What kind of worship does Amos criticize?
Answer. Empty or false worship in which rituals of praise and sacrifice are not sincere and backed up with just actions toward others

Question. How is Hosea's relationship with Gomer similar to God's relationship with Israel?
Answer. Gomer has deserted Hosea for other lovers, just as Israel has deserted God for the Canaanite god Baal. And just as Hosea wants to punish his wife but then be reunited with her, God will put Israel through a time of exile that will eventually bring Israel back into its loving relationship with God.

Question. How did the northern kingdom come to an end?
Answer. Palace revolutions, assassinations of kings, and worship of Baal weakened the nation, and instead of trusting in God, Israel turned more and more to making deals with foreign powers for security. After a long siege of Israel's capital of Samaria, the Assyrians conquered the city and deported thousands of Israelites.

Text Activities: Amos and Hosea in the North

- Who are the people in your life who keep calling you back to goodness? Name two such persons and describe in writing what message they communicate to you. Do they express this message by their words or by their actions? Explain.
- Write your thoughts on the following statement: *In our society we sometimes enjoy luxuries at the expense of those who are poor.*
- Explain in writing how God's Law can serve to protect poor people in our society from going hungry or rich people from becoming greedy. Name two other ways God's Law can protect people.
- Many poets and songwriters say their writing is sometimes inspired by heartbreaking experiences. Find a poem or a song that is an example of this, and write a paragraph about what the writer seems to have learned from his or her suffering.
- If Hosea were to name his children to symbolize corruption in our time or in our country, what names do you think he might choose? List them and explain their significance.
- Have you witnessed or experienced cultural, racial, or religious prejudice? What do you think people have learned about this problem since the time of the Samaritans? Write your thoughts in a brief essay.

 ## Additional Activities: Amos and Hosea in the North

Amos and Conspicuous Consumption

This activity can be used with the second activity on page 155 of the student text to further reflect on how overconsumption affects people who are poor. Amos's picture of the rich Samaritan women is drawn as a caricature, like political cartoons that exaggerate the features of their subjects in order to satirize them. Amos wanted the women to reform their lives.

Tell your students to either draw or bring to class a political cartoon that captures the "fat cattle" of today. That is, what typifies or symbolizes modern outlandish consumption at the expense of the poor?

Give each student a turn to explain the cartoon to the class.

Empty Worship

False worship continues to be a problem in modern times, not just because of discrimination, but also because of hypocrisy.

1. Remind the students that the Old Testament condemns rituals of praise and sacrifice to God that are not backed up with just actions toward others.

2. Divide the class into groups of three or four to discuss how false, or empty, worship can still be a problem today. Then select two teams of students to prepare to debate this point: No one is perfect, so worship is not always backed up by just actions toward others. But that doesn't mean that it is false, or empty, worship. Conduct the debate, using the fishbowl technique discussed in the introduction of this manual.

Praying Our Experiences

1. Tell your students something like the following:
♦ We often forget that God speaks in tiny breezes, in the seemingly mundane events of our life. Consequently, we may believe that God is present to us only at special, "sacred" times or in the obviously significant issues of our life. But God speaks and is revealed constantly. Authentic prayer can be a conversation with God about everyday realities like our feelings for another person, confusion about a decision, anger over a hurt, joy at an accomplishment, and so on. Amos learned from God while working and watching locusts. His experience taught him divine lessons.

2. Instruct your students to do the following, either as a homework assignment or in class:
♦ Create four lists, each on a half sheet of paper. Title the lists "People I met today," "Things I did today," "Situations that concern me right now," and "Hopes I have for the immediate or distant future." Include at least five items in each of your lists.
♦ Pick out one item from each list and tell God, in writing, what you think and feel about it.
♦ For each of the items you prayed about in writing, write down what you believe is God's response to your prayer.

3. When the students have finished writing, discuss the activity by posing these questions:
♦ How do you feel about this type of prayer?
♦ Where or when could a person use this method of prayer?
♦ Do you think that God appreciates this type of prayer more than formula prayers? Explain.

Reflections on Betrayal

To be betrayed (as Hosea was by Gomer and as God was by Israel) is terrible, especially when the betrayer is someone we love. Most students have been hurt by betrayals.

1. To help the class understand God's infinite mercy in contrast with our human problems with forgiving, assign the following:
♦ In a paragraph or two, describe a time when you were betrayed by someone, when your trust was shattered by a person who was special to you. Describe how you felt, what you did, and how you were different after the betrayal.

2. When the students have finished writing, pose these questions for discussion if you sense that the class would be comfortable discussing them:
♦ Could someone tell their story of betrayal? [Ask for several examples.]
♦ [Follow-up questions for each story:] How did you feel? What did you do? How were you different afterward?

3. Next, divide the class into small groups that will discuss and compose answers to these questions:

- ◆ Considering the human reaction to betrayal, what do you think about God's forgiving Israel and commanding that Hosea forgive Gomer? Did Israel and Gomer deserve forgiveness?

4. Ask each group to report its answer to the whole class. Close with comments such as these:

- ◆ When we are in the midst of a painful situation, such as being betrayed, it is hard to understand that anything good could come out of it. It seems devastating. We may wonder, "Why me, God? Why do I have to hurt so much?"
- ◆ The story of Hosea and Gomer reminds us that some of our greatest insights and growth come out of painful situations. Without his tragic marriage to Gomer, Hosea would never have understood God's passionate love for Israel or God's forgiveness of the betrayer. Out of Hosea's pain came some of the most beautiful and moving insights and images in the Judeo-Christian tradition. When we wonder what our pain is all about, we should try to remember Hosea.

7

Concept D: Isaiah in the South: The Greatest Writing Prophet

Pages 161–171

Review Questions: Isaiah in the South: The Greatest Writing Prophet

Question. What three major parts make up the Book of Isaiah? In what context was each part written?

Answer. First Isaiah, or Isaiah of Jerusalem, who pleaded with Judah's kings and people before the Babylonian Exile, chapters 1–39. Second Isaiah, who spoke during and at the end of the Exile, chapters 40–55. Third Isaiah, who was with the people when they returned to Judah from exile, chapters 56–66.

Question. What is Isaiah's response to the vision in the Temple?

Answer. Overwhelmed by his own sinfulness, Isaiah fears he will die because he has seen God. But after an angel cleanses his lips and a voice asks, "Whom shall I send?" Isaiah answers, "Here am I; send me!"

Question. What does the name Immanuel mean? How do Christians understand Isaiah's prophecies about a child to come who will be the ideal king?

Answer. Immanuel means "God is with us." For Christians, Jesus is the Messiah, the one to whom Isaiah's prophecies pointed; in him, "God is with us."

Question. How is Jerusalem saved from the Assyrian invasion? How does this event foster a sense of complacency and a refusal to listen to the prophets' warnings in a later generation?

Answer. An "angel of the Lord" strikes down the Assyrian army just before it is about to storm Jerusalem. This sense of divine protection makes the Judahites complacent, refusing to acknowledge that Jerusalem can ever fall to its enemies and turning a deaf ear to prophets who warn them otherwise.

Question. What does Isaiah see ahead for Judah?

Answer. Isaiah sees the day when Jersualem will be overcome by its enemies because the people's hearts are far from God. But also, on the other side of defeat, Isaiah sees hope for new life to bloom for Jerusalem out of the desert of exile.

Text Activities: Isaiah in the South: The Greatest Writing Prophet

- List three prophetic messages of our time, that is, messages that challenge us—beyond what is comfortable—to be faithful. In writing, respond to these questions:
  - Do people listen to modern prophecies?
  - Why or why not? Give examples.
- Find an article that presents an issue in our times that a prophet might address. Write a paragraph explaining what you think the prophet's message would be.
- Find or create a symbol of God's majesty and goodness and bring it to class.
- Read Matthew 21:33–41. Jesus frequently quoted from the Book of Isaiah. In writing, compare the symbols and message of the parable of the vineyard with those of the Vineyard Song.
- If you could bring together in peace two enemies—two groups or persons who are typically hostile to each other—who would they be? Explain in writing how the world would be better if they were at peace.
- Respond in writing to the following questions:
  - Is the knowledge of God's willingness to forgive an encouragement to laxity and sin? Or does it inspire deeper love and gratitude?
  - What about the opinion that a little fear never did anyone any harm—meaning that the fear of hell and damnation is an inducement to avoid sin. Is it? Explain your view.

Additional Activities: Isaiah in the South: The Greatest Writing Prophet

"Here I Am, Lord"

The lovely, stirring song of commitment "Here I Am, Lord," by Dan Schutte (*Glory and Praise Comprehensive*), is based on the call of Isaiah from chapter 6 of the Book of Isaiah. (The song is recorded on *Lift Up Your Hearts* [Saint Louis Jesuits, 1981].) Play the song for the students or sing it with them, and then ask them to write a reflection on the following:

- ◆ Imagine that the secretary-general of the United Nations has sent for you. When you arrive at the U.N. headquarters, the secretary-general tells you that you have been specially chosen to carry out a mission that will benefit the entire world. Imagine what that mission might be. How might you react when you learn of your significance to the mission? Can you picture yourself saying, "Here am I; send me!" as Isaiah did?

The exercise is significant because the students have been chosen for a mission to benefit the world. Each Christian today is called by God (not the U.N. secretary-general) to fulfill a special purpose that will make a difference to humankind. Like Isaiah, the students may not feel worthy or up to the task, but they have been chosen nonetheless and have been blessed by God for the mission that is particularly theirs. Ask the students to share some ideas about what their missions might be, or invite them to journal about this.

7

God Have Mercy on Dead Men Walking

The prophetic message of Sr. Helen Prejean, whose ministry to death row prisoners and to prohibit the death penalty became famous in the movie *Dead Man Walking,* is hard for many to hear. And yet it is a most healing message: no one is beyond the reach of God's infinite mercy. One of the songs from the film's sound track, "Dead Man Walking (A Dream Like This)," by Mary Chapin Carpenter (Columbia Records, 1995), can be used as a springboard for discussion that extends the textbook activities on pages 167 (on modern-day prophets) and 171 (God's forgiveness) and that ties together many of the Exile's themes.

1. Either show the movie *Dead Man Walking* to your class (see the following note about its rating), or offer this brief summary of Sr. Helen Prejean's ministry and her book *Dead Man Walking,* from which the movie was inspired:
- ◆ In 1982 Sr. Helen Prejean became the spiritual adviser to a death row inmate and helped him accept responsibility for his crime. She continues to work against the death penalty, in accord with Catholic teaching, and has offered spiritual support to both prisoners and families of victims. She believes it is wrong for anyone, including the state, to kill. She wants people to see death row prisoners as human beings, still children of God despite the heinous crimes they have committed.

2. Review the themes of the Exile with the students. Remind them that despite the prophets' warnings, Israel made many evil choices. But God kept forgiving and bringing good out of evil. Eventually, Israel was exiled, and that painful time helped Israel realize its need to change and grow. Out of the desert of exile, hope for new life bloomed for the ancient Israelites. Note that a death row prisoner can be said to be in exile for making a choice for evil.

3. Play Carpenter's song, highlighting the image of "beggars asking for redemption," perhaps by writing the phrase on a chalkboard or overhead projector. Discuss it briefly in class, and then play it again.

Handout **7–A**

4. Distribute handout 7–A, "Exile and Redemption," and direct the participants to gather into groups of three or four to discuss the handout questions. (If you have shown the movie *Dead Man Walking,* you may wish to add questions about the death row prisoner's attitude and how it changes.)

5. Ask a member of each group to report the highlights of her or his group's discussion to the entire class. Then, as a homework assignment, direct the students to write a one-page reflection on this question: How are we all like beggars asking for redemption—"dead men walking"?

Note: The film *Dead Man Walking* is rated R and contains some violence, profanity, and sexual content. Such elements are not gratuitous—rather, they serve the plot and issues of the film. It is important for you to view the film and to assess the maturity of the students before using it in class or assigning it. If the presence of such elements will overshadow the students' understanding of the substance of the film, it may be unwise to use that film as an educational tool. Students who are ready to discern the value of the various aspects of the film's content, however, will find their experience of learning enriched by attentive viewing of this film.

The Vineyard Song

Invite students to bring to class and play a country-western, folk, soul, or rock song that expresses the sense of betrayal that is apparent in the Vineyard Song.

The Assyrian Colonial Policy: Origins of the Samaritans

Direct the students to the sidebar "The Assyrians" on page 162 of the student text. The following additional information may be of interest to your students and may help them better understand Jesus' parable of the good Samaritan. Go over this material with the students:

In 2 Kings 17:24–29, we read of the colonial policy of the Assyrians at the time that they captured Samaria (the capital of the kingdom of Israel) and destroyed the kingdom. In earlier wars the Assyrians had followed a fierce policy of genocide when they conquered a people. With Israel it was different. The new Assyrian policy was to deport the conquered inhabitants, scattering them, thus disrupting their culture and ensuring that they would never come together again to rebel. This policy worked well with the kingdom of Israel; the ten tribes of that kingdom became scattered and are known as the ten lost tribes of Israel.

In order to repopulate the land, the Assyrians imported other conquered foreigners, who replaced the scattered Israelites. The origins of the people who would later be called Samaritans (after the name Samaria, which was applied to the whole territory, not just to the former capital of Israel) is revealed in 2 Kings 17:24.

As the passage from the Second Book of Kings indicates, the Assyrians had an interest in making sure that the imported foreigners knew how to worship the god of the conquered territory (the one God). The Assyrians assumed that without proper worship, the new inhabitants of Samaria would be killed off by lions, which the Assyrians believed were sent by God. So a captive Israelite priest was sent back to Samaria to teach the people how to worship God properly. However, this arrangement did not totally convert the Samaritans to belief in the one God. They mixed the worship of their own gods with worship of God. Thus the Samaritans were, in a way, "cousins" of the Jews of later times, including those of Jesus' time—but they were distant and despised cousins. The mixing of the worship of God with devotion to pagan gods was the origin of the prejudice and animosity that the Jewish people held toward all Samaritans. That animosity was an essential ingredient in the parable of the Good Samaritan, told by Jesus centuries later.

Ask the students this question:
◆ Why did Jesus choose a Samaritan, rather than simply another Jew, to portray the compassionate person who lovingly cared for a beaten man on the highway?

Stories of Our Hard Hearts

Ask your students each to write a short narrative about a time when they hardened their heart to some truth about themselves or some advice that would have saved them a lot of trouble. You may use these written reflections in the closing prayer for this chapter, perhaps at some point having the students tear up their stories as an act of resolution to stay open to the truth.

Isaiah in Our Own Time

To make the character of Isaiah more real to the students, pose these questions for discussion:
 ◆ If Isaiah of Jerusalem came back to us right now, how would he dress? What would he look like? Where would he live?
 ◆ With which of these groups would Isaiah be most comfortable: rich people, the clergy, factory workers, homeless people, children, or refugees? [Ask the students to explain their answers.]
 ◆ What would be Isaiah's main message to us?

7

Concept E: Micah in the South: Sympathy from the Bottom of Society

Pages 172–174

Review Questions: Micah in the South: Sympathy from the Bottom of Society

Question. What experience makes Micah especially sympathetic to the poor?
Answer. His own experience near the bottom rung of society's ladder—probably as a farmworker

Question. For what image of peacemaking is Micah well known?
Answer. When nations "shall beat their swords into plowshares" (4:3)

Question. According to Micah, what does God require?
Answer. "To do justice, and to love kindness, / and to walk humbly with your God" (6:8)

Text Activities: Micah in the South: Sympathy from the Bottom of Society

• Some Scripture scholars consider Micah 6:8 to be the most powerful passage in his book. Write a one-paragraph response to this question: *Is Micah 6:8 a complete statement of what God requires of Christians?*

- Research one other group or person who works for peace, and write an essay about those efforts. Include your reflections on this question: *Do you think it is possible to have world peace—with no threat of war? If so, tell how you imagine this can come about.*

 ## Additional Activities: Micah in the South: Sympathy from the Bottom of Society

Do Rich People Really Scheme?

Micah accused the rich people of concocting schemes for depriving poor people. Tell a group of your students to find a list of the ten wealthiest persons in the country. Then tell the students each to research a different person on the list to find out how he or she made his or her fortune and if that person had to step on people to do so. Allow time for oral reports by the researchers.

What Are We Called to Do?

This exercise is an extension of the first activity on page 173 of the student text, which explores Micah 6:8.

1. To remind the class of the verse, play "We Are Called," by David Haas, from the album *Give Your Gifts: The Songs* (GIA Publications, 1999).

2. As a springboard to a discussion, invite the students to share with the class their answers to the question in the activity on page 173: *Is Micah 6:8 a complete statement of what God requires of Christians?* If so, does that mean the New Testament has nothing to add to our understanding of what God requires of us? If not, what more does God require of Christians?

The Remnant in Amos, Micah, and Isaiah

The remnant theme (which also appears in chapters 8 and 9 of the student text) is introduced by Amos 3:12; Micah 5:6; and Isaiah 10:20–22; 37:31–32. Each of these passages alludes to the fact (or the hope) that one day, after the inevitable punishment for sin is over for Israel and Judah, a small band of faithful people will begin anew, recommitting themselves to the Covenant. Direct the students to the above passages and then ask them these questions:
- ◆ Why was the notion of the remnant crucial to the people of Israel? [It offered them hope.]
- ◆ When modern-day people are in their darkest times—say they have just been evicted from their apartment or have just lost their job or even recently experienced a loved one's death—how do they keep going? What little (or not-so-little) things give them hope?

Closing Prayer

1. Begin the closing prayer by reminding the students that God is present with them. Then invite them to pray together Psalm 139:1–12.

2. If your students wrote stories of hardness of heart (see "Stories of Our Hard Hearts" on p. 154 of this manual), they might at this point tear up the stories and each say a silent prayer for an open and truthful heart in the future. Play some soft music as they do this.

3. Ask the students to offer prayers of petition for people who are prophets today.

4. End by praying Psalm 139:13–14 aloud together.

Closing Teacher Prayer

Call to prayer. Be still within and without. Center yourself in the God of hope.

Reflect. What have you learned in the process of teaching this chapter? Was it a learning of the head or the heart? Does this reveal God more fully to you? How? What effect could this learning have on your life?

What gift did you receive from your students? Which students do you feel are especially in need of God's tender care today?

Pray.
Gracious God,
may our deepest yearning
meet the ardent impulse
of your love and your will.
Loving God,
nourish the seed of hope
that is dormant within us.
I eagerly await the fullness of life
that only your spirit can give.
Come, Spirit of Life. Amen.

(Bergan and Schwan, *Taste and See:
Prayer Services for Gatherings of Faith*)

Exile and Redemption

Discuss the following questions in your group. Have one person take notes in order to report your responses to the class later.

1. How is Sr. Helen Prejean a prophet? Is her message well received?

   _____

   _____

   _____

2. What should be the consequences of evil choices like murder? Is the death penalty just?

   _____

   _____

   _____

3. Can someone be forgiven if he or she does not accept responsibility for his or her decisions and actions?

   _____

   _____

   _____

4. If the Israelites had not gone into exile, or if murderers are not imprisoned, do you think they could still have the same motivation to change? In what way were the Israelites like beggars asking for redemption? How about those who commit murder?

   _____

   _____

   _____

5. How did knowing that God is merciful help the Israelites during their exile? How would that knowledge help death row prisoners? How does it help us in our everyday lives? If we are in need of such mercy from God, why is it so difficult for us to forgive others?

   _____

   _____

   _____

   _____

CHAPTER 8

The Exile:
Prophets of Warning, Consolation,
and Hope

Major Concepts

A. Judah's Slippery Slope: Heading for Disaster. Despite the prophets' warnings and King Josiah's great reforms, Judah continues its downward slide to ruin. The Babylonians capture Jerusalem, destroy the Temple, and exile the Judahites. Josiah, however, inspires in his followers zeal for the Covenant. This leads to the Deuteronomists composing the history of Israel, which is part of the Bible. Zephaniah prophesies that the poor will become the remnant from whom God will build the new Israel. Nahum, prophesying during Josiah's reign, says Assyria will fall to Babylon, but doesn't dream that Judah will meet the same fate. Habakkuk is the first to question God, wondering why he has not punished Judah for its injustice and violence. *See* the *Catechism,* nos. 33, 37–38, 158, 164, 314 (attempting to understand God's ways); 401 (Israel's infidelity); 702 (the prophets); 710–711, 714 (God's remnant—the poor); 2060–2063 (the Covenant).

B. Jeremiah: Persecuted for God's Sake. More than any other prophet, Jeremiah communicates God's message not only through words but also through his own suffering. A reluctant prophet, he warns Judah to change its evil ways or face destruction. But the Judahites are convinced that God would never allow Jerusalem to be destroyed. They persecute Jeremiah, who despairs of, but remains faithful to, his calling.

Jeremiah tells the people to go willingly into the first Babylonian exile because God will purify them through this means and offer the hope of return. The people consider Jeremiah's message to be treason and try to kill him. Jeremiah prophesies that God will make a new Covenant with the people, writing the Law on their hearts. Israel's acceptance of exile will bring hope for an entirely new, living relationship with God. But a second Babylonian exile begins after Jerusalem is destroyed in 587 BC. Jeremiah's contemporaries see him as a complete failure. But the exiles and succeeding generations of Jews see that the "failure" in both the experiences of Jeremiah and of the exile holds seeds of transformation and hope. The Jewish religion came to birth during the exile. The Book of Lamentations contains five hymns of Judah's grief after Jerusalem's fall, and the Book of Baruch was written centuries after the exile to nurture the faith of the

Jews of the Dispersion. *See* the *Catechism,* nos. 201, 212, 2112–2114 (the one God); 220 (Jeremiah); 312 (good resulting from suffering); 612 (Christ's agony); 715, 762, 1965 (the new Covenant).

C. **Ezekiel: From Hearts of Stone to Hearts of Flesh.** Like Jeremiah, Ezekiel prophesies in Jerusalem before the exile, using drama, symbols, and story-telling. But the people ignore his message that they should repent, and Jerusalem falls. Ezekiel accompanies the people on their deportation to Babylon and becomes their counselor. He continues to prophesy, inspiring hope in God's forgiveness. He has a vision of a valley of dry bones that represents Israel mistakenly having lost hope that God will save them. Ezekiel prophesies a return to Jerusalem and to faithfulness and the rebuilding of the Temple. *See* the *Catechism,* nos. 652–655 (Christ's Resurrection); 702, 715 (prophecy); 710 (the exile); 715, 1965 (renewed hearts).

D. **Second Isaiah: Toward a Joyous Return.** This prophet (or prophets) lived in Babylon toward the exile's end. Many exiles had grown comfortable in Babylon. During the exile the Jewish religion focused more on the Word of God and the community, and less on the place of worship. Jewish customs developed to remind the people of who they were. The challenge for Second Isaiah was to raise the people's hopes for the day when they would return to Jerusalem. The Persian Cyrus overthrows Babylon and allows Israel to return home. Second Isaiah introduces the suffering servant, an innocent man who suffers greatly to save the people from their sins. The identity of this suffering servant is unclear; sometimes he appears to be Israel. Christians see in him a prophetic image of Christ.

After the exile Judaism becomes a portable religion, which enables Jews to be faithful wherever they are. *See* the *Catechism,* nos. 345–348, 2168–2172 (the Sabbath); 523, 719 (John the Baptist); 524 (Advent); 580, 601, 608, 615 (Jesus as the suffering servant); 710 (the return from exile); 713 (servant songs).

Opening Teacher Prayer

Call to prayer. Be still within and without. Sit with the God who unsettles us at times.

Read. Psalm 107

Reflect. What words or phrases in Psalm 107 are challenging to you? In what areas of your life do you need to make a return to God? Where and how are you called to be a prophet?

Hold in your heart. "He satisfies the thirsty, / and the hungry he fills with good things" (Ps. 107:9).

Pages 177–180

Concept A: Judah's Slippery Slope: Heading for Disaster

Review Questions: Judah's Slippery Slope: Heading for Disaster

8

Question. What types of reform does King Josiah lead and inspire?

Answer. He leads the people in a renewal of the Covenant and a celebration of the Passover, and then commences his reforms. First, he destroys pagan altars and executes pagan priests and temple prostitutes. Then, driving north, he reclaims territory lost to Judah for a hundred years. He also inspires the Deuteronomists to assemble and edit Israel's ancient texts of its history before, during, and after the exile. Josiah also inspires the prophets Zephaniah, Nahum, Habakkuk, and Jeremiah.

Question. What people does Zephaniah say will become the remnant, through whom God will build the new Israel?

Answer. The unfortunate and impoverished, the "humble of the land, will become the remnant."

Question. What kind of questioning did the Book of Habakkuk introduce?

Answer. The questioning of God by asking him why. Habakkuk introduces questions such as the following: Why, if God is present, does he seem not to be? Why, when God says prayers will be answered, do they seem not to be? Why does God not stop human evil?

Text Activities: Judah's Slippery Slope: Heading for Disaster

- Write a story or news report about an imaginary society where the poor and lowly people are treated as the most important citizens. Then answer this question in a separate paragraph: *Why is this situation so different from our reality?*
- Imagine that Habakkuk is a friend of yours who has asked why some misfortune has happened to him. In writing, explain what you would say to him.

Additional Activity: Judah's Slippery Slope: Heading for Disaster

The Remnant: A Radical Notion Then and Now

Explain to the students that Zephaniah's notion of the remnant of Israel further developed the concept as it was first introduced by Amos, Micah, and First Isaiah. (The meaning of the remnant in the work of those three prophets is addressed in the activity "The Remnant in Amos, Micah, and Isaiah" on p. 155 of this manual.)

Zephaniah's interpretation of the remnant included more than the promise that a small band of faithful would survive and be the hope of Israel's restoration. As the student text notes on page 178, the remnant took on an additional, deeper meaning: this surviving band would be made up of the unfortunate and impoverished of the land—those who, in Zephaniah's time, were considered the least worthy to carry on the mission of Israel. The remnant would not be composed of the "righteous elect," who kept all the rituals and religious rules, but of the poor, who could not afford to be "religious."

As the student text hints, Zephaniah's notion of the remnant pointed toward Jesus' proclamation of the Beatitudes six centuries later. For both Zephaniah and Jesus, poor and humble people were not only deserving of justice and charity (already a familiar theme in the Old Testament). More significantly, they were the chosen ones, the elect ("Blessed are you who are poor, / for yours is the kingdom of God" [Luke 6:20]), who would carry out God's will in the world. In other words, the people who were the signs of hope for Israel were not the ones who "had it all together" according to the standards of success in that society.

Ask the students to consider this additional meaning of the remnant in terms of attitudes toward poor people today. Distinguish for the class two approaches toward the poor:

◆ Many good people believe that the poor should be treated with justice and charity. Basically, though, they see poor people as a drag on society, and they hope that by treating the poor justly and charitably, these poor might become less of a drag. This approach certainly does not see poor and hurting people as chosen by God for a special mission in the world.

◆ Another approach, consistent with Zephaniah and Jesus' outlook, says that among the poor and unfortunate people in our society, we will find the Reign of God. In other words, God is particularly present among the poor, and they are a blessing, not a drag on society.

Ask the students:

◆ Which view of poor people do you think is more popular?
◆ In our society who are typically considered "chosen" and a sign of hope for the future?
◆ How might poor and unfortunate people—people who are suffering (including perhaps ourselves)—be a blessing and a sign of hope?

Remind the students that in Matthew 25:31–46 (the Last Judgment), Jesus completely identifies himself with the hungry, thirsty, sick, lonely, and forsaken ones of society.

 ## Concept B: Jeremiah: Persecuted for God's Sake

 ## Review Questions: Jeremiah: Persecuted for God's Sake

Question. What is Jeremiah's reaction to God's calling him to be a prophet?

Answer. He is frightened and not eager to respond to the call. He cries out, "I am too young!" God tells him not to fear, that he will put the right words into Jeremiah's mouth. And Jeremiah gives in to God.

Question. Why are the Judahites so confident in ignoring Jeremiah's message that the time of disaster is coming?

Answer. They had convinced themselves that God would never allow Jerusalem to be overcome. They thought this because the holy Temple was located there and also because of an apparent miracle during Hezekiah's reign a century earlier when a mysterious "angel of the LORD" (2 Kings 19:35) killed the Assyrians who were attacking the city. Add to this the pledge that God would be with David's royal line forever, and the Judahites were sure they were safe.

Question. What aspects of Jesus' life and ministry reminded the early Christians of Jeremiah?

Answer. Jesus' sufferings. Like Jeremiah, Jesus was sent to teach God's ways but was despised, plotted against, and entrapped by his enemies. Jesus, too, felt abandoned by God on the cross.

Question. What is Jeremiah's message to the people after the first Exile?

Answer. Basically, it is "Do not resist Babylon. Go willingly into exile, and make the most of this sad situation. It will be a time for something new to happen in you."

Question. How will the new Covenant differ from the old, according to God's message to Jeremiah?

Answer. It will be written on people's hearts instead of on stone tablets. The Law will no longer be merely a matter of external practices and norms imposed from outside the person. Each individual will know God and what he wants from deep within.

Question. What happens to Jerusalem and its people in 587 BC?

Answer. The Babylonians return, breach the city's walls, and torch its buildings; the Temple is destroyed, and many of the people are deported to Babylon. King Zedekiah is captured, forced to see his sons slain, and then blinded and hauled off in chains to Babylon.

Question. What understanding did later Jews come to have about the "failure" of Jeremiah's life?

Answer. They saw it, like the sorrow and humiliation of the exile, as a seed of hope and transformation.

Question. How did the Book of Lamentations help Judah?

Answer. It seems to have given Judah a way to grieve—recalling its agony, lamenting, and asking for healing.

 ## Text Activities: Jeremiah: Persecuted for God's Sake

- Write your opinion on this question: *Why would someone be faithful to God despite of his or her suffering?*
- Find an article about a child or a teenager who has said or done something that inspired and taught an important lesson to adults. Write your reflections on this article in a paragraph or two.
- Write your responses to these questions:
  - What behaviors do you regularly see or hear about that are unsafe?
  - Are people generally aware of the risks and consequences of such behavior?

- - If so, why would they choose to engage in dangerous behavior? If not, what would it take to raise their awareness?
- Write a paragraph about how the challenges of being a prophet in Jeremiah's time might differ from the challenges of being a prophet in our time.
- Often our response to approaching pain or disaster is to try to avoid it at all costs. Jeremiah's message is different. He advises that we go with the pain and accept it as a time for changing and growing. Can you think of an experience from your life or that of someone you know when embracing pain might have been more beneficial than fighting it? Share your thoughts on this in writing.
- Answer these questions in writing:
  - How do you know the truth when you hear it?
  - What can stand in the way of your hearing the truth?
  - If possible, give examples of your experience with hearing or not hearing the truth.
- We follow some laws or rules simply because that is what is expected of us *and* we know we might be punished for disobeying them. Think of a law or rule that is instead "written on your heart"—one you follow because, in your heart, you know it is right and good.

  Create a sign or poster that states the law or rule and illustrates it, if possible, with symbols, photos, or other artwork.
- A piece of spiritual wisdom heard in our times is "We are not called to be successful. We are called to be faithful." Write about how this relates to the experience of Jeremiah and about how it relates to your life.
- Write a character sketch of Jeremiah, responding to these questions.
  - Is he like a person you know or know about?
  - What is his most outstanding trait?
  - Whom would you cast as Jeremiah in a movie?
  - What will you remember about him?
- Do you know of someone who is far from home and needs support and encouragement? If so, write a letter to that person.

 ## Additional Activities: Jeremiah: Persecuted for God's Sake

Jeremiah on the Reforms of King Josiah

Remind the students that Jeremiah was called by God during King Josiah's reign. Explain that Josiah's intentions were honorable. He desperately wanted to rid Judah of the influence of the idolatrous Canaanites, and he took extreme measures to do so, inspired by the newly discovered Book of the Law. His reform at least moved Judah away from idolatry, and for this reason Jeremiah initially supported Josiah's plan. But eventually Jeremiah became disillusioned with the reform because, in a way, it backfired. The reform focused the people's attention more and more on prescribed ritual. Of course performing all the proper ceremonies was easier than repenting of injustice and was more reassuring than relying on God alone—and not on foreign powers, like Egypt—for security. So the Judahites under the reform began to think that by following the rules, they were doing everything they needed to do to be favored by God; surely God would not let anything terrible happen to those who kept all the ritualistic laws!

Unfortunately, Josiah's reform did not go far enough; it did not touch the inner lives of the people; it did not challenge them to change their hearts. Josiah intended to call the people back to God by eliminating idolatry in the kingdom, but the people had a limited definition of "returning to God." Josi-ah himself died on the battlefield in a vain attempt to save Judah by allying with other nations, rather than by repenting of the kingdom's wrongdoing.

Ask the students to complete this assignment in writing:

◆ Have you ever known of a reform attempt that failed because it did not go far enough? Describe the situation that needed reform, the changes that were attempted, and why the reform failed. What would have been a more effective reform?

A Stubborn Judah Faces Off with Babylon

From our perspective twenty-six centuries later, it is difficult to imagine why the Judahites and their last kings thought that Judah—a tiny, weak nation—had the slightest chance to prevail against the mighty empire Babylon and King Nebuchadnezzar's powerful army. Judah was foolishly stubborn.

Ask the students to consider this:

◆ Jerusalem was under siege by Babylon for eighteen months. Even dur-ing that time, the people ignored Jeremiah's warnings that they must surrender or be crushed. Why?

If the students do not offer an answer, remind them that the Judahites were lulled into complacency by their own rigid emphasis on ritualistic piety (see the previous activity, "Jeremiah on the Reforms of King Josiah"). And as mentioned in chapter 7 of this manual, the people assumed that God's Covenant with David assured them of everlasting divine protection for their land, their king, and their Temple.

In addition, the Judahites remembered what had happened about a cen-tury earlier when Jerusalem was under a similar threat: the Assyrian army un-der Sennacherib had been struck down by an "angel of the LORD" (2 Kings 19:35) the night before its planned attack on Jerusalem. The prophet Isaiah had told the people of Jerusalem to trust in God, and sure enough, God did not fail them in their hour of need. Certainly, the Judahites thought, this was a sign that Jerusalem was under God's protection and would never be con-quered!

The Judahites' stubbornness in rebelling against Babylon is a remarkable example of people's persistence in believing what they want to believe—a re-fusal to acknowledge any reality that does not square with what they want to hear. On this theme ask the students:

◆ Have you ever seen an instance of people refusing to face reality be-cause the facts did not fit what they wanted to hear? What were the circumstances?
◆ What typically happens to someone who tries to present the facts to people who do not want to hear the truth?

Headlines: Read All About Jeremiah

Direct your class in preparing a newspaper front page with stories that are contemporary versions of Jeremiah's concerns.

1. Divide the class into six groups. Assign each group a theme from Jere-miah's life, making that theme the headline of a news story. These are the sug-gested themes:

• Deal justly with your neighbor.
• No longer oppress the resident alien.

- Show mercy to widows and orphans.
- Stop shedding innocent blood.
- Do not worship strange gods.
- Are we safe from harm because we are God's people?

2. Tell the groups to find a recent news story that reflects their theme and headline. Mention that later they may have to edit (shorten) or add to the story for a front-page fit.

3. Use a computer program, if you have one, that can arrange the stories in a column and page format, complete with bold headlines. In any case have the stories typed up and pasted together like a front page, which may be posted in the classroom. The groups should read their story to the class so that each story can be discussed in terms of how it reflects its respective theme from Jeremiah.

A Jeremiah Collage

1. Lead a brainstorming session to come up with a list of ten key episodes from Jeremiah's life.

2. Instruct your students each to construct an 11-by-17-inch collage from news clippings, photos, and headlines, showing that the problems or realities that Jeremiah addressed are still common today.

3. Divide the class into small groups. Instruct the group members to take turns explaining their collages to one another.

4. Display the collages in your classroom.

Charting the Exile to Babylon

One of the great tragedies of war is the plight of refugees or exiles. They become strangers in faraway, strange lands. This exercise helps to connect the agony of the exiled Judahites with the experiences of people today who are victims of war, racial strife, or injustice.

Select a group of students to do research on the following:

◆ How many miles did the biblical exiles have to walk when they traveled from Jerusalem to Babylon? What were the roads like? How did the people carry their possessions?

◆ Research the plight of several groups of modern refugees throughout the world and calculate the number of miles that they have had to travel to find safety.

◆ Describe the living conditions that modern refugees have while traveling and once they arrive in a refugee camp.

The research team should report its findings to the class, using maps as part of its presentation.

8

Lamentations: The Need to Grieve

Focus on the Book of Lamentations by telling the students that these hymns are instructive for us today—representing, as they do, our need to grieve our losses and tragedies before we can go on to have hope, to regenerate our spirit, and to grow to a new depth of humanity.

1. Explain to the students that the ancient Jews, earthy and real and honest, had no inhibitions about expressing their grief. By "getting it all out," the devastated Judahites were eventually able to move on to a new faith in God's love for them. ("Getting it all out" included the remembrance of horrors such as the starvation of children in besieged Jerusalem and the cannibalism among their starving mothers [Lam. 2:19–20].) Deep sorrow and grief united with unquenchable hope in God is the prophetic vision.

2. Point out that the prophetic vision is relevant to us today as we struggle with our personal and global losses and tragedies—some of them more serious than others, but all of them worthy of grieving. Often counselors help people who have lost a loved one or a familiar way of life (through death, divorce, a move to a new place, the loss of a job, the failure to attain a goal, the breakup of a friendship, etc.). For their clients the counselors emphasize the need to grieve adequately before trying to pick up the pieces of life and move ahead. In this respect the Judahites were quite insightful about what they needed to do for their own mental health and future; to them, lamenting came naturally.

Suggest to the students that humankind might be better off if personal and global tragedies were publicly lamented. Wakes and funerals give us some opportunity, but unfortunately many people suffer through these occasions stoically rather them using them as a way to share grief.

3. Ask the students to brainstorm a list of personal, community, national, or global tragedies that teenagers are likely to be concerned about; write these on the chalkboard as the students call them out. Encourage the students to offer both personal losses and those relevant to the wider society (e.g., losing a boyfriend or girlfriend; the World Trade Center attack; the suicide of a classmate; the depletion of the rain forests; the spread of nuclear weapons; the divorce of one's parents; failing in school; being put down by peers, parents, or teachers; the AIDS epidemic; the devastation of communities and lives through drug addiction and drug pushing; child abuse).

4. Ask the students each to choose from the list one tragedy that is meaningful to them and to write a lamentation (at least fifteen lines) about it. When the lamentations have been completed, invite volunteers to read their work. You might also use some of the lamentations in the closing prayer for this chapter.

8

Concept C: Ezekiel: From Hearts of Stone to Hearts of Flesh

Review Questions: Ezekiel: From Hearts of Stone to Hearts of Flesh

Question. What were Ezekiel's gifts that he used in prophesying?
Answer. Drama, symbol making, and storytelling.

Question. Give three examples of Ezekiel's dramatic actions and the message he tries to convey through each of them. What is the people's attitude in response?
Answer. [In response to the first question, any three of the following bulleted items are correct.]

- Ezekiel makes a model of Jerusalem, using sticks and stones around it to signify a siege. He wedges a large iron griddle into the ground behind the "city," and he lies down and gazes at it for over a year. This symbolizes God watching Nebuchadnezzar's siege of Jerusalem but doing nothing about it.
- Ezekiel cuts off his hair and beard, burns one-third of it within his model city, strews a third around the city and strikes it with a sword, and tosses to the wind all but a few hairs of the final third. He keeps the few remaining hairs in the hem of his garment, but even some of these will be burned. This pantomime signifies that Jerusalem will be cut down, with some people dying of pestilence, some being slain, some being exiled, and only a few returning.
- Ezekiel packs his baggage, leaves his house, and goes through an elaborate pantomime of escaping from the city. Later he explains that his actions represented King Zedekiah in disguise escaping the city. But the king will be caught, blinded, and taken to Babylon, where he will die. Ezekiel stands in front of the people and trembles as he eats bread and water—as they will do when they are captives.
- Ezekiel tells the whole history of Israel through an allegorical love story reminiscent of the prophet Hosea's, in which Jerusalem proves to be God's vain and faithless spouse. Only when Jerusalem has shamed herself entirely—taking countless lovers, paying for their services, destroying her beauty, and behaving worse than her sisters Sodom and Samaria—only then will God forgive her and renew their marriage.
- Ezekiel's wife, the delight of his eyes, dies and he is told by God not to show his grief. His silence embodies a message to the people. Ezekiel tells them that the delight of *their* eyes—the Temple, Jerusalem, and all its people—will also be taken from them. Ezekiel's failure to mourn outwardly for the loss of his wife symbolizes the people's not mourning their lost relationship with God.

The people respond to Ezekiel by continuing in their hard-heartedness, brushing him off and not wanting to be bothered.

Question. What passage in Ezekiel echoes the new Covenant prophesied by Jeremiah?
Answer. "A new heart I will give you, and a new spirit I will put within you; and I will remove from your body the heart of stone and give you a heart of flesh" (36:26).

8

Question. How does Ezekiel's vision of the dry bones relate to Israel? to Jesus?

Answer. His vision is about a kind of spiritual resurrection—the raising up of a nation that has lost hope. Israel has tried to manipulate its own fate and has failed lamentably; now it is God, whom they have betrayed and rejected, who alone can save them—and will. Christians have seen in Ezekiel's vision of dry bones come to life an image of Jesus' Resurrection and the new life his rising brings to those united with Christ.

Text Activities: Ezekiel: From Hearts of Stone to Hearts of Flesh

- Where do you find comfort and hope when you are in trouble? Think of one such source and write a poem, prayer, or reflection about it.
- Ezekiel says that the scroll describing God's mission for him tastes as sweet as honey. Write a half page about your own discovery that doing what is right, even if it is difficult, could be said to taste sweet.
- List symbolic actions—like Ezekiel's—that people might take to get across a message about one of the following issues:
  - nuclear waste disposal
  - air pollution
  - endangered lifeforms
  - destruction of water supplies
- Ezekiel uses the image of dry bones to describe the Israelites, who have become lifeless and faithless. Think of something in your life that appears lifeless. What kind of image would you use to describe it? Draw or describe the image and write a paragraph explaining it.

Additional Activities: Ezekiel: From Hearts of Stone to Hearts of Flesh

Prophecy by Pantomime

If you wish to extend the activity on page 192 of the student text, you may invite the students to select a few of the symbolic actions they devised and act them out in pantomime. The students may also wish to create pantomimes for issues other than those listed in the activity. After each pantomime let the class guess which issue is being addressed. Then ask:
- Which is more effective—words alone or pantomimes—in getting across a prophetic message? Explain.
- What might be some other ways to effectively communicate prophetic messages today?

Ezekiel's Vision

Help your students create a contemporary version of Ezekiel's vision of God. Divide your class into triads and ask each to illustrate Ezekiel's vision of God with drawings, magazine clippings, and other symbols. Perhaps present the option of writing a song about Ezekiel's vision of God.

Allow time for each group to explain its illustration or perform its song.

True Prophets Versus False Prophets

Many true prophets, such as Ezekiel and Jeremiah, warned the people against believing in "false prophets," who were leading Jerusalem astray (see Ezek. 13:1–12).

1. Give your students some insights about both types of prophets and what motivated them.

◆ The false prophets were any of the professional, or guild, prophets who had deluded themselves into thinking that they were expressing God's will or God's view, when in fact they were really expressing their own. Usually the false prophets did not consciously try to deceive the people; rather they unconsciously deceived themselves into thinking that their own voice was God's. (Evil often has an unconscious source; rarely is the deception of others completely conscious or rationally planned. Self-deception usually precedes leading others astray. That is why people who are not good for us often seem sincere.)

◆ The court prophets, of course, were professionals. The main criteria for their employment generally were that they be willing to tell the king whatever he wanted to hear and, even better, that they believe it themselves.

◆ Not all the professional prophets were false prophets. We can expect that some of them were speaking truth to the people, but we have no record of that. However, the true prophets of the Scriptures—for example, Micah, Amos, Jeremiah, Ezekiel—did not come from the ranks of the professionals.

◆ Although the Scriptures convey a sense that the true prophets were totally alone, with no community support whatsoever, this probably was not so. There were always faithful people who listened to the true prophets and followed them because they recognized in these prophets the truth and the original spirit of the Sinai Covenant, the faith of Israel. If Jeremiah, Ezekiel, and so on, had no followers, we today would not have a record of their messages, preserved by Judahites who kept their words alive for succeeding generations.

Handout **8–A**

2. Distribute handout 8–A, "A True Prophet Versus a False Prophet." Direct the students to examine the lists on the handout, which contrast the characteristics of a true prophet and a false prophet. Then ask them to answer the questions at the bottom of the page. They may discuss their answers either in small groups or as a class.

God's Role in War

Show the class some pictures of war and its horrors—for example, picture books on the war in Vietnam, Goya's drawings of the Napoleonic Wars, Mathew Brady's photos of the U.S. Civil War, or some video coverage of the Gulf War. Then pose these discussion questions:

- ◆ What is God's role in these slaughters? Does God plan them or allow them to happen, or are they simply the result of human evil?
- ◆ Could God have saved ancient Jerusalem even though the people did not repent? Could God have performed a miracle?
- ◆ Could God miraculously stop today's wars?
- ◆ Can God stop all wars? If so, will God stop them?
- ◆ Will people and nations let God put an end to war?
- ◆ Is Ezekiel's plea for repentance still relevant today? In other words, would a conversion of our hearts and minds put an end to war?

Allegorical Cartoons

Ask the students each to draw a political cartoon illustrating one of Ezekiel's allegories. (Allow them to adapt figures from current political cartoons.) Set up a classroom exhibit of the cartoons.

Dry Bones

The scriptural excerpt about the vision of dry bones (Ezek. 37:1–14) shows Ezekiel at his most inventive. His message is that only God can save the disheartened, hopeless exiles, who have ignored and betrayed God.

Discuss the hopelessness and anxiety around us today. Here are some questions with which to begin:

- ◆ What is the message of Ezekiel's dry bones vision?
- ◆ How can that message be applied today?
- ◆ What current situations prompt people to say, "What difference can one person make?"
- ◆ What happens when people are hopeless and anxious and feel that they cannot make a difference?
- ◆ A great temptation today is to think that it is too late to make peace, repair the damage to the planet, help the poor, feed the hungry, clothe the naked, or protect our children. Is this a serious temptation? Do you see any evidence of our succumbing to this temptation?
- ◆ Do you agree with this statement: "Our greatest sin is when we refuse to believe that God can help us do anything"?

Ezekiel and Jeremiah: A New Covenant

In your own words, go over the following information with the students, giving them a sense of the significance of the new Covenant proclaimed by Jeremiah and Ezekiel.

Both Ezekiel and Jeremiah were heralds of a new Covenant between God and the people. In two passages (Jer. 31:31–34 and Ezek. 36:26–27), we hear about this new, interior relationship between God and the people of Israel. It is described in moving, poetic terms.

God said to Jeremiah, "I will put my law within them, and I will write it on their hearts" (31:33). The Sinai Covenant had always been about a loving relationship between God and the people; since the great events at Sinai, God had been trying to teach them how to love through the Law. But the old Covenant was no longer enough because the people had not kept their part of it. They had fallen into idolatry and hypocrisy over and over again. According to Jeremiah, God would now be active within the heart of each person. The new Covenant would be not only with the people as a whole but with every member of Israel individually.

Ezekiel prophesied about the same new Covenant in the heart of each person: "A new heart I will give you, and a new spirit I will put within you; and I will remove from your body the heart of stone and give you a heart of flesh. I will put my spirit within you" (36:26–27).

Both of these prophets, aware of the coming destruction of Jerusalem and heartbreaking period of exile, knew that the exile would be an opportunity for the people's hearts to be turned from "stony" to "natural." Bitter though their suffering would be, the people would come to experience God in an interior way, not just in a way of life that depended on having a certain land, a certain temple, a certain ritual. The people had misinterpreted the Sinai Covenant; they thought that it was about keeping the externals and, what's more, that in meticulously keeping these externals, they would earn God's love and protection.

The true prophets, of course, had always known what God intended; they knew that the Sinai Covenant was about how to live a moral life in union with God. The prophets were continuously calling the people away from mere externals to a genuinely moral ethic. Ezekiel and Jeremiah, however, did not simply call the people back to a moral way of life; they told the people that God would be at work within each of them in an intimate, enlivening way. This was the new Covenant, and it gave the people great hope and the willingness to persevere through the exile, knowing that God was intimately with them.

Jeremiah and Ezekiel, like the rest of the exiles, were expecting that Judah and Jerusalem would be restored to their former glory. Even these visionary prophets did not realize that Israel had a far more wonderful destiny in store for it than being a powerful religious nation with a king and a temple they could be proud of. In fact after the exile Israel would never be the same; it would never experience the "glory days" of old. True, Israel would recover the land and rebuild the Temple under the tolerant Persians; however, it would never again be its own powerful nation nor have its own king. But neither would it fall deeply into idolatry ever again. Eventually (in AD 70) the second Temple and Jerusalem would be destroyed by the Romans, and the Jews would have no homeland again until the twentieth century. Meanwhile, they would be dispersed throughout the known world.

Although this history of geographical scattering sounds like a destiny of failure, the irony is that in order for Judaism to become the universal religion that it was destined to become, Israel had to be transformed from a nation with land, king, Temple, and rituals into a religious people that was not tied to externals. Israel became a religion rather than a nation. Its essence was spiritual, and its great moral-religious vision would come to have a profound effect on the rest of history. If the new Covenant between God and the Jews had not been written on the people's hearts, the Exile would very likely have destroyed the last vestiges of a land- and Temple-based religion. Instead, the Exile (which the people came to believe had been arranged by God to purify them) created the opportunity for the flowering of a world religion. What was first experienced as a profound loss became the medium for making a tremendous gain, in spiritual terms.

During their grief in exile, many faithful Jews met in homes to study and to pray, although they could not offer sacrifice as they had in Jerusalem. What emerged was a focus on their Scriptures; many parts of the Old Testament were compiled, edited, and rewritten by priests and scholars in exile. People began to concentrate on the word, and out of study and prayer groups, the concept of the synagogue developed after the Exile. Synagogues would become (as they are today) the major vehicles for supporting the faith of Jews scattered throughout the world and for converting those drawn to the faith. Jews became known as the people of the book because of their scriptural focus within the synagogues.

A major lesson of the Exile, then, was that the nation of Israel could be separated from the religion of Israel and the religion could still survive—even flourish. Judaism did not have to depend on land, Temple, king, or sacrifices. Rather, it depended on how the people received the Word of God into their hearts and lived that word.

Handout **8–B**

As a way of demonstrating for the students what the new Covenant was all about, give them handout 8–B, "Which Marriage Is More Promising?" This handout compares a marriage covenant that is based on externals with one that is rooted in the heart. The marriage covenant based on externals parallels the Israelites' misinterpretation of the Sinai Covenant. The marriage covenant rooted in the heart parallels the new Covenant. Have the students examine the two lists and then answer the questions on page 2 of the handout, first in writing (distribute loose-leaf paper for this) and then aloud in a class discussion.

Handout **8–C**

A Map of the Empires

Handout 8–C, "Empires of the Ancient Near East," offers a map exercise, which you can assign as homework. Suggest that the students consult a world atlas that shows the empires of the ancient Near East. On the handout map, they must sketch in the approximate boundaries of the following empires and label them, using a different color of pencil for each: Egypt, Assyria, Babylon, Persia, Greece, Rome. (The latter two have not yet come up in the student text, but they will be mentioned in the last chapters.) Some boundaries will overlap because some empires held the same territory at different times.

Pages 194–203

Concept D: Second Isaiah: Toward a Joyous Return

Review Questions: Second Isaiah: Toward a Joyous Return

Question. Where and when did the prophet (or prophets) known as Second Isaiah live?
Answer. In Babylon toward the end of the exile, around 550 BC.

173

Question. In what ways was the Exile a time of religious renewal for the Jews? What tensions and compromises did they face?

Answer. Because the Jews were not allowed to build a temple or practice their religious rituals in public, they carefully preserved the words of the prophets and the Torah. The people gathered as families or in community to read the Scriptures, pray, and chant their hymns and psalms. Also, customs such as the Sabbath as a day of rest, male circumcision, and kosher dietary restrictions became significant during the Exile. Although this religious renewal drew many in the Jewish community closer, Babylon with its sophisticated ways was alluring to many Jews, especially the younger ones. As the decades went on and Jerusalem seemed farther away, people must have wondered whether God had forgotten them or was simply a weak God. So Jews of that time varied in their faithfulness to God. Some blended in with the Babylonians. Even some faithful Jews were content to remain in Babylon indefinitely.

Question. What was Second Isaiah's challenge?
Answer. To raise the hopes of the people for the day when they would make a joyous return to Jerusalem.

Question. Why does the suffering servant suffer? How have Christians understood the image of the suffering servant?
Answer. Not as punishment for his own sins but in order to save the people from theirs. Christians have always seen a prophetic image of Christ in the suffering servant.

Question. What images does Isaiah, chapter 55, use to convey hope?
Answer. A feast that will satisfy, water that will quench thirst. Also, God promising peace, mountains that break into song, trees that clap their hands, cypresses instead of thornbushes, myrtle instead of nettles.

 ## Text Activities: Second Isaiah: Toward a Joyous Return

- When we are separated from someone or something that means a great deal to us, we may try to keep alive memories of that person or thing through familiar rituals, symbols, and so on. Write a brief reflection about a time you experienced this.
- Is there something in your religious or ethnic heritage that your family values deeply—that is, passionately? If so, bring in a symbol or story about it. If not, ask your parents or grandparents if they have had such a feeling or experience in their family.
- Among your acquaintances, family members, and neighbors, identify someone who is a bruised reed. Write a note to that person, expressing your concern.
- Write about three examples from the Old Testament in which God shows the Israelites that he will never forget them.

8

➡ Additional Activities: Second Isaiah: Toward a Joyous Return

Ambivalence About Regaining Freedom

After decades of living in a place that has grown comfortable, it can be difficult to muster the will to leave, even to return to one's home and customs.

1. Remind the students:
◆ After several decades in Babylon, many of the exiles had grown prosperous and comfortable there. Many were drawn to Babylon's sophisticated ways. The drawbacks of being in Babylon—not being free to leave or to conduct public worship—perhaps began to fade in importance compared to many of the benefits. When the exiles are free to return to Judah, only a fraction go.
◆ Babylon is not unlike rich countries today where the standard of living is high and, at times, quite indulgent. One can be lured by the riches and comforts, and fall into a consumeristic mind-set that values things over people. Yet, just like many Israelites were loath to leave Babylon, so people today are loath to give up their comforts and prosperity to return to a simpler, more spiritual way of living.

2. Ask the students to imagine they are Jews living at the time of the Babylonian Exile and have just received word that they are free to leave. Instruct them to write a first-person story defending their decision to stay in Babylon or explaining why they chose to leave and what was hardest about leaving.

Isaiah and the Advent Readings

Isaiah 40:1–11 is one of the Advent readings because it urges people to prepare the way for the Lord. The musical *Godspell* and Handel's *Messiah* feature this beautiful and famous passage. Go over the passage with your students in the following way. (By the end of the activity, your students may better appreciate Second Isaiah's importance in the Christian tradition.)

1. Assign these parts to seven strong readers:
• Isaiah 40:1–2
• Isaiah 40:3
• Isaiah 40:4–5
• Isaiah 40:6a
• Isaiah 40:9–11
• Luke 3:1–4a
• Luke 3:4b–6

2. Tell your class that the reading they will hear from the Book of Isaiah is used during Advent. Ask them to reflect quietly on this question as they listen to the reading and two musical renditions:
◆ Why is this passage from Second Isaiah used during the season of Advent?

8

3. Have your student readers perform their parts. Then play "Prepare Ye the Way of the Lord," from *Godspell,* and any of the following from Handel's *Messiah:* "Comfort Ye," "Every Valley," "And the Glory of the Lord," and "He Shall Feed His Flock."

4. After the music has ended, discuss the students' reflections on the question from step 2.

Cyrus: A Report

Persia plays an important role in the events described in this chapter; Cyrus is a hero and, for Second Isaiah, a kind of prototype of the Messiah. Assign to one or two students a brief oral report about Cyrus and the Persian Empire. Require that the report include a map and at least three illustrations.

Suffering Servants of Today

The servant described by Second Isaiah is to be a light to the nations (Isa. 49:6). Jesus, of course, is called "the light of the world" (John 8:12), and every Christian is urged to be a light to the world.

Most of us are not great prophets about whom books will be written to inspire future generations. However, all who consider themselves Christian are called to be the light of God in whatever they do.

To discuss how ordinary folks can be prophets in small, ordinary ways, pose these questions to your students:
- ◆ What qualities of personality and what skills does a person to help create the Reign of God, to be a light to the world?
- ◆ Describe how each of the following people could be a light to the world: a comedian, a rock star, a lawyer, a doctor, a banker, a politician, a factory worker, a teacher, a florist, a prison guard, a janitor, a professional athlete. [You may want to add to the list or substitute different occupations.]

Closing Prayer

1. Remind your students that God is present. Then divide the class into three groups, who in turn will pray aloud these passages:
- *Group 1.* Isaiah 40:12–14
- *Group 2.* Isaiah 40:21–22
- *Group 3.* Isaiah 40:25–31

2. Next have five student lectors (selected beforehand) read in turn these passages:
- Isaiah 55:1
- Isaiah 55:2
- Isaiah 55:3
- Isaiah 55:8–9
- Isaiah 55:10–11

8

3. Invite the students to share petitions or reflections. Then end the time of prayer by singing "On Eagle's Wings," by Michael Joncas (*Gather Comprehensive*). Or pray Psalm 91 as a class, with alternate sides of the room taking verses. Or close with the lamentations that the students wrote in the activity "Lamentations: The Need to Grieve" on page 166 of this manual.

 ## Closing Teacher Prayer

Call to prayer. Be still within and without. Center yourself in the God of justice.

Reflect. What have you learned in the process of teaching this chapter? Was it a learning of the head or the heart? Does this reveal God more fully to you? How? What effect could this learning have on your life?

What gift did you receive from your students? Which students do you feel are especially in need of God's tender care today?

Pray.
Gracious God, may your love,
like water,
pour over our thirsty spirits,
cleansing, refreshing, renewing us.
Be present as we seek
to know you, to love you, and to respond
to your unconditional love for us. Amen.

(Bergan and Schwan, *Taste and See:*
Prayer Services for Gatherings of Faith)

8

A True Prophet Versus a False Prophet

The two lists below contrast the characteristics of a true prophet and a false prophet. Examine the lists.

A True Prophet . . .

1. usually is reluctant to speak for God
2. listens to the authentic voice of God within him or her and then communicates God's message
3. tells people the truth, even if it hurts
4. is a realist
5. conveys a message that is consistent with the faith of Israel, the Sinai Covenant
6. is unpopular, holds no official position, and suffers for telling the truth
7. offers people hope and a means of surviving suffering and devastation
8. lives the message preached
9. has a message that stands the test of time

A False Prophet . . .

1. eagerly takes on the job of speaking for God
2. listens to his or her own opinions and wishes, communicating those as God's thoughts
3. says what people want to hear
4. is an optimist
5. conveys a message that is consistent with most people's inclinations
6. is popular, often holds an official position, and leads a comfortable lifestyle
7. offers people no way to make sense of suffering and loss
8. talks a lot without taking action
9. has a message that does not hold up over time—is not confirmed by historical developments

Answer these questions on loose-leaf paper:

a. Using the characteristics listed above, name some modern-day people who could be described as false prophets. Why are they false?

b. Name some modern-day people who could be described as true prophets. Why are they true?

c. In what situations is it easier for teenagers to tell people what they want to hear rather than the truth?

Which Marriage Is More Promising?

Imagine that you know two engaged couples and that each couple has decided to write down the terms of their marriage agreement. The couples show you their "covenants," which are offered below. As you read, consider the pluses and minuses of each type of agreement.

Agreement 1

1. Each of us will be allowed to go out without the other only one night a week.

2. Each of us will wear a wedding ring.

3. If one of us becomes seriously ill, the other will stay home two days a week to help out.

4. We will divide our property in half so that if we divorce some day, each of us can take an equal amount.

5. We will not have sex with anyone but each other.

6. If one of us is left without a pension at retirement, the other will give one-fourth of her or his pension to the pensionless one.

7. Each of us will cook three evening meals a week. One night each week we will go out to dinner.

8. If children are born from this marriage, we will split the child-care responsibilities exactly in half, both of us working at a job for the same number of hours and caring for the children for the same number of hours.

Agreement 2

1. Each of us will be the other's closest companion.

2. We will let others know by our attitudes and behaviors how important we are to each other.

3. We will compassionately care for each other in times of need.

4. We will completely share our belongings.

5. We will be faithful to each other in mind, heart, body, and spirit.

6. We will look after each other's well-being in our old age.

7. We will share our household tasks in a spirit of equality.

8. If children are born from this marriage, we will do whatever is necessary to care for them while allowing for each other's growth as a person.

Answer these questions on loose-leaf paper.

a. What are the advantages and disadvantages of each agreement?

b. Which agreement will be easier to keep? Why?

c. Under which agreement will it be harder to know if the partners are doing their part? Why?

d. Is anything wrong with agreeing on definite, external signs of love, such as in agreement 1? Under what circumstances would such an agreement help a marriage? Under what circumstances would it hinder a marriage?

e. How do each of the marriage agreements correspond to the Israelites' misinterpretation of the Sinai Covenant?

f. How do each of the marriage agreements correspond to the new Covenant proclaimed by Jeremiah and Ezekiel?

Empires of the Ancient Near East

On this map draw in the boundaries of the following ancient empires. Then label the empires, using a different color of pencil for each.
- Egypt
- Assyria
- Babylon
- Persia
- Greece
- Rome

Note: Some boundaries will overlap because some empires held the same territory at different times.

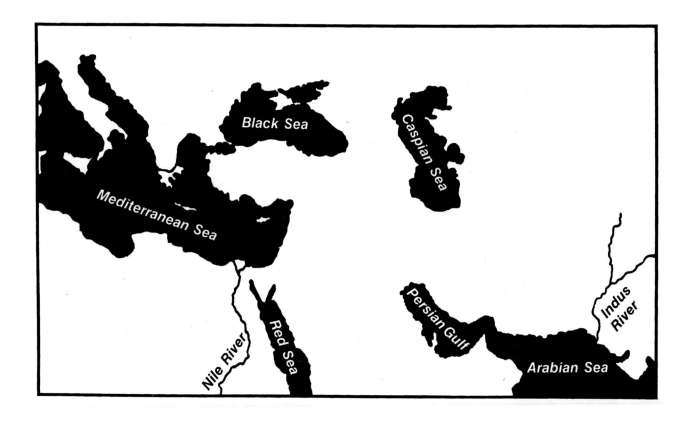

CHAPTER 9

The Remnant:
Making a Home After the Exile

Major Concepts

A. **Chronicles: History as It Should Have Been.** The period of restoration
when the exiles returned to Judah began in 538 BC. The exiles set spiritual boundaries that defined who they were and allowed their faith to survive in foreign lands. The two Books of Chronicles, written after the
rebuilding of the Temple, retell Israel's history, emphasizing the ideals of
David and Solomon but omitting their sins. They reminded the Jews that
they were called to be a holy nation, not an empire. *See* the *Catechism*, nos.
2578–2579 (David); 2580–2581 (Solomon and the Temple).

B. **The Return: Discouragement and Struggle.** The Book of Ezra and Third
Isaiah describe the exiles, who expected a glorious homecoming, being
disappointed to find Jerusalem in ruins and resentment from the poor residents there. The exiles begin to rebuild the Temple, but after they rebuff
the Samaritans' offer of help, the Persian king halts construction for eighteen years. The Jews of the south consider the Samaritans to be inferior because of their weakened tribal identity and religious fidelity through
marriages to foreigners. Third Isaiah says true fasting is acting compassionately toward those in need. Third Isaiah tries to stir the community
out of its religious apathy, promising one who will bring all God's glory to
earth and make Israel a light to the nations. This notion, called universalism, envisions all nations coming together under God's Reign. In Luke's
Gospel Jesus proclaims that he is the fulfillment of Isaiah's prophecy. The
overall theme of the Book of Isaiah is God's love for Israel and tender care
for Zion. *See* the *Catechism*, nos. 710–711 (the Remnant); 714, 716 (Jesus
as the Messiah).

C. **The Second Temple: A Focus for Faith.** The prophet Haggai urges the Jerusalem community to rebuild the Temple in order to preserve its faith
and religious identity. But the people focus on the building project instead
of their need to recommit themselves to God's call. Zechariah foresees the
coming of a messiah, a Davidic king who would unite all nations in peace
and justice under God. First Zechariah sees Zerubbabel, the heir to David's
throne, as a messianic figure. Second Zechariah expects the messiah not to
be a rich and powerful king but a peaceful messiah of the poor who will
ride a white donkey. Early Christians and perhaps Jesus himself saw this
and Zechariah's image of a shepherd as referring to Christ. Malachi criticizes the priests for offering blemished sacrifices in the Temple, and the

people for their infidelities. He tells them to tithe and repent. Contrary to the people's hopes, the Second Temple is no guarantee of righteousness. *See* the *Catechism,* nos. 559 (a messiah and the riding of a donkey); 2401, 2449 (tithing).

D. Renewal: Drawing the Community's Boundaries. Nehemiah, a Jew who served the Persian king as Judah's governor, involves the entire Jerusalem community in rebuilding the city's walls. He is a model public servant, who insists on justice and leads by serving. He sets strict boundaries, sealing the city gates to prohibit trade on the Sabbath and condemning Jews who marry foreigners, in order to preserve the people's religious commitment and unity.

Ezra, a faithful priest and scribe who lived in Babylon, leads the Jews in Jerusalem to reject their past sins and commit themselves to the Law. On another visit to Jerusalem years later, he tells the Jews they must abandon their foreign wives and children, reinforcing Nehemiah's boundaries to ensure the survival of Judaism.

Scripture scholars speculate that the Books of Ruth and Jonah critique the exclusivist policies of Nehemiah and Ezra. The Book of Joel focuses on a locust plague that symbolizes the coming of God's judgment on the unfaithful Jews. Obadiah, the Bible's shortest book, condemns Edom for its fratricide. *See* the *Catechism,* nos. 401, 709–710 (Israel's infidelity); 2060 (the Law).

E. Keeping the Faith Alive Under Fire. After Alexander the Great conquers the Persian Empire in 330 BC, the Greek Empire dominates and often persecutes the Jews in Judea. King Antiochus Epiphanes persecutes the Jews, many of whom remain faithful. Eleazar won't even eat meat that looks like pork for fear of scandalizing the young, and pays the price with his life. The Second Book of Maccabees describes the same period of persecution, including the martyrdom of a mother and her seven sons. This story and the Book of Daniel point to belief in resurrection. The Maccabees wage a military campaign against the Greeks, win a degree of independence for Judea, and regain control of the Jerusalem Temple. The Jewish feast of Hanukkah originated in the eight-day celebration that followed the rededication of the Temple. The author of the Book of Daniel, an apocalyptic writer who used Babylon at the time of the Exile as the setting, inspired the Jews to nonviolent resistance against the Greeks. The Romans conquered the Greeks in 63 BC. *See* the *Catechism,* nos. 297, 992 (Maccabean martyrs); 436, 439, 711–716 (a messiah); 440 (Jesus—Son of Man).

Opening Teacher Prayer

Call to prayer. Be still within and without. Center yourself in the God who calls us to holiness.

Read. Psalm 19

Reflect. What does it mean to you to be one of God's holy people? What words in Psalm 19 could help you live out the call to holiness?

Hold in your heart. "Let the words of my mouth and the meditation of my heart / be acceptable to you, / O LORD" (Ps. 19:14).

Pages 207-208

Concept A: Chronicles: History as It Should Have Been

 ## Review Questions: Chronicles: History as It Should Have Been

Question. What kind of boundaries did the returning exiles need to set?
Answer. Not the geographical kind, but the spiritual kind that defines the limits of a person or group

Question. What did the Chronicler's history emphasize about David and Solomon? Why was the history written this way?
Answer. The Chronicler presented David as a liturgist and leader in worship, in order to inspire the Jerusalem community to return to a vibrant religious life. Chronicles' story of Solomon is told with emphasis on his wealth, his building and dedication of the Temple, and his wisdom—no mention of his idolatry.

 ## Text Activities: Chronicles: History as It Should Have Been

- Think of a group to which you belong—such as a church, a family, a club, a team, a school—that has a strong sense of identity. Then write a paragraph that describes who you and the other members are as a group.
- The Chronicler rewrote Israel's history the way it *should* have happened. Try doing the same: rewrite an incident in your life to make it come out as you wish it had.

 ## Additional Activity: Chronicles: History as It Should Have Been

David as a Leader of Worship

As the student text points out, the Chronicler portrayed David as a leader of worship, the originator of the Temple, a hymn writer—in general, a religious leader more so than a political leader. Explain to the students that many scholars doubt that David functioned in such a priestly capacity. Then ask them this question:

◆ After the Exile, Israel no longer had a king, let alone an empire. Why would the Chronicler downplay David's political role and highlight (even exaggerate) his religious role? [As a defeated nation under foreign domination, Israel needed to realize that it did not need a political king to carry on David's concerns. Rather, according to the Chronicler, being faithful to Judaism would put Israel right in line with David's concerns, which centered on worship.]

9

Pages 208–212

Concept B: The Return: Discouragement and Struggle

Review Questions: The Return: Discouragement and Struggle

Question. What do the exiles find when they return to Jerusalem?
Answer. They find nothing but a miserable little village perched on a pile of rubble—its wall and Temple in ruins—and ahead of them a future promising nothing but hardship. Judah is an impoverished land, and its residents resent the exiles.

Question. Why are the exiles prejudiced toward the Samaritans?
Answer. The exiles consider themselves to be the true Israel. Because the Samaritans are descendants of not only the Jews but also the foreign settlers of the north, the Jews of the south regard them as inferior.

Question. According to Third Isaiah, what is the true fasting that God desires?
Answer. Working for the release of the unjustly imprisoned, freeing the oppressed, sharing bread with the hungry, sheltering the homeless, and clothing the naked

Question. What is meant by the notion of universalism in Second and Third Isaiah?
Answer. The dream that God's love for Israel will make it a light to the nations, ultimately bringing together all nations and peoples of the earth under his Reign

Text Activities: The Return: Discouragement and Struggle

- Are you surprised to find so much prejudice in the Bible? Write a one-paragraph answer to this question: *Is prejudice more prevalent in society today than it was in biblical times?*
- What do you think it means to bring together all nations and peoples of the earth under God's Reign? Is it possible to unite all people? Find an article that illustrates a step toward this vision and write a one-paragraph reflection about it.

Additional Activities: The Return: Discouragement and Struggle

Going Home Again

Ask the students if they have ever experienced moving away from a home they loved and then longing to go back to live there again. Such an experience of moving is a kind of exile. If the students who have been in that posi-

9

tion are willing, ask them to describe to the class their grief at being away from the place they considered home. Urge them to share their dreams about going back, especially their imaginings about what it would be like if they could return to the loved place and pick up where they left off. Perhaps one or more of those students did go back for a visit or even moved back after some period of time away. What was that experience like?

Relate these ordinary, twentieth-century experiences to the exiles' return to Judah. Although most of the returning exiles had never even seen Judah (they were not alive when the Exile began), they carried in their heart a longing for Judah, the land of their roots and their identity as a people.

Refer the students to the map on page 218 of the student text, which shows the route that the exiles likely took on their way from Babylon to Jerusalem in 538 BC (later on, Nehemiah and Ezra would travel a similar route). Encourage the students to imagine the anticipation and joy of the exiles as they traveled the hard and dangerous journey home—some six hundred miles on foot or by donkey.

Point out to the students Psalm 126, the song of the returned exiles, a beautiful and heart-lifting account of what it feels like to come home after a difficult time away ("When the LORD restored the fortunes of Zion, / we were like those who dream" [vs. 1]). Read the psalm aloud with the class.

Remind the students that although the exiles felt deep joy at returning, this emotion was tempered with the realization that things would never be the same as they had been before the Exile—that is, the Jews would not have a king nor their own nation. For years they would be frustrated in their attempts to build a Temple; Jerusalem would be in ruins for a long time; and the people's lot would be one of hardship and discouragement. Ask the students who have visited or moved back to a loved home if they also found that things would never be the same again. How would things be different? Why?

9

True Fasting

In order to examine "true fasting," as it is defined by Third Isaiah, use this activity:

1. Tell your students to draw four columns on a full sheet of loose-leaf paper. At the top of the paper, they should label the first column "The Afflicted," the second column "The Brokenhearted," the third column "Captives," and the fourth column "Prisoners." Urge them to think about each category in terms of a broadened meaning of the word involved: for example, captives could include those who are illiterate or drug-addicted; prisoners could mean people who are locked into impossible situations.

2. In each column the students should list people they know who fit that particular category and the specific way that each person is afflicted or brokenhearted, a captive or a prisoner. The students may use initials instead of full names for purposes of confidentiality.

3. After the students have completed their lists, ask them to choose one person from each category and to write down ways in which they might help that person. Remind the class that "true fasting" means helping those in need.

Concept C: The Second Temple: A Focus for Faith

 ### Review Questions: The Second Temple: A Focus for Faith

Question. According to the Book of Haggai, when the people finally get around to building the new Temple, what do they focus on? What should they focus on?

Answer. They focus on the building project's size and furnishings, instead of the state of their lives and their worship.

Question. How does the image of the Messiah differ between the first half of Zechariah and the second half?

Answer. First Zechariah sees Zerubbabel, the heir to David's throne, as a messianic figure. Second Zechariah expects a peaceful messiah of the poor, not a rich and powerful king.

Question. What behaviors does the prophet Malachi object to among the priests? among the people?

Answer. Malachi objects to the priests' offering blemished, lame, and blind animals as sacrifices in the Temple. He objects that the exiles have divorced their Jewish wives and married rich pagan women in order to live more prosperously, and that the offerings in the Temple storehouses have been stolen.

Text Activities: The Second Temple: A Focus for Faith

- Imagine an ideal building for worship. Explain in writing what it looks like and why.
- Why was there no reason for the Jews to feel ashamed of the second Temple? Write your answer as if you were a Jew who helped rebuild the Temple.
- The spirit behind tithing is that we give the first 10 percent of our income to charity and to our church, trusting that God will take care of our needs, no matter what financial struggles we might meet. The giving should happen before we buy anything or pay our bills, not from leftover money. Tithing is an act of justice and an act of faith. Answer the following questions in writing:
  ○ If you were to tithe each month, to whom would you want to give your money?
  ○ What things might you have to give up in order to tithe?
  ○ What is your opinion about tithing? Do you think you could do it?

 ### Additional Activities: The Second Temple: A Focus for Faith

Research on the Apocalypse

The Book of Zechariah concludes with a vision of the apocalypse. As the student text notes, we should avoid reading such passages with the belief that they refer to specific events or persons of our time. In fact, the students may already have been exposed to this interpretive mind-set—that is, to people who have taken ancient apocalyptic texts (whether Judeo-Christian or otherwise) and tried to draw out of them predictions of specific events.

Explain to the students that the genre of Judeo-Christian apocalyptic literature (the Books of Daniel and Zechariah, from the Jewish tradition; the Book of Revelation, from the New Testament) is concerned principally with the cosmic struggle between good and evil. The writers saw earthly conflicts as simply symbolic of the universal, spiritual conflict between good and evil. Their writings are about taking sides in the struggle, and the highly symbolic fashion of the works is not intended to be interpreted in terms of specific historical events.

Give your students some perspective on what happens when we take apocalyptic literature literally instead of symbolically: Have a few of them research and report to the class on groups of people in the last century or so who, because of what they had read in the Bible, thought that the world was ending. (Many of those people sold everything and then were surprised to find out that they had been mistaken in their interpretation.) Some other students could find out what some religious sects predicted in relation to the world's ending.

A New Earth

Using this activity will encourage your students to imagine what an ideal or messianic age would be like.

1. Divide your class into small groups. Give the groups instructions along these lines:
- ◆ Imagine that the end of the world is coming now. God is giving you two weeks' notice. Only one thing can change God's plan: you must come up with a good plan for changing the world. This plan for a New Earth (a new age for the earth) must create a world that would please Jesus. As a group decide what this New Earth will be like. Include in your outline for the New Earth some description of how people in society will work, take leisure, govern themselves, treat the environment, feed themselves, and so on.

2. When the groups have finished developing their scenario, ask each group to present an oral report of the New Earth plan that it would present to God. Let all the class members critique each plan as they think Jesus would.

3. Now here is the clincher: Ask your students if it is possible to build a New Earth without the threat of the end of the world hanging over humankind. Discuss this issue in terms of how Christians are called to build the Reign of God even within our own lifetime—especially within our own lifetime, for that is the only time that we (personally) have to bring that dream about.

Tithing

The following can be used to promote a class discussion of tithing in conjunction with the individual reflections called for in the activity on page 215 of the student text. Malachi, in berating the people for their stinginess toward God and the Temple, can sound like a modern-day pastor scolding his congregation for its lack of generosity to the parish building campaign. Explain to your class that actually Malachi was not as concerned with the amount of offerings in the Temple storehouses or with the quality of the sacrificial animals as he was with an inner attitude that put God first in the believer's life. That was why he called on the people to tithe. Tithing was a way for the people, who had come to admire material wealth more than goodness, to set their priorities right.

Ask the students if they have heard of tithing in their own parish. The practice is more common among Protestants than among Catholics, but its use is growing in Catholic churches, with an emphasis on the donation of time and talent as well as monetary treasure. The concept of stewardship is that Christians ought to be responsible stewards (caretakers) of their resources—time, talent, and treasure—and give a fair portion of these to their church.

Concept D: Renewal: Drawing the Community's Boundaries

Pages 215–224

9

Review Questions: Renewal: Drawing the Community's Boundaries

Question. When Nehemiah arrives in Jerusalem, what is the first project he calls the people to work on?
Answer. Rebuilding the walls of Jerusalem

Question. Give three examples of characteristics that make Nehemiah a model public servant.
Answer. [Any of the following items are correct.]
1. He involves the whole community in rebuilding the city walls.
2. He insists on justice for all, ordering rich people to repay poor people they have cheated.
3. He refuses to use an expense account, to benefit from taxes, or to take land for himself.
4. He sets a table with food and wine for the workers rebuilding the walls, at his own expense.

Question. What two reforms does Nehemiah enforce? Why were these important boundaries?
Answer. After he discovers the Jerusalem farmers and merchants conducting trade on the Sabbath, he orders the city gates sealed before the Sabbath and opened only when it is over. He curses and orders beaten the Jews who married foreign women and whose children cannot even speak Hebrew. He warns the other Jews not to allow their children to marry foreigners. The boundaries were important in order to preserve a clear Jewish identity so that the Jews could go forward with undivided hearts and as a united people.

Question. What was Ezra's greatest gift to Judaism? How has this gift helped Judaism to survive?
Answer. His preaching of the Law, or Torah, provided a kind of constitution for the Jews to root their lives in a common faith and common code of be-

havior. Judaism has survived because it is centered in the Bible. As people of the book, they could continue faithfully even after the Temple was destroyed in AD 70.

> **Question.** What does the plague of locusts in the Book of Joel symbolize?
> *Answer.* It symbolizes the coming catastrophe of God's judgment on the people for their continuing infidelity.

Text Activities: Renewal: Drawing the Community's Boundaries

- Find or write a story about a person or a group that possesses perseverance and inner strength in the face of great difficulty. What or who do you think inspires the person or members of the group to keep struggling for what is important to them?
- Think of someone who is a leader, but leads in a servantlike way, that is, she or he does not act superior but tries to serve the people rather than dictate to them. Describe the person in writing.
- Write a paragraph that expresses what the prophets might say to our society about our attitude toward money and profit.
- Answer these questions in writing: *When you recall your past, what are you grateful for? What do you regret about your own actions?*
- Have you ever had a teacher who was passionate about the subject he or she taught? Write about that teacher and tell how you were affected as a student.
- Write a paragraph about what you think this passage from Joel could mean for our day.

Additional Activities: Renewal: Drawing the Community's Boundaries

---

Work: Never on Sunday?

Remind the students that in Nehemiah's time, people did not have the work schedule patterns that are common today: shift work around the clock, rotating schedules, or regular work on the Sabbath. Whenever the Jewish people did break the Sabbath for commercial purposes, the prophets, including Nehemiah, loudly condemned putting money and profit before religious commitments. Jesus' priorities were consistent with the prophets' (see Matt. 6:24), but he was not legalistic about the Sabbath (see Mark 2:23–28).

The issue of working on the Christian Sabbath is worth discussing with your students. In a multireligious society such as our own, where different people observe different days of rest (and some observe no day of rest at all), it would be unreasonable and insensitive to try to legislate laws that prohibit work on Sundays. Ask the students to identify the Sabbath days of various other faiths and religions in our society—for example, Saturday for Jews, Friday for Muslims. In the absence of laws that allow only essential businesses to operate on Sundays (laws that until a few decades ago were enforced in many U.S. states), what guidelines should Christians follow about working on Sundays?

1. Direct the students to the following Gospel passages, in which Jesus is concerned with the keeping of the Sabbath:
- Mark 2:23–28
- Matthew 12:9–14
- Luke 13:10–17

2. Then ask these questions:
- ◆ What are the advantages—psychological, physical, social, and spiritual—of observing the Sabbath every week on Sunday? ("Observing the Sabbath" means that the day is not spent in employed labor; rather, it is dedicated to renewing the self and relationships through whatever ways seem best for the individual.)
- ◆ What are some reasons that people have for not observing the Sabbath? [Exclude from your discussion essential employed work, e.g., hospital work, public-safety jobs, telephone jobs. You will only sidetrack the discussion by debating whether people should work at those jobs on the Sabbath. Concentrate instead on nonessential work, e.g., sales work at a shopping mall, factory work, work in a fast-food restaurant.]
- ◆ What are some disadvantages of not observing the Sabbath?
- ◆ Would people be better off if they regularly observed the Sabbath?

Option. As an alternative approach to considering the Sabbath, have the students debate this resolution:
- ◆ Resolved: People in our society, including teenagers, should observe the Sabbath every week.

9

Mixed Marriages

Nehemiah and Ezra condemned the Jews of their time who married outside the Jewish tradition. But today mixed marriages are so common that the issue is seldom controversial. Indeed, many of your students may be the children of mixed marriages. To provide both a better understanding of Nehemiah and an opportunity to think about mixed marriages today, lead a discussion with these questions:
- ◆ Why did Nehemiah and Ezra condemn mixed marriages? [It is important for the students to know that in Nehemiah and Ezra's time, a marriage created a political and religious alliance between two families. Thus intermarriage tied Israel to other faiths in ways that weakened the faith of the Jewish people. Judaism was still a fledgling religion; only recently had the people given up their flirtations with idolatry. The firm monotheistic faith of the Jews was just emerging, and they were constantly tempted to believe that other gods might be more powerful than the one God. Intermarriage only increased that temptation.]
- ◆ Most of you probably know of marriage partners who come from different religious traditions. What problems, if any, result from their mixed marriages?
- ◆ Do mixed marriages tend to lead one or both partners into compromising their faith?
- ◆ Are there advantages to mixed marriages?
- ◆ The Catholic Church recognizes marriages between Catholics and persons of other denominations or faiths. Should it?

Option. The students might interview a husband and wife who come from different religious backgrounds to learn more about the struggles, benefits, and ways that the couple has come to practice their faith. Have the students present their findings to the class.

The Program of Nehemiah and Ezra

Recall for the students an activity from chapter 8: "Ezekiel and Jeremiah: A New Covenant" (pp. 170–172 of this manual). The activity highlights the notion that after the people's exile in Babylon and the prophets' transforming that tragedy into a growth point, Israel became more than a nation; it became a universal religion. The Jews had found that they could live without their land and the Temple. They had discovered how to keep their faith alive through the written word. These discoveries enabled the people to spread throughout the world and to faithfully worship God in synagogues wherever they settled. Furthermore, Jeremiah and Isaiah's insistence that God was the only God, the God of all the nations, made Judaism a potentially evangelizing religion, one with a mission to bring faith in the one God to everyone.

Nehemiah and Ezra, however, may appear to have been taking a step backward from the universalizing trend of Judaism. Their program attempted to make the practice of Judaism more restrictive and orthodox. These men, one a governor and one a priest, were dedicated to making Judaism pure and exclusive. They wanted to rebuild the identity and image of Judaism by getting back to the basics; their method was to insist on standards by which authentic Jews would be known. Review these standards with the students:

◆ Jews had to share the same ethnic background—that is, intermarriage with foreigners was forbidden.
◆ Jews had to be supportive of the Temple and look to the Temple as the center of their religious life.
◆ Jews had to be devoted to the Law, the Torah.

The students might wonder how Nehemiah and Ezra's program could have been consistent with a religion that was destined to become ever more universal—nonexclusive. In fact the two reformers had plenty of Jewish critics in their own time, people who thought that these leaders were going too far by pulling Judaism back to a highly orthodox position. Remind the students that some scholars today think that the story of Ruth, set in the era of the judges, was actually composed after the Exile as a refutation of rigid standards for who was Jewish and who was not. After all, in the story Ruth—the great-grandmother of the beloved David—is a Gentile, a Moabite woman! According to the scholarly hypothesis, the point of the writer is clear, and it points right at Ezra and Nehemiah's program: If David himself was of mixed ancestry, do the leaders of Judaism have the right to be so harsh about mixed marriages?

Regardless of critics' opinions in the postexilic era or our own opinions today, scholars do believe that Judaism would not have survived without the bold action of Ezra and Nehemiah. Judaism was still in a fledgling, vulnerable stage. It needed a phase of exclusivity in order to consolidate its identity as firmly monotheistic. Judaism could survive to become a world religion (and later to give birth to Christianity) only if it became absolutely sure of who and what it was.

Draw a parallel for the students by pointing out the need for identity in one's personal life: A young person should establish his or her identity before getting married. Likewise, people must have a sense of who they are before they can make a major contribution to society. As the old saying goes, "You can't give what you don't have."

So the Jewish community under Ezra and Nehemiah was in the somewhat painful stage of identity formation—and that identity, the people grew to realize, was firmly established in the Law, the Torah. The Word of God was so central to the postexilic Jews that when their city and their Temple were finally destroyed by the Romans in AD 70, they simply expanded into the known world, basing their faith on the Word of God, which could never perish. The Jews have been identified ever after as the people of the book, which testifies to the centrality of the Word in their faith.

The irony of Ezra and Nehemiah's exclusivist program is that it ultimately brought about the flowering of Judaism as a world religion—by preserving it and rooting it in the Law at a time when it was shaky and unsure of itself.

You may wish to ask these discussion questions:
◆ Can you name any religious groups today that are exclusivist?
◆ Is this exclusivism necessary to the flourishing of the group, similar to the result of Ezra and Nehemiah's exclusivist program?
◆ Can exclusivism be dangerous, such as in certain cults? Give examples [the People's Temple in Jonestown, Branch Davidians, Heaven's Gate, etc.].
◆ How can it be determined whether a group's exclusivism is dangerous or not?
◆ Do you view the Catholic Church or other Christian Churches as exclusive or inclusive? Explain.

9

Swarms of Locusts

Assign some students to find out about locusts: their size, eating habits, potentially destructive effects, and so on. Tell the researchers to bring in pictures of locusts (or even a live one). Oral reports by the researchers should help your class comprehend why the locust plague that Joel wrote about was devastating to Judah—why it would have been viewed as a terrible punishment for sin and as a symbol of the coming Day of the Lord.

Another way to convey the devastation of a locust plague would be to read to your students the following quotation, by W. M. Thomson:
◆ "Their number was astounding; the whole face of the mountain was black with them. On they came like a living deluge. We dug trenches, and kindled fires, and beat and burned to death 'heaps upon heaps'; but the effort was utterly useless. Wave after wave rolled up the mountainside and poured over rocks, walls, ditches and hedges—those behind covering up and bridging over the masses already killed. It was perfectly appalling to watch this animated river as it flowed up the road, and ascended the hill above my house. For four days they continued to pass on." (Quoted in *The Student Bible*, p. 787)

A Summary of the Prophets

Chapter 7 of this manual offers the activity "A Map Exercise: Prophets to Israel and Judah (p. 147)." Referring to the map entitled "Prophets to Israel and Judah" on page 146 of the student text, the activity calls for the students to look over the names of the prophets listed on the map and to underline each prophet's name as he is studied in chapter 7, 8, or 9. The activity also suggests that on a separate sheet of paper, the students should keep a running list of all the prophets studied, with a one-sentence summary of each prophet's message.

Handout **9–A**

At this point in the course, the students are concluding their study of the prophets. To consolidate their learning and to assist them in remembering the prophets, distribute handout 9–A, "The Prophetic Tradition," a summary chart of the prophets. Explain to the students that although Samuel and Nathan are not listed on the map on page 146 of their text, they are called prophets. Also, the first four prophets listed on the chart are the nonwriting prophets; all the others left a literary tradition. Baruch is not included in the chart because scholars assume that the book bearing his name was written long after he lived, as a retrospective account of the Exile.

A caution: The messages listed in the column "What?" do not fully summarize the prophets' works. Although the information provided does represent significant, distinguishing features of the prophets' messages, each prophet certainly dealt with other themes as well. So allow the students to come up with messages other than those offered.

In addition, the dates given on the chart are approximate, and many are still under dispute by scholars. The dates will help, however, in giving the students general points of reference.

Pages 224–233

Concept E: Keeping the Faith Alive Under Fire

Review Questions: Keeping the Faith Alive Under Fire

Question. Besides the Greeks' persecution of the Jews, what aspects of Greek domination threatened traditional Jewish life?

Answer. The allure of the sophisticated Greek lifestyle and bold new way of thinking, including the language, philosophy, and customs

Question. In what ways does King Antiochus Epiphanes persecute Jews in Jerusalem?

Answer. He sends soldiers to burn houses, kill people, and build a citadel for housing a continuing military presence and for the protection of apostate Jews. When these measures fail to counter Jewish resistance, he orders everyone in his realm to embrace his religion under penalty of death. The Temple is also defiled.

Question. Why does Eleazar not eat meat that looks like pork, even though doing so would save his life?

Answer. He didn't want to scandalize all the young who were watching him; that is, he felt it would compromise his faith if he even pretended to eat pork, and he did not want to set that kind of example for the young.

Question. What story in the Second Book of Maccabees gives testimony to the belief in a resurrection and afterlife?

Answer. The story of a mother and her seven sons who were arrested for refusing to eat pork. As the sons go to their deaths, they proclaim their belief that they will live again after death.

Question. What event in Jewish history is celebrated each year on the feast of Hanukkah?

Answer. The rededication of the Jerusalem Temple after the Greeks had defiled it

9

Question. Contrast the Maccabees' strategy of resisting the Greeks with that of the author of the Book of Daniel.

Answer. The Maccabees focused on human power and might to set things right; the author of Daniel held out God's love and justice as the ultimate power that saves.

Question. In whom do Christians see fulfilled Daniel's prophecy of the coming reign of "one like a son of man" (Dan. 7:13, NAB)?

Answer. Jesus Christ

Question. Why does apocalyptic literature, like that in the Book of Daniel, use strange symbolic images and code language? What is the intent of the authors of this type of literature?

Answer. To keep the true subject of the writing secret from the oppressors. The authors' intent was not to predict real events in the future but to give hope and inspiration to those oppressed by powerful forces.

 ## Text Activities: Keeping the Faith Alive Under Fire

- Think of an example of persons or groups who are in conflict because one side wants to take on the new and the other wants to hold on to the old. Then share your opinion on this question: *Is it possible to accept and adapt to the new and yet remain faithful to the old?*
- If you were told by the government that you no longer are allowed to express your faith or practice your religion—under threat of death—what effect would that have on your life? Describe in writing what you would do and how you might feel about the situation.
- Eleazar, the teachers from Norway, and the mother and her seven sons all showed incredible faithfulness and integrity. The choices they made were not just for themselves, but more important, for the people who were watching them. Through our choices we may teach or influence others toward good or away from it. Write about a situation when you might have influenced another person by the choices you made.
- Write your thoughts on these questions:
  - Is violent resistance the only way to overcome oppression?
  - If so, why do you think that way?
  - If not, what are other solutions?
- The biblical Jews wanted to preserve their heritage—a desire we can all share. Write a paragraph detailing your ethnic background and describing any family customs and stories associated with it.
- Martyrs are people who are persecuted and killed because they refuse to abandon their faith and religion. Find out about a martyr and write an essay about her or him.
- Write a letter—you can send it if you wish—to someone who is going through a time that seems overwhelming and defeating. What words of hope can you offer?

 ## Additional Activities: Keeping the Faith Alive Under Fire

Daniel, Martyrdom, and Resurrection

The following background information may help you in providing your students with insights about the Book of Daniel.

Many of the martyrs of Antiochus IV's persecution of the Jews were tortured and suffered a terrible death, and no saving angel intervened as in the story of Daniel and the lions or the story of the three faithful young men in the fiery furnace. Constancy in faith—willingness to die for what is right and true—is the lesson of the Daniel stories (even though the heroes do not actually die). The Book of Daniel is set in the time of Babylonian captivity, but it was composed in the second century BC to sustain Jews who were living under Greek domination and knew that they might die for their faith.

Remind the students that the writer himself had to take precautions so that he would not be executed by Antiochus (we do not know if he ever was). He protected himself and those who listened to his stories by disguising his message of hope and courage in the form of inspiring tales about the folk hero Daniel. The writer was drawing a direct parallel between the oppression by Nebuchadrezzar in the sixth century BC and that by Antiochus in the second century BC—but he did not dare breathe Antiochus's name or mention the cruelty of the Greeks!

Also note for the students that Jesus could have escaped death if he had been willing to return to Nazareth and cease stirring up the people with his teachings about truth, freedom, dignity, and eternal life. Perhaps like the Jews of Antiochus's persecution, Jesus remembered the Daniel stories, told to him as a child by his mother. Inspired and sustained by these tales of courage, he could believe in the ultimate triumph of good over evil.

As the student text mentions, the Book of Daniel articulates the belief in resurrection that had been growing in Judaism since the third century BC. Certainly the message in Daniel, like that in the Book of Wisdom, is that suffering is not necessarily the result of sin. Given the notion of resurrection, the Books of Daniel and Wisdom assert that there is hope in suffering and martyrdom because God is with us even beyond the grave. This crucial insight prepared the way for the teachings of Jesus and the early Church's proclamation that Jesus is "the resurrection and the life" (John 11:25).

The Book of Daniel, as mentioned in the student text, contains pieces of apocalyptic writing. This style of writing, which uses symbols and visions, is intended to show its readers, in times of distress, "how it will all turn out." In other words, the writing shows that in the end, goodness will triumph over evil, God will win the struggle with the power of darkness. Remind the students that this is the message, too, of the Book of Revelation, in the New Testament. It is a message of hope, one that all believers need to cling to in the face of suffering and oppression in a world that at times does not seem to make any sense. Although apocalyptic writing may sound bizarre to us, it is important to look past its strange symbolism to its unshakable conviction that love is stronger than death, that good will triumph over evil, and that we need to be on the side of love and goodness, not death and evil. This conviction has sustained the martyrs of Judaism and Christianity through the centuries and continues to give hope and fortitude to people who live in oppressive situations. (See also the chapter 9 activity "Research on the Apocalypse" on pages 186–187 of this manual.)

To help the students think about martyrdom in personally relevant terms, ask these questions:

◆ What are some "small deaths" or persecutions that people go through when they stick up for what they believe is right and true?

◆ In what sense can we say that people who suffer "small deaths" for the sake of goodness also experience "small resurrections" while they are still living?

◆ Do we have to wait until the end of the world to see good triumph over evil? In other words, can we see good triumph in our own time in small ways?

◆ What happens inside people when they turn their backs on their values and beliefs in the face of social pressure?

Daniel in the Lions' Den

Several familiar metaphors are rooted in the story of Daniel in the lions' den: saved from the jaws of the lion, rescued from the lions' den, or entering the lions' den. Ask your students:

◆ Have you ever been "saved from the lion's jaws"? Describe what it was like when you were about to be "devoured" and then realized that you were being rescued.

In the story of Daniel in the lions' den, those who conspired to have Daniel thrown to the lions suffer the fate they themselves had devised for him, and their families are thrown to the lions as well. This "massacre" approach to justice is a holdover from the early folk origins of the tale. The Jewish law of "An eye for an eye, a tooth for a tooth" was meant to prevent unmerciful vengeance and to limit the escalation of violence when an injustice or injury occurred. An eye for an eye called for one life for one life only, not the massacre of whole families for the crime of one member. The person who edited the tale in the second century BC may have simply neglected to omit the massacre of the families. Or possibly he retained this gory scene in order to show how barbaric the Babylonians were.

9

Ancient Jewish Beliefs About the Afterlife

Most people who believe in an afterlife wonder what it will be like. For centuries, the ancient Jews believed that the dead resided in Sheol, a shadowy, dusty, melancholy nonworld of utter inactivity. It was not a place of punishment but simply the state of nothingness. Many other ancient Near Eastern cultures had similar beliefs about the afterlife.

The belief that the good go to be with God did not appear until the third century BC. After the idea of an afterlife became connected with reward and punishment, concepts of a Heaven and a hell developed, although these concepts varied. Sometimes Heaven and hell were understood as actual places; sometimes they were understood as states or conditions of the dead, with the good being in a happy state in God's presence and the evil being in despair.

Up until the references to resurrection in the Books of Wisdom and Daniel, however, we do not see in the Old Testament any conception of what happens after death besides Sheol. Here are some references to Sheol, or the netherworld, for your students to look up and discuss:

• *Genesis 42:38.* Jacob will go to Sheol if Benjamin is taken from him.
• *Psalm 88:4–9.* Sheol is a pit and a dark abyss.
• *Isaiah 14:9–11.* Isaiah describes Sheol, to which the king of Babylon will go.
• *Job 10:21–22 and 17:13–16.* Sheol is a land of darkness and gloom.
  Ask the students:
  ◆ How would you feel about the prospect of your life ending if you thought that everyone who died ended up in Sheol?

Who Was Alexander the Great?

Select one or two students to prepare an oral report outlining the career of Alexander the Great, the territory he conquered, his methods of conquest, how he treated a vanquished people, his religious views, and so on. Encourage the researchers to use a map in their report to the class.

The Jews in a Hellenistic Culture

Throughout the Hellenistic world, the Jews were considered strange and exclusive because of their religion. Many Jews who lived in the Greek-speaking empire downplayed their differences in order to live side by side with their Gentile neighbors. The Maccabees, however, did not tolerate that approach to living in the Greek culture.

Even the Greek sporting events were religious in nature, so loyal Jews were not supposed to participate in them. The Olympic Games were held to honor the god Zeus; during the opening and closing ceremonies, prayers and sacrifices to Zeus were offered. The winners of the games received crowns of olive leaves, but the greatest honor was the glory of having competed for the gods.

After explaining these facts about the Jews in the Hellenistic world, ask your students:

- ◆ Why did Greek-sponsored athletic events pose a threat to the Jewish way of life?
- ◆ What modern tyrant matched Antiochus IV in his oppression of the Jews? How were the two alike? different?
- ◆ What does the career of Antiochus tell us about trying to force a set of beliefs down people's throats? Is it ever justifiable?

9

A Guest Speaker on Hanukkah

Invite a rabbi or a religious educator from a local synagogue to speak to your class about the story and celebration of Hanukkah.

Becoming a Dispersed People

Remind your students that when the Romans took Jerusalem in AD 70 and forbade the Jews to enter the city, the Jews became a landless people. The Dispersion, which had begun with the Assyrian and Babylonian exiles, became a reality for all Jews. They remained without a homeland until the formation of the modern state of Israel in 1948. Even today, the vast majority of Jews live outside Israel.

Assign a few students to look into where the Jews settled over the centuries after they were driven from Jerusalem. The students might also research how other peoples related to the Jews, including a history of persecutions and pogroms inflicted on the Jews into the twentieth century.

Ironically, the Babylonian Exile taught the Jews that they could still be Jews, worship their God, and keep their Law without land, the Temple, ritual, or sacrifices. They had to find God's Word written in their hearts and in their community, and that they did. Thus Judaism became one of the world's great religions.

Closing Prayer

This prayer centers on the postexilic community's dream of an age of peace and prosperity in Jerusalem. Tell the students that they can think of Jerusalem (also called Zion) symbolically as well as literally, viewing it as the Reign of God that Jesus said was already among us.

1. Remind your students of God's loving presence.

2. Ask one student to read Zechariah 8:1–8,11–13, which tells of the messianic age in Jerusalem.

3. Introduce a brief period of reflection by asking the students to think about how the returning exiles must have longed for peace, harmony, and prosperity after the years of disruption and exile.

After a few moments, remind the students that Jesus longed for "Jerusalem"—the Reign of God—to be among all of us. He ushered in that Reign with his life and death. Encourage the students to reflect for a few more moments on where they have seen glimpses of "Jerusalem" in their own life or community or world. If they are comfortable with spontaneous prayer, invite them to offer their reflections aloud.

4. Recite Psalm 87, alternating verses with the right and left sides of the classroom, with all joining for the last verse.

5. Close the time of prayer by listening to or singing together one of the following: "City of God," by Dan Schutte or "Sing a New Song," by Dan Schutte, both of which can be found in *Gather Comprehensive*.

 Closing Teacher Prayer

Call to prayer. Be still within and without. Remember the God who gifts us with fresh beginnings and new life.

Reflect. What have you learned in the process of teaching this chapter? Was it a learning of the head or the heart? Does this reveal God more fully to you? How? What effect could this learning have on your life?

What gift did you receive from your students? Which students do you feel are especially in need of God's tender care today?

Pray.
Gracious God,
soul of life and of all creation,
your healing spirit hovered over the primeval chaos,
and comes to rest over our yearnings and our desires.
Anoint us with your love,
mend our brokenness,
heal our woundedness. Amen.

(Bergan and Schwan, *Taste and See:
Prayer Services for Gatherings of Faith*)

9

The Prophetic Tradition

Who?	When? (all BC)	To whom?	What?
Samuel (nonwriting)	1040–1020	The tribes of Israel	Anoints Israel's first two kings, Saul and David, but warns the people of the dangers of having a king.
Nathan (nonwriting)	1000	David	Tells David that he and his family will suffer because of David's sins of adultery and murder.
Elijah (nonwriting)	875–850	Israel	Challenges belief in the god Baal.
Elisha (nonwriting)	850–820	Israel	Performs miracles and cures.
Amos	750	Israel	Condemns empty ritualism and the oppression of poor people.
Hosea	750	Israel	Compares Israel's betrayal of God to his own wife's infidelity.
Micah	725	Israel and Judah	Looks ahead to a time of justice and peace.
First Isaiah	742–700	Judah	Prophesies about Immanuel.
Zephaniah	630	Judah	Tells of a time of judgment for unfaithful Judah; preaches the idea of a humble remnant.
Jeremiah	626–570	Judah	Condemns idolatry, injustice, and foolish defiance of Babylon; offers hope of a new Covenant, which will be "written on the hearts of the people."
Nahum	612	Judah	Rejoices over the coming destruction of Assyria.
Habakkuk	609–598	Judah	Asks why God does not stop human evil by punishing Judah.
Ezekiel	600–570	Judah and the Babylonian exiles	Performs pantomimes of Jerusalem's coming destruction; later offers the exiles hope of restoration and a new Covenant.
Obadiah	after 587	The Babylonian exiles	Condemns Edom for "fratricide" in helping Judah's enemies.
Second Isaiah	550	The Babylonian exiles	Consoles the exiles with the joyous expectation of returning home; tells of a suffering servant who will save the people.
Third Isaiah	540–510	The postexilic community	Calls for true fasting—that is, works of justice and mercy; proclaims God as the God of all the nations.
Haggai	520–515	The postexilic community	Spurs the people into rebuilding the Temple.
Zechariah	520	The postexilic community	Describes the messianic age; portrays the messiah as a king of peace.
Malachi	500	The postexilic community	Condemns sacrilegious offerings and materialism.
Joel	400	The postexilic community	Calls for fasting and prayer after a plague of locusts.

CHAPTER 10

Wisdom and Wit: Seeking the Ways of God

Major Concepts

A. **Life According to Proverbs, Job, and Ecclesiastes: What's It All About?** Biblical wisdom literature inspires moral integrity. The Jewish sages saw the world as full of God's wisdom. The Book of Proverbs gives practical advice on how to live virtuously, which brings prosperity. The Book of Job questions why good people suffer. It concludes that evil is a mystery and that we must trust God to never stop caring for us. Qoheleth in the Book of Ecclesiastes also concludes that he cannot solve life's mystery. *See* the *Catechism,* nos. 164 (suffering); 223, 239, 303, 370 (the nature of God); 227, 309–314 (the problem of evil); 275 (Job); 295, 299, 1805, 2500 (wisdom); 721 (Mary); 1007 (earthly life).

B. **Wisdom, Sirach, and the Song of Songs: Life with God.** The Book of Wisdom asserts that the soul's life can carry on after bodily death, a concept introduced to Judaism by the Greeks. The Book of Sirach says that wisdom is found in the teachings God gave Israel. Sirach, like Proverbs, depicts wisdom as a woman who was with God at Creation. Song of Songs is a collection of love poems that early interpreters saw as a religious allegory of God's passion for Israel. *See* the *Catechism,* nos. 164 (suffering); 219, 1040, 1604, 1611, 2331 (God's love); 295, 2500 (God's wisdom); 363–366 (soul); 992–993 (afterlife); 1611 (Song of Songs); 2215, 2218, 2223 (Sirach—respect for parents).

C. **Stories of Encouragement: Faith and Goodness Triumph.** The stories told during the centuries following the Babylonian Exile inspired courage and faith in times of trial, reminding the people that goodness will ultimately triumph. The Book of Tobit tells of God rewarding Tobit and his family for their faithfulness and goodness. The Book of Judith tells of an Israelite woman who saves her people from destruction by trusting God to work through her talents. The Book of Esther was written to praise the goodness of God and to explain the origin of Purim. The Book of Jonah is a satirical prophetic book that reminds people that God's mercy extends to all. *See* the *Catechism,* nos. 29 (fleeing God's call—Jonah); 64, 489 (Judith and Esther); 162–165, 314 (perseverance in faith); 336 (angels); 1611 (Tobit); 2300, 2447 (respect for the dead); 2361 (Tobias and Sarah).

Opening Teacher Prayer

Call to prayer. Be still within and without. Center yourself in God, our source of all wisdom.

Read. Psalm 27

Reflect. What comes to your mind when you think of "mystery"? For what or whom in your life do you seek God's wisdom?

Hold in your heart. "Wait for the LORD" (Ps. 27:14).

 Pages 236–241
Concept A:
Life According to Proverbs, Job, and Ecclesiastes: What's It All About?

 ## Review Questions:
Life According to Proverbs, Job, and Ecclesiastes: What's It All About?

Question. What was the main goal of the biblical teachers of wisdom?
Answer. To inspire moral integrity.

Question. Give three examples of quotations from the Book of Proverbs that give practical advice.
Answer.
- *Parenting.* "Discipline your children while there is hope; / do not set your heart on their destruction" (19:18).
- *Communication.* "A soft answer turns away wrath, / but a harsh word stirs up anger" (15:1).
- *Attitudes.* "Pride goes before destruction, / and a haughty spirit before a fall" (16:18).
(See pp. 237–238 of the student text for other answers.)

Question. According to Proverbs, what is the reward for a virtuous life?
Answer. Success, prosperity, honor, dignity, and a good name.

Question. What is meant by the problem of evil?
Answer. The dilemma of why the good suffer and the wicked prosper in this life.

Question. What is the message of the Book of Job?
Answer. Although we may never rationally understand the existence of evil in the world, we can trust that even in the darkest moments, God is in charge, loving us through it all.

Question. What conclusion does Qoheleth come to in Ecclesiastes?
Answer. He concludes that life is a mystery he cannot solve. He says the sensible thing is to accept it from the hand of God and enjoy it as well as one can.

10

Text Activities:
Life According to Proverbs, Job, and Ecclesiastes: What's It All About?

- Choose one of these proverbs and write about an experience from your life that illustrates its meaning.
- Write three proverbs that would be good advice for today's world.
- Write about someone you know who is wise. Give an example of a circumstance in which he or she demonstrated wisdom.
- Have you ever asked *why* in the face of something terrible and undeserved? If so, write a brief reflection about it.
- What do you think of God's "answer" to Job? Write your own response to God.
- Write a reaction to Qoheleth's attitude toward life. Do you agree or disagree with him? Why?

Additional Activities:
Life According to Proverbs, Job, and Ecclesiastes: What's It All About?

Images of God

God transcends sexual categories. Stress this point with the students. One way of doing this is to briefly explain some of the names for God.

The three names most often used for God in the Old Testament are Yahweh, El or Elohim, and Adonai.

1. *Yahweh* is the name that God revealed to Moses as most fitting. Meaning "I am the One who is always present," it comes from the Hebrew verb "to be" or "to be actively present." Many devout Jews will not use this name because they consider it too sacred. In fact the original pronunciation of the Hebrew has been lost; Yahweh is a modern version of the original word. Obviously, "the One who is always present" is neither masculine nor feminine. That is because God completely transcends sexual categories.

2. *El* is an ancient Semitic term meaning "the Deity" or "God." The plural form, *Elohim,* can also be used for a single divine being, "the One who completely possesses all the divine attributes." Thus, once again, God (El or Elohim) is complete and is not bound by masculinity or femininity.

3. *Adonai* is most frequently translated "LORD." Adonai grew in usage as the name Yahweh became so sacred that devout Jews ceased using it, out of respect. Only with the use of Adonai was any sex-specific name given to God. The word was taken from common Hebrew usage to denote a master or sovereign who, because of the culture at the time, was inevitably male. The Jews' use of Adonai must not be taken to mean that they limited their understanding of God to a masculine figure; for the Jews, such a limitation would have been sinful. A masculine image would have been considered inadequate to describe the nature of God.

10

4. Then tell the students:

◆ Though God is neither man nor woman, biblical writers did use male and female images to describe God because that was what they knew from their human experience. Write a paragraph or two on your image of God and how it developed.

Wisdom Literature: A Debate on the Meaning of Divine Fairness

Before discussing the wisdom books with your students, you might want to become familiar with the following background information and synthesis. This material covers the origins of Jewish wisdom literature and how the wisdom books "debate" one another's points about whether goodness is rewarded and evil is punished. Specifically, the wisdom books included here are Proverbs, Job, Ecclesiastes, Sirach, and Wisdom. (The Song of Songs differs in major themes from these other wisdom books and so is not treated in the background material.)

To even the casual reader, the wisdom books sound quite different from the other books of the Old Testament, both in style and in theme and content. Wisdom literature does not address the history of a people (the communal dimension found in most of the rest of the Old Testament). Rather, it deals with the meaning and conduct of a person's life (the individual dimension). Wisdom literature is the product of a tradition different from the tradition that produced the historical books. The wisdom books came from the sages, or thinkers.

The sages had a rather cosmopolitan view. They studied the wisdom literature of other cultures, such as Egypt's, and integrated sophisticated philosophical outlooks with Israel's belief in the Law and the one God. (The sages' openness to the wisdom of other cultures would probably have put them at odds with Ezra and Nehemiah.) Thus the writings of the sages reflect philosophical concerns such as the reasonableness and orderliness of reality and the fate of the individual—which were not major preoccupations for the rest of the scriptural writers.

The sages, however, were not all of one mind. The following numbered sections show how the thinking of various authors of the wisdom books differed on the issue of divine fairness and the destiny of the individual.

1. Proverbs. The original intention of Proverbs was probably to help young men learn how to live decently and honorably so that they could take up a respectable career in the administration of the monarchy. On the whole, the collectors of these wise sayings accepted at the individual level the notion of divine retribution that was espoused by the Deuteronomists (who saw God's retribution—or dispensing of reward and punishment—operating at the communal level). The notion of divine retribution is this: Those who are virtuous will be rewarded, but those who are wicked will be punished.

This idea of divine retribution at the individual level certainly squared with the long-standing belief in a just God who would not let virtue go unrewarded or wickedness go unpunished. (At the communal level, the Deuteronomists had asserted that when the nation or the king rebelled against God, the people as a whole were punished. Likewise, when the nation or the monarchy repented and returned to God, all the people of Israel were saved.)

Until very late in Judaism's scriptural history, Judaism included no concept of a life after death (except for the nonworld of Sheol), so the sages expected that the rewards and punishments for an individual's conduct would come about during the person's lifetime. This view became distorted, however, to the point that many followers of the sages began assuming that goodness automatically led to prosperity, health, good fortune, and long life, and correspondingly, that sin automatically led to poverty, sickness, ill fortune, and an early death. Many proverbs could be misinterpreted to mean just that. The warped notion of divine justice led to a kind of "vending machine" mentality about God: put in the "coin" of virtuous behavior, and out pops the "candy bar" from God—wealth, luck, long life. In this view God was predictable and, in a way, subject to human control. (Incidentally, this view is not far removed from the approach to God that many modern Christians have. It is humorously referred to as the "gospel of health and wealth.")

2. Job and Ecclesiastes. The Books of Job and Ecclesiastes responded to the distorted view of divine retribution in Proverbs. The authors said, in effect, "It's not so simple. You can't figure out God and life so easily. You can't simply order the kind of fate you want from God. God's ways are mysterious, and we are arrogant if we expect God to conform to our ways and expectations. The real meaning of things like suffering is hidden from our eyes. Poverty and suffering are not punishments for sin, nor are prosperity and health rewards for goodness. God is beyond our attempts to understand and control."

Though the authors of Job and Ecclesiastes differed from the sages of the Proverbs in their outlook on divine fairness, they were alike in that they had no concept of an afterlife where good would be rewarded. So the authors of Job and Ecclesiastes simply called for humility in the face of realities that human beings cannot grasp.

3. Sirach and Wisdom. The author of the Book of Sirach probably had read Job and Ecclesiastes, and he too was skeptical of the neat arrangement that matched up goodness with a prosperous, honorable life and connected sinfulness with a life of suffering. The author of the Book of Wisdom, however, went beyond all the other sages by articulating a belief in an afterlife. Wisdom, probably the latest-written Jewish book incorporated into the Catholic canon of the Scriptures, asserts that the good are not necessarily rewarded in life, nor are the wicked punished. But God is just, because the reward for a good life is immortal union with God, which is the soul's destiny.

This late development in Jewish thinking yielded deeper insight into the idea of divine retribution. Later it opened the way to a Christian understanding of the cross and the Resurrection. (Imagine trying to make sense of Jesus' life, ministry, and Crucifixion using the limited concept of reward and punishment offered in Proverbs!) The belief in life after death was also asserted in another late work, the Book of Daniel (see pp. 231–232 of the student text and major concept E in chapter 9 of this manual).

Thus, within the development of wisdom literature, a kind of debate went on, which led to an ever more refined understanding of God's justice and the meaning and purpose of an individual's life.

A recommendation. Do not present the above material directly to your students. Rather, as your class studies the Books of Proverbs, Job, Ecclesiastes, Sirach, and Wisdom, try to draw out the students' understandings of how the insights of the wisdom literature developed; then fill in with additional information as needed.

When you conclude the study of concept B, summarize it by reviewing with the students this development in Jewish theology. Consider using handout 10–A, "Images of God, Understandings of Life," which illustrates the development of the sages' thinking. Ask the students which image of God is closest to their own image of God.

Handout **10–A**

Proverbs Abound

Tell your students to write down one "proverb" from each of these sources:
- advertisements
- home
- school
- athletics

Remind the class that proverbs are short, easily remembered phrases used to give practical advice or moral guidance.

Later urge the students to orally report the proverbs that they found. Then discuss proverbs, using these questions:
- ◆ Almost all cultures have a set of proverbs that are passed from generation to generation. For example, one Chinese proverb is, Fool me once, shame on you; fool me twice, shame on me. In the United States, Benjamin Franklin came up with hundreds of proverbs: A penny saved is a penny earned. A stitch in time saves nine. No pain, no gain. These proverbs are so ingrained in people that they assume the sayings are timeless truths. Why do almost all cultures have proverbs?
- ◆ Are proverbs popular in our culture today?

Applying Proverbs

In a brainstorming session with your class, list on the chalkboard recent happenings in the school, in your community, in the nation, or in the world. Then assign one event to each student, requiring him or her to find a proverb from the Book of Proverbs that would shed light on that event or that would provide moral guidance to the people involved in the event.

After the students have found fitting proverbs, invite them to read their choices.

Proverb Challenge

This activity aims to help students become familiar with the Book of Proverbs and with some of the individual proverbs. Structured as a game, it requires the students to find proverbs with messages that are the same or similar to those of other proverbs.

1. In advance select about twenty-five proverbs from the Book of Proverbs to use as "the challenge proverbs." Because many themes recur throughout Proverbs (the value of friendship, the problem of laziness, the importance of honesty, the need to listen to and obey authority, etc.), each of the twenty-five proverbs you select will no doubt match a theme that comes up in other scriptural proverbs. Hold on to your list of proverbs and do not let the students see it before the game starts.

2. Appoint three students to be the judges for the game. Divide the rest of your class into four or five teams. Give each team a different kind of noisemaker—such as a bell, a clicker, or a kazoo.

3. Tell the class that the object of the game is that they become familiar with the Book of Proverbs. Explain these steps:
- ◆ I will read a proverb aloud only once.

10

- ◆ The teams will look for a proverb that matches—or says something similar to—the one I have read. For example, if I read, "What is desirable in a person is loyalty, / and it is better to be poor than a liar" [19:22], a team might find, "Better the poor walking in integrity / than one perverse of speech who is a fool" [19:1].
- ◆ When a team locates a matching proverb, it will make noise with its noisemaker. In the case of close calls, the judges will decide which team made a noise first. The team that makes a noise first will read aloud the proverb that it found, and the judges will decide if the proverb is similar to the one read aloud by me. If the proverb qualifies, the team will earn a point.

4. Warn the groups to get their Bibles ready. Then begin the game by reading the first proverb on your list. (Clearly, you need to control the pace of the game; keep it moving. Some students may want to dispute the judges on close calls. One way to avoid such protests is to go on to the next proverb as soon as the judges' decision is made.)

5. Arrange for a judge, or a scorekeeper, to record the team points on the chalkboard. The duration of the game depends on you, of course. You may want to award a novelty prize to the winning team. The judges, who will probably work hard at being fair, might also be given a prize.

A Proverbial Bible Bookmark

10

Have your students each create a proverbial bookmark for their Bible. The bookmark may be made of cloth, heavy paper, or leather, but it must bear a favorite scriptural proverb of the student. Perhaps display these bookmarks in the classroom before they are used by the students.

Role-Playing Scenes from Job

Ask for volunteers or select students to role-play each of these passages from Job:
- *Job 1:1–12.* Characters: narrator, God, and Satan
- *Job 1:13–22.* Characters: narrator, four messengers, and Job
- *Job 3:1–6; 4:7–9; 6:8–10,24–25; 8:3–7; 11:2–6; 13:1–5,15–16; 27:3–6.* Characters: Job and his friends Eliphaz, Bildad, and Zophar
- *Job 38:1–7 and 42:1–6.* Characters: God, narrator, and Job

The students can either read the passages directly from their Bibles or paraphrase the passages in their own words. (Humor is not out of place.)

A Cartoon of Job

Tell your students each to draw a cartoon based on a passage from the story of Job and to use that passage as a caption; encourage the use of humor. Display these cartoons in the classroom.

As an alternative you could tell your students to cut out a picture from a magazine or newspaper and to superimpose on the picture a cartoon bubble containing a quote from the Book of Job. For example, if a picture shows a football player missing a pass, the bubble could say, "Perish the day I was born!" Or if it shows a person dressed up in fancy clothes, a voice (bubble) from Heaven could say, "Who is this, obscuring my intentions?"

Humorous as the cartoons can be, they can also be a highly effective way to focus on the message of Job.

"Turn, Turn, Turn"

Play a recording of the well-known folk song "Turn, Turn, Turn" for your class. Ask the students to compare the message of the song (based on Eccles. 3:1–8) to the way things go in life.

The Inconsistencies We Live With

Qoheleth holds before us the constant turning of life. Medieval poets called it the Wheel of Fate—sometimes we are up, and sometimes we are down. Qoheleth's advice is to accept the mystery of life and enjoy what is good.

Ask your students to jot down five of life's inconsistencies that they or people they know have experienced. Request that volunteers share their stories of surprise or inconsistency. Finally, ask your class these questions:
- How do most of us act when we are faced with a twist of fate?
- In the experiences you jotted down, did anyone who was affected by the situations want to blame God?
- Do people in general—and you in particular—find mystery, surprise, and the up-and-down nature of life hard to accept? [Ask the students to explain their answers.]

10

Concept B: Wisdom, Sirach, and the Song of Songs: Life with God

Pages 241–245

Review Questions: Wisdom, Sirach, and the Song of Songs: Life with God

Question. According to the Book of Wisdom, what is our destiny as humans?
Answer. Life forever with God.

Question. How does the Book of Sirach differ in its concerns from other wisdom literature?
Answer. Sirach is deeply concerned with the history of Israel, its heroes, and its institutions.

Question. What is the Song of Songs? According to early Jewish and Christian interpreters, what is it meant to symbolize?

Answer. It is a collection of love poems in which a bridegroom and a bride speak of their love and longing for each other. For both Jews and Christians, the bride and groom's mutual love was an image of God's love for and passionate devotion to Israel. For Christians it was also a figure of Christ's love for his "bride," the Church, and also for the soul of an individual believer.

Text Activities: Wisdom, Sirach, and the Song of Songs: Life with God

- If you were to personify wisdom, would it be young or old? male or female? human or another animal? Create a written portrait of wisdom. Once you have thoroughly described wisdom, let it speak: What is its wisest saying?
- Do young people today see virginity as positive for someone who is not married? Give your opinion in a paragraph.

Additional Activities: Wisdom, Sirach, and the Song of Songs: Life with God

10

The Song of Songs: Many Levels

The Song of Songs has been interpreted in various ways by spiritual writers and scholars over the centuries. The student text mentions some of those interpretations. But scholars really do not know the context in which the poems were written or their original purpose. It is most likely that they were created simply as celebrations of the earthly joys of marital union. Share with the students some of the following ways that the Song of Songs has been understood:

- as an erotic love poem about the goodness and holiness of marriage and the marriage act
- as a memory of Solomon's wedding with one of his many wives
- as a conversation between wisdom and the soul
- as a description of the contemplative experience, in which God seeks union with the soul
- as an allegory of the relationship between God (the bridegroom) and God's people (the bride)
- as an allegory of the relationship between Christ (the bridegroom) and the Church (the bride)

Ask the students:

- Are any of these interpretations definitely wrong?
- Is it possible that they are all right? If so, how? [The Scriptures can always be interpreted at many levels. That is one source of their richness—that they speak to us as individuals and as a community in different ways at different times, according to our needs and the movement of the Spirit in us.]
- In what other books of the Old Testament have we seen the relationship between God and the people pictured as a marriage? [Hosea and Ezekiel]

◆ If the only purpose of the Song of Songs were to celebrate the sanctity and joys of marital union, would this book still belong in the Bible?
Why or why not?

The Four Cardinal Virtues

Christian tradition teaches that there are four cardinal virtues: prudence, self-
control, justice, and courage. According to Wisdom 8:7, these virtues are
taught by Wisdom (personified as "she"). Direct the students to define each of
the cardinal virtues and to compose for each virtue a short fictional case in
which a character shows evidence of either having or lacking that virtue.

Concept C: Stories of Encouragement: Faith and Goodness Triumph

Pages 246–253

Review Questions: Stories of Encouragement: Faith and Goodness Triumph

Question. What does the Book of Tobit remind us about?
Answer. In the end, faithful goodness and trust in God are rewarded with
blessings.

Question. What did the author of Judith try to emphasize?
Answer. Judith trusted completely in God as she used her considerable
wits and charm. God worked through her particular talents and gifts.

Question. What story is remembered and celebrated in the Jewish feast
of Purim?
Answer. Purim honors the courage of Esther, who overcame her fears to
save her people. The feast gets its name from the lot—the *pur*—that Haman
drew to determine the date of the slaughter of the Jews.

Question. What was the author of the Book of Jonah trying to tell his au-
dience?
Answer. That God's mercy extends to all, not just to the "insiders" (Israel).

Text Activities: Stories of Encouragement: Faith and Goodness Triumph

- In Tobit we see the model of a faithful Jew in ancient Israel. In writing, create a model of a faithful Christian today.
- Judith combines personality traits often referred to as feminine with others
seen as masculine. Do males and females tend to be more alike or more different in qualities of mind and heart? Explain your answer in a one-page essay.

- In the last century, a "Haman" killed six million Jews in Europe and millions of other Europeans. Who was he? Explain in writing how such crimes can evolve within a community or a country.
- Have you ever "run away" from a difficult situation like Jonah did? Did running away work? Write down your story and include the consequences of your running away.
- Answer the following question in writing: *What do you think could have been Jonah's answer to God's question at the end of the Book of Jonah?*

Additional Activities: Stories of Encouragement: Faith and Goodness Triumph

Judith as Heroine

After your students have read the story of Judith, tell them to list all the qualities of character that they find in Uzziah and the elders, and those that they find in Judith. Then pose these questions for discussion:

- ◆ What are the sources of Judith's wisdom and vision?
- ◆ What is lacking in the character of Uzziah and the elders? Why?
- ◆ If Judith were a historical figure instead of a fictional character, would she be considered a prophet?
- ◆ Judith uses her beauty to deceive Holofernes. Do the circumstances make it okay for Judith to use her beauty to deceive, or do you think she is wrong?

A Courageous Role Model

Remind the students of the story of Esther and how she overcame her fears to save her people. Her courage, in risking her life, is still celebrated today in the Jewish feast of Purim. To get the students to reflect on times they, too, have been courageous, ask them to write a one-page reflection on a time when they were scared to do something they were called to do. They should describe the circumstances, their feelings, and the outcome. Tell the students that the situation does not need to be as dramatic, or call for as much courage, as Esther's situation. Even little acts of bravery are exemplary.

Purim

If possible, ask a rabbi or a religious education teacher from a local synagogue to talk with your class about Purim.

The Book of Jonah as a Warning Against Prejudice

Chapter 9 of the student text describes the program of strict and exclusive Judaism promoted by Nehemiah and Ezra. The background material provided in the activity "The Program of Nehemiah and Ezra" on pages 191–192 of this

10

manual says that many critics of Ezra and Nehemiah's reform thought that they were going too far with their exclusivist approach to Judaism. Scholars have proposed that the Book of Ruth was written by those critics to counter the prejudice against Gentiles that the critics saw as an inherent part of Nehemiah and Ezra's reform. Note for the students that scholars have speculated that the Book of Jonah may have had a similar purpose. Ask the students:

♦ What aspect of Jonah's story could be considered a criticism of Ezra and Nehemiah's program? [God insists on being merciful to the enemy city of Nineveh, despite Jonah's complaints and prejudice against the Ninevites. The story's point is that God loves the Gentiles as well as the Jews.]

Closing Prayer

This prayer service celebrates God's wisdom.

1. Before the service invite one student to practice reading John Henry Newman's reflection entitled "He Knows What He Is About" on page 243 of the student text. (He or she will be asked to read it later during the service.) Place a candle and a Bible in the prayer environment. Play quiet instrumental music in the background.

2. Invite the students to gather in a large circle with their Bible. Begin by asking God to bless the group and to help them be open to God's wisdom. Then tell the students to think of a time that they, or someone they knew, showed wisdom. Ask them what the difference is between wisdom and intelligence.

3. Then direct the students to turn to Sirach, chapter 24, in their Bible. Let the students take turns prayerfully reading the verses. Allow a brief time of meditation afterward.

4. Say this prayer:
♦ O Lord of all wisdom, we praise you and thank you for giving us a taste of your wisdom. Please continue to fill us with your fruits and bless us as we seek the ways of your truth. Amen.

5. The student reader may then introduce the John Henry Newman reflection and read it slowly, so the words can sink in.

6. After a brief period of meditation, invite the assembly to share any petitions, especially any that may relate to wisdom. Then pray:
♦ God, in your wisdom, you know not only our needs but also what is best for us. Please hear our prayer and give us wisdom for ourselves and for others, so we may serve you better. Amen.

7. End with a hymn, either something mellow like "Open My Eyes," by Jesse Manibusan, or something more rousing like "Sing of the Lord's Goodness," by Ernest Sands (both of which are available in *Today's Missal*, Breaking Bread edition [Portland, OR: Oregon Catholic Press, 2002]).

Closing Teacher Prayer

Call to prayer. Be still within and without. Center yourself in the God of mystery.

Reflect. What have you learned in the process of teaching this chapter? Was it a learning of the head or the heart? Does this reveal God more fully to you? How? What effect could this learning have on your life?

What gift did you receive from your students? Which students do you feel are especially in need of God's tender care today?

Pray.
Dear God, at the center of life
is the mystery of trust and surrender.
It is the heart of love,
the spring of new life and all creative effort,
and the touchstone of true freedom.
Help me join my heart to the psalmist's words,
"Whom shall I fear?" (Ps. 27:1). Amen.

(Bergan and Schwan, *Taste and See: Prayer Services for Gatherings of Faith*)

Images of God, Understandings of Life

The sketches below represent the different images of God and understandings of life that were held by the Jewish wisdom sages. Beneath each sketch, list the wisdom books that correspond to that image.

God as a Judge

Living well brings rewards in this life; sinning brings punishment in this life.

Wisdom books represented: _____

God as a Mystery

Life has ups and downs; we know not why.

Wisdom books represented: _____

God as the Goal of Existence

Living means moving toward eternal union with God.

Wisdom books represented: _____

CHAPTER 11

The Psalms:
Pouring Out Heart and Soul to God

Major Concepts

A. The Psalms as **Songs of the Heart.** The Psalms, central to Jewish and Christian prayer, express deep feelings that people of all times can identify with. Most psalms focus predominantly on one of three sentiments: lament, thanks, or praise. Though about half of the Psalms are attributed to King David, he likely did not write many. But they were written in his spirit, and many refer to David's experiences. The Psalms were composed to be sung in public worship. Some point to specific events in Israel's history. The Psalms play an important role in the Mass and in the liturgy of the hours. They express the same idea in several poetic ways and use concrete, metaphorical, and active language that helps us to sense God's power and makes them easy to remember. The Psalms are ideally suited to group or solitary prayer. *See* the *Catechism,* nos. 288, 304, 2579, 2585–2589 (prayer and the Psalms); 1093, 1096, 1176–1177 (the Psalms in church worship).

B. **Psalms of Lament: Crying Out in Suffering.** Most psalms of lament tell God of great suffering, plead for help, affirm that he is trustworthy, and end up praising him. They console and gradually transform the suffering one who prays to become more centered in God. The language of these psalms is often bluntly angry, helping us bring our whole selves to God and let go of our negative feelings, entrusting them to him. The psalms of lament often rail against enemies, which can be particular people, oppressive systems, or even evil within ourselves. God wants to transform all these "enemies" by love. *See* the *Catechism,* nos. 215, 227 (trust in God); 301, 303, 410 (God never abandons us); 407–409 (the human tendency to sin); 708, 716 (the lamentation psalms); 2438 (oppressive systems).

C. **Psalms of Thanks and Praise: Celebrating Who God Is.** The psalms of thanks and praise focus on God's goodness and spring from a humble attitude. They recognize that God brings us through suffering and death into new life and hope. These psalms celebrate God's wonderful deeds and the beauty of creation that He sustains with love. Psalms of thanks and praise are filled with a sense of wonder and awe. They are a marvelous school of prayer, showing us the way to a genuine relationship with God. *See* the *Catechism,* nos. 223–224 (gratitude to God); 299–301 (God sustains creation); 2589, 2639, 2641 (prayers of praise).

Opening Teacher Prayer

Call to prayer. Be still within and without. Open your deepest emotions—joy, longing, fear, grief, anger, hope, gratitude, confusion—to God.

Read. Psalm 139

Reflect. What feelings come to you as you read the psalm? Can you share these completely with God?

Hold in your heart. "O LORD, you have searched me and known me" (Ps. 139:1).

Pages 258–267

Concept A: The Psalms as Songs of the Heart

Review Questions: The Psalms as Songs of the Heart

Question. Name and define the three major types of psalms.
Answer. Psalms of lament, which express grief and complaint to God for suffering and beg for help; psalms of thanks, which express gratitude for God's good deeds, and psalms of praise, which celebrate the wonder and majesty of God.

Question. When were the Psalms composed?
Answer. Scholars believe the psalms were composed from about 1000 to 300 BC.

Question. How were the Psalms originally intended to be used?
Answer. They were composed to be sung in public worship.

Question. How are the Psalms used in the Christian liturgy?
Answer. They are used in the liturgy of the word (a responsorial psalm follows the first reading of God's Word) and in the liturgy of the hours.

Question. Describe two poetic features of the Psalms.
Answer. They are structured with repetition and contrast, and they use concrete language. They are full of metaphors that help us sense the power of God, and they are full of action.

11

Text Activities: The Psalms as Songs of the Heart

- Imagine how Psalm 116 could apply to your own situation or that of someone you know, and describe that situation in writing. Remember that being rescued from death does not have to be taken literally: "death" can mean the painful loss of someone you love, the heartbreak of enduring parents' separation, or the anguish of being rejected by others.

- Compare Psalm 104 to chapter 1 of Genesis and make a collage that tells the glorious story of God's Creation.
- Psalms were often written as reflections on biblical events that happened many years earlier. Choose a story from the Old Testament and find a psalm that captures the spirit of the event or persons featured in the story.
- Can you recall a time when your whole school went through something very significant together? Perhaps it was the death of a student or a faculty member, the closing of your school, or a major victory in a contest or sports event. The community liturgy at such times may seem more heartfelt than usual because everyone has shared in the major event and brings strong feelings about it to the worship. People seem more open to God.

    Consider such a significant event in your school's life, either real or imaginary, and write a description of it. Suppose you have been asked to choose a psalm, or an excerpt from a psalm, for the schoolwide liturgy centered on that event. You hope it will express people's strong feelings and help them be open to God. What psalm, or psalm verses, would you choose and why? Explain in writing.
- Find three metaphors about God in the Psalms that you find comforting or disturbing. Write each down and explain how it makes you feel and why.
- Write your thoughts on what the "desolate pit" and "miry bog" could mean in a young person's life.

Additional Activities: The Psalms as Songs of the Heart

Using the Psalms for Prayer Before Class

For each day that your class studies this chapter, designate one student to read aloud one psalm as an opening prayer for the session. The other students can follow along in their Bible or pray every other verse aloud. Here are some short psalms or psalm excerpts to use: 1; 3; 4; 6; 8; 13; 23; 25:1–7; 29; 33:1–8; 41; 42; 54; 66; 67; 79; 81; 91; 96; 100; 111; 121; 131; 148; 150. *Pray Your Heart: Contemporary Songs from the Psalms* (OCP Publications, 2001) is another resource for daily prayer. The *Pray Your Heart Resource Manual* (Saint Mary's Press, 2001) provides music-based sessions and prayer experiences for teens for the songs on this CD (see appendix 3).

The Honesty and Passion of the Psalms

In the Book of Psalms, we find the Jews' deepest emotions and their religious beliefs brought together in one source. The Psalms were (and still are) the everyday prayer of the Jews, and they were most well developed and used after the Babylonian Exile, in the second Temple. Remind the students that the Psalms arose out of many specific historical contexts, most of which we do not know about today but can only imagine. Throughout the course, in connection with certain themes or historical episodes, this teaching manual has recommended the praying or reading of particular psalms.

Reading the Psalms or listening to them being sung is like listening in on the intense, honest, emotional conversation of lovers who are not afraid to be themselves with each other, even when being themselves does not present a lovely, pleasant picture. These hymns express praise, thanks, wonder, joy, struggle, guilt, doubts, fears, anger, even hatred, as the psalmists share everything about their life and experiences with their God.

In his book *Praying the Psalms,* Walter Brueggemann describes ways the honesty and passion of the Psalms may be better understood. Read over the following excerpts from his book as background for helping your students see why some psalms do not convey a "pretty" picture of those who pray them.

I suggest, in a simple schematic fashion, that our life of faith consists in moving with God in terms of

a. being securely *oriented,*
b. being painfully *disoriented,* and
c. being surprisingly *reoriented.*

This general way of speaking can apply to our self-acceptance, our relations to significant others, our participation in public issues. Most of all, it may provide us with a way to think about the Psalms in relation to our common human experience, for each of God's children is in transit along the flow of orientation, disorientation, and reorientation. The first situation in this scheme, that of being securely oriented, is one of equilibrium.
. . .

. . . The Psalms mostly do not emerge out of such situations of equilibrium. Rather, people are driven to the Psalter's poignant prayer and song precisely by *experiences of dislocation and relocation.* The experiences of being overwhelmed, nearly destroyed, and then surprisingly given life empower us to pray and sing.

. . . Thus, the Psalms reflect such passionate and eloquent events that occur when experience presses us to address the Holy One. . . .

The Psalms thus propose to speak about human experience in an honest, freeing way. This is in contrast to much of human speech and conduct, which is in fact a cover-up. . . .

. . . The speech of the Psalms is abrasive, revolutionary, and dangerous. It announces that our common experience is not one of well-being and equilibrium. Life is instead a churning, disruptive experience of dislocation and relocation. (Pp. 14–17)

. . . The Psalms are awkward in their *concreteness.* . . . Psalmic rhetoric is concrete about commandments and punishments, about angers, loves, and hopes. . . .

. . . There is no mediation to "clean up," censor, or filter what is going on. . . . Since there are no secrets hidden from God, there is less self-deception at work in these prayers. . . .

. . . The robustness and candor of the Psalms are especially evident in the *articulation of hatred and anger.* . . .

. . . But Israel is not only able to rage with abandon; it has equal *passion for hope.* Elie Wiesel, that most remarkable storyteller from the Holocaust, has said that what makes a Jew a Jew is this inability to quit hoping. . . . The structure of hope is the conviction of a new world. . . .

. . . Even the lament psalms are acts of hope. . . .

. . . The practice of concreteness and candor, of anger and hope . . . prepare us for the most striking and problematic element of Jewish prayer, the *readiness to seek vengeance.* (Pp. 49–53)

. . . *The yearning for vengeance is here, among us and within us* and with power. It is not only *there* in the Psalms but it is *here* in the human heart and the human community. . . . The Psalms do "tell it like it is" with us.

It is important to recognize that these verbal assaults of imagination and hyperbole are *verbal.* They speak wishes and prayers. But the speaker doesn't *do* anything beyond speak. . . .

The speech of vengeance is characteristically offered to God, not directly to the enemy. . . .

. . . This full rage and bitterness are yielded to God's wisdom and providential care. (Pp. 58–60)

Oftentimes, the Psalms honestly communicate what we are already feeling. In being honest with God, we are honest with ourselves. Such sharing can dissipate our hurt, anger, and desire for vengeance.

Contemporary Songs and Psalms

Many of today's songs reflect accurately and passionately the thoughts, feelings, and concerns of young people. Tell your students each to write down the lyrics of a song that, to them, is a modern psalm. Then have them answer these two questions in writing:

- ◆ What message does the song express?
- ◆ Why do you consider this song a contemporary psalm?

To prepare for this activity, you could develop a list of ten or so contemporary songs that you see as psalms. To keep current with the youth music culture and to receive regular commentaries on popular music from a Christian perspective, you can subscribe to *Top Music Countdown,* which is a quarterly publication. Another source of music reviews is the "Ministry and Media" feature in the magazine *Group.* This magazine, published six times a year, is oriented to youth ministry. See appendix 3 for more information on both of these publications as well as for information about other relevant music resources.

11

Illustrating the Psalms

Before class gather materials for this art project on the Psalms. Begin the project by telling the students each to select one psalm or part of a psalm and to copy it neatly onto poster paper, leaving a 2- to 4-inch margin on all four sides. Then instruct them to position around the printed psalm images or pictures that illustrate the ideas in the psalm. These pictures will form a border or frame for the psalm. Display the posters in class or around your school.

Concept B: Psalms of Lament: Crying Out in Suffering

Pages 268–273

Review Questions: Psalms of Lament: Crying Out in Suffering

Question. What are the five elements found in most psalms of lament?
Answer. (1) An address to God; (2) a complaint or account of the misery suffered; (3) a plea for help; (4) an affirmation of trust in God; and (5) a statement praising God.

Question. Is it acceptable to have in our own heart the kind of brutally honest language and sentiments that are in the psalms of lament? Why or why not?

Answer. Yes, because to feel negative emotions and bring them to God is not the same as acting on those emotions. The greatest gift one can bring to God is the gift of one's whole self—honest, true, uncensored, even flawed with sin.

Question. How should "the enemies" in the Psalms be understood?

Answer. "The enemy" is rarely just the "bad guys" out there. The enemy is also all those negative parts of ourselves that we have not yet turned over to God's transforming love. The enemy can also be oppressive, cruel systems that cause injustice and misery for poor people in the world.

 ## Text Activities: Psalms of Lament: Crying Out in Suffering

- Find a newspaper or magazine article that tells of a situation of great suffering. Using the five elements listed on the previous page, tell about the story in the style of a psalm of lament.
- Choose a verse from Psalm 77 that is meaningful or interesting to you and write a reflection about it.
- Write your thoughts on these questions:
  - How do you feel about being completely honest with God?
  - If a person is not able to be honest in relationships with other people, is it possible to have an honest relationship with God?
- Describe three insights or lessons you have learned in your life about how to treat "enemies." From whom did you learn these lessons?

 ## Additional Activities: Psalms of Lament: Crying Out in Suffering

No Pain, No Gain

To engage your students in reflecting on how voicing the experience of suffering can move people to a deeper faith, explain to them:

- Often it takes a very painful experience or a "bottoming out" to make people realize how much they need God in their life. When life goes smoothly, it is easy to forget about God or to take God for granted and spend little time in prayer. Spend the next 5 minutes or so thinking of a particular person's painful experience that resulted in her or his growing in faith. It can be your own experience, or the experience of someone you know, or even that of a character in a movie, a book, or a song. Then write a one-page reflection, describing that person's experience and how voicing it moved her or him to a deeper faith.

Once the students have finished writing, their reflection may be shared with the class.

11

Singin' the Blues

The Psalms can be reminiscent of the lamentations found in contemporary music. In this exercise the students can compare and contrast the two. You may wish to use this activity if you did not use the activity "Contemporary Songs and Psalms" under concept A, or if you wish to focus exclusively on psalms of lamentation.

1. Before class select either a blues or a country-western song to play for the students. You may wish to copy the words onto a handout and distribute it for the students' reference. The song should convey a message of lament.

2. Before playing the song, address the class as follows:
◆ As you listen to the song I am about to play, keep in mind these questions: What is the problem posed by the songwriter, and does it ever get solved? If so, how? Does God play any part in it? What are the images and feelings described in the song?

3. Play the song and hold a class discussion on the questions above.

4. Divide the students into groups of three or four and have them find a psalm of lament in their Bible. Ask the students to compare and contrast the psalm with the song you played. Tell each group to appoint someone to take notes on its discussion to report to the class.

5. After the small groups have made their findings, have each group report by first reading the psalm it chose, then offering the class one way the psalm and the song are alike and one way they are different.

11

A Clean Sweep

The text discusses how the Psalms sometimes address God in what could be taken as an offensive manner. In this exercise the students will take a psalm with what could be considered to be brutal language and "clean it up" by taking out the language that they think might offend God. Then they will compare the revised psalm to the original and discuss which is more prayerful. Although any psalm of lamentation could be used, you may wish to focus on Psalms 38, 44, and 88.

1. Assign one-third of the class to look up Psalm 38, another one-third Psalm 44, and the rest Psalm 88. Then tell the class:
◆ The psalm you have located contains language that you might consider offensive to God. Your job is to rewrite this psalm so that the offensive language is removed.

2. After the students have rewritten their psalms, read each original psalm aloud, followed by a few students from each group sharing their "cleansed" versions.

3. Then pose these questions to the class:
◆ When we are terribly upset about something, whom do we talk to? How do we talk about the pain we feel? Are the words and the tone we use always polite and calm?

◆ What do you suppose God thinks of the original psalms?
◆ Which psalms—the originals or the cleaned-up versions—do you think are more prayerful? Why?
◆ What does this imply about how we can pray to God?

An Eye for an Eye?

This activity explores two different approaches to evil—"smashing" one's enemies versus God's way of transforming one's enemies by love.

1. Remind the students:
◆ Though we are often tempted to return evil for evil, God suggests another way to deal with our enemies. Recall that the text says, "God does not want to smash the enemies 'out there' [or] to smash the sinful tendencies within us but to transform them by love." You are to write a fictional account comparing how two characters treat an enemy—one by smashing, and the other by transforming by love—and the results of such treatment. You can either contrast how each character treats a common enemy, or how each character treats his or her own enemy.

2. Because this activity could be lengthy, you may wish to have the students start writing in class and finish it for homework.

3. After you have evaluated the assignments, choose a few students to read theirs to the class. After each reading ask the class these questions:
◆ Which approach do you think is more effective? Why?
◆ Which approach do you think is the right one? Why?
◆ Is the "transforming by love" approach realistic in today's world? Why or why not?
◆ What did Jesus have to say about how we are to treat our enemies?

Concept C: Psalms of Thanks and Praise: Celebrating Who God Is

Review Questions: Psalms of Thanks and Praise: Celebrating Who God Is

Question. What are the elements of psalms of thanks and praise?
Answer. An introductory word or statement of praise; the reason for the praise, or what the person praying is grateful for; and another statement of praise.

Question. What did "Sheol" and the "Pit" mean to the ancient Jews?
Answer. They thought that all who died, whether good or bad, entered a shadowy underworld, Sheol, which, in their belief, was a void (the Pit). Sheol's inhabitants were basically in a state of nonexistence.

Question. What themes come up in the Psalms as reasons for praising God?

Answer. God's wonderful deeds and goodness to the people again and again, and the beauty and intricacy of all creation, which he has brought into existence and sustains with love.

 ## Text Activities: Psalms of Thanks and Praise: Celebrating Who God Is

- Rewrite Psalm 136 to include the people, things, events, and so on, for which you are most grateful to God. For example: *"Who provides me with a safe home, for his steadfast love endures forever."*
- Find a picture that expresses a feeling of praise and write a brief reflection, poem, or prayer about it.
- Take an experience from your life and tell about it in the style of a psalm of lament, thanks, or praise.

 ## Additional Activities: Psalms of Thanks and Praise: Celebrating Who God Is

Choose Your Favorite

Inviting the students to pick a favorite psalm can help them to both review the Book of Psalms and identify psalms they would like to return to in prayer. You may wish to reflect on this yourself before class and share your favorite psalm with the students after they have done the assignment.

1. Say to the students:
- In the 150 psalms, probably many appeal to you. However, I would like you to select one favorite psalm and explain in some detail why you like it and what it means to you. Some of you may know right away which psalm is your favorite; if so, begin writing immediately. Others may wish to take about five minutes to review the Psalms before starting.

2. After everyone has completed the assignment, form the participants into groups of three or four to share what they have written.

3. After the sharing time, reconvene the whole class and take a poll of the class's favorite psalm; if two or more students chose the same psalm, ask them to share why that psalm is meaningful to them. Add yours to the mix and explain what it means to you.

Praying a Psalm from Different Viewpoints

This activity extends the students' understanding of how a psalm can be prayed from different viewpoints. In the sidebar on page 274 of the student text, a psalm of lament is prayed from three viewpoints. In this exercise the students are asked to pray a psalm of thanksgiving from the same three viewpoints.

1. Review the material in the sidebar and elicit the three viewpoints from the students (our own viewpoint, the viewpoint of others, and the viewpoint of Jesus). Write each on the chalkboard or an overhead projector. Then direct the students as follows:

♦ Find Psalm 138 in your Bible. What type of psalm is it? Your assignment is to write three brief prayers, based on this psalm, from each viewpoint we have discussed. Clearly label each point of view as a heading above each prayer.

Alert the students that their prayers will later be shared with the class.

2. After the students have finished writing, have them turn in their papers. Then randomly distribute them among the class and call on students to read the prayer in a particular viewpoint category, alternating among the three categories.

Closing Prayer

In the course of this chapter, the students have read many psalms, examined them, reflected on them, and written some psalms of their own. To prepare for this prayer service, ask the students to locate—either in the Bible or from their homework—one psalm that has been particularly meaningful to them, and choose one or two verses of it that they want to share with the rest of the class. For the prayer service they should have that psalm, a piece of paper, and a pen.

1. Begin the time of prayer by asking the students to close their eyes. Remind them that God is in our midst. Invite them to rest in that presence for a few moments of quiet. You may wish to have soft music playing in the background.

2. Ask the students to begin reading aloud, one person at a time, the verses they chose, slowly and prayerfully—allow them to speak in random order or direct them regarding the order in which they should speak. They should pause for five seconds or so between readings so that the words can sink in. Tell them it is all right if the same verse is recited by more than one student. As the students are reading their verses, slow them down to a prayerful pace if necessary.

3. Ask your students to reflect on this course and to write down at least three insights they have gained from it—insights about themselves, the Scriptures, their faith, or life in general. Urge the students to talk silently with God and to offer a personal prayer of thanksgiving for this growth.

4. If your class is comfortable with shared prayer, invite students to offer aloud prayers of petition or thanks.

5. Close with the Lord's Prayer.

Option. Ask a group of students to volunteer planning the prayer service. Meet with them and have them each find two psalms (encourage variety, that is, praise, lament, etc.) that are meaningful to them. Then tell them to choose one or two verses from each that they will share with the students. Help them prepare a slide show to express visually the meaning of the psalm verses they have chosen. This would replace step 2 above. The rest of the prayer service can proceed as suggested, or perhaps the students will create something different.

 ## Closing Teacher Prayer

Call to prayer. Be still within and without. Center yourself in God, the ever present companion in your every experience.

Reflect. What have you learned in the process of teaching this chapter? Was it a learning of the head or the heart? Does this reveal God more fully to you? How? What effect could this learning have on your life?

What gift did you receive from your students? Which students do you feel are especially in need of God's tender care today?

Pray.
Take, my God, receive all of me.
Lead me into the deep trust that depends totally on you.
Gift me with the grace of surrender
and full awareness of your presence
within the reality of my everydayness. Amen.

(Bergan and Schwan, *Taste and See:
Prayer Services for Gatherings of Faith*)

11

The New Testament: God's Love Story Fulfilled in Jesus

Major Concept

A. **The New Testament.** The Story of God's love for us starts with Creation and culminates in Jesus, God's Son. About ninety years after the Roman Empire took over Palestine, while the Jews long for a messiah, Jesus announces that he is the savior who has fulfilled all that God has promised. The Gospels tell of Jesus' life, execution, and Resurrection, and of Jesus' proclaiming God's mercy and calling people to love as his Father does. The New Testament records the faith testimonies of Jesus' early followers. The Old Testament and the New Testament form one continuous story, so one cannot be appreciated without the other. *See* the *Catechism,* nos. 50–65, 102, 436–440, 522, 652, 714, 763, 1065, 1286 (Jesus as the fullness of God's Revelation and fulfillment of God's promise); 121–123 (the Old Testament); 124–127 (the New Testament); 128–130 (the unity of the Old and New Testaments).

Opening Teacher Prayer

Call to prayer. Be still within and without. Center yourself in the God of our journeys.

Read. Psalm 136

Reflect. How has God's steadfast love endured in your life? For what things are you most grateful?

Hold in your heart. "[God's] steadfast love endures forever" (136:1).

Concept A: The New Testament

Pages 279–281

Text Activity: The New Testament

- Leaf through the chapters of this book to recall the course contents. Also read over some of your responses to the reflection activities presented in the margins of this book. Then answer the following questions in a one-page essay:
  - What is one significant idea about the Old Testament that you learned in this course?
  - What is one significant personal insight—a lesson about yourself—that you gained through this course?

Epilogue

Additional Activities: The New Testament

All Part of the Same Story

In this exercise the students compare and contrast a major concept from the Old Testament with its counterpart in the New Testament.

1. As a way of reviewing the course, remind the students that Christianity is built on the shoulders of Judaism and the Old Testament. The two testaments, which each shed light on the other, are to be read as one continuous story. Review the following two concepts with the students by saying:

- ◆ God's covenant with humankind was first established with Noah, and was renewed time and again throughout the Old Testament. Jeremiah and Ezekiel speak of a new Covenant that will be written on and will change people's hearts. The New Testament recalls Jesus' death, the sacrifice of the new Covenant that reconciles all people to God through the forgiveness of sins for all time.

◆ Jesus has been considered by some to be portrayed as the new Moses. For example, as babies, both Moses and Jesus narrowly escaped being killed by the authorities. Moses and Jesus both freed people from slavery; both experienced a mountaintop experience that left them dazzling; both proclaimed the will of God at a mountain site.

2. Assign the students to choose one of the above concepts and, in writing, compare and contrast them as to how each is presented in the Old and New Testaments. If the students choose God's Covenant, direct them to use the text and the following biblical books or texts to back up their statements: Genesis, Exodus, Deuteronomy, Jeremiah, Ezekiel, the Gospel accounts of the Last Supper, and the Letter to the Hebrews. If they choose to compare Jesus and Moses, instruct them to use the text and the Books of Exodus and Matthew.

3. Evaluate the papers and select one on each topic to be presented by its author to the class.

Handout
Epilogue–A

Scriptural Connections Between the Old and New Testaments

Distribute handout Epilogue–A, "Making Connections," to help the students make connections between the Old and New Testaments. The students may use their textbooks and the Bible to look up answers.
Answers. 1. f, 2. i, 3. e, 4. h, 5. a, 6. g, 7. c, 8. j, 9. b, 10. d

Handout
Epilogue–B

The Story Continues

As a way of bringing closure to the course and bringing home to the students Jesus' roots in the Old Testament, use handout Epilogue–B, "One Day in the Synagogue." This handout is a fictionalized version of the story about Jesus in the synagogue. Distribute the handout to the students, asking them to prepare to act it out. After the students have acted out the story, reflect on the questions that follow the story. Then lead a discussion of those questions.

Prayer Service

This prayer service could be built around the previous activity, using Luke 4:19 (Jesus quoting Isa. 61:2). Invite the students to reflect on what "the year of the Lord's favor" would be like. Who are the poor today who need to hear good news? the captives who need release? the blind who need sight? the oppressed who crave freedom? Songs like "City of God," by Dan Schutte (*Glory and Praise Comprehensive*), or "Song of the Body of Christ," by David Haas (*You Are Mine—The Best of David Haas,* vol. 2), would be appropriate to use in the service. You could also use quotes from a prophetic voice such as Dorothy Day. Perhaps the students could help plan this closing service by finding readings and songs to fit the theme.

Closing Teacher Prayer

Call to prayer. Be still within and without. Center yourself in God's peace.

Reflect. What have you learned in the process of teaching this course? Was it a learning of the head or the heart? Does this reveal God more fully to you? How? What effect could this learning have on your life?

What gift did you receive from your students? What blessing will you ask God for on behalf of your students as they move on from this course?

Pray.
Loving God, radiance of our life,
you are the light to our darkness,
hope to our despair,
promise to our dreams.
Gift our life
with an unfolding awareness of your life within us.
Let us live in the joyful surprise
of your transforming work,
continually creating us anew,
reaching out to all the world
with your healing, hope, and boundless love. Amen.

(Bergan and Schwan, *Taste and See: Prayer Services for Gatherings of Faith*)

Epilogue

Making Connections

Complete the matching exercise below, using your textbook and the Bible to help find the answers.

_____ 1. The number of Israel's tribes and Christ's Apostles (Luke 6:12–16).

_____ 2. Jews celebrate this from sunset Friday to sunset Saturday; Christians celebrate it on Sunday (Exodus 20:8–11).

_____ 3. This person quoted Deuteronomy 6:5 and Leviticus 19:18 in teaching the great commandment (see Mark 12:28–34).

_____ 4. The Passover seder, recalled in Exodus 12:1–14, is the model for this Christian sacrament (Mark 14:22).

_____ 5. In Matthew 21:13 Jesus uses these words from Jeremiah 7:11 to describe what people had made of the Temple.

_____ 6. This birthplace of the Messiah is prophesied in Micah 5:2; see also Matthew 2:1.

_____ 7. The words of the sanctus in the Catholic Mass, taken from Isaiah 6:3.

_____ 8. Christians interpret Isaiah 40:3–4 to refer to this man (Luke 3:2–6).

_____ 9. The meaning of Immanuel (Isaiah 7:14 and Matthew 1:23).

_____ 10. This man used Isaiah's passage about the suffering servant (53:7–8) to evangelize the eunuch in the Acts of the Apostles 8:32–38.

a. den of robbers
b. "God is with us"
c. "Holy, holy, holy is the Lord of hosts"
d. Philip
e. Jesus
f. twelve
g. Bethlehem
h. the Eucharist
i. Sabbath
j. John the Baptist

One Day in the Synagogue

Read this story. Then reflect on the questions that follow it.

It was a dusty path that meandered from the marketplace of Nazareth to the squat old synagogue outside of town. A breathless young man hurried along the path on a hot summer day, anxious to make it to the synagogue for afternoon prayer. The Jews in the village observed the customary practice of praying in the morning, at noon and in the afternoon. The young man arrived a few minutes late.

Old Eleazar, the leader for the week, cocked an eyebrow and observed the late arrival. "Very unusual," he thought. "He's usually the first one here and the last to leave."

A few other men turned their heads as their townsman wrapped himself in his *tallith*—prayer shawl—and moved toward a seat.

The congregation had already completed the great *Shema!* and had paused before beginning its next round of prayers. As in all synagogues in Palestine, the men faced Jerusalem as they prayed. Slowly Eleazar began to intone the words to the first psalm of the afternoon. The rest of the men followed his lead:

Yahweh my God, I take shelter in you;
from all who hound me, save me, rescue
　　me. . . .

(Psalm 7:1)

Eleazar noticed old Phineas dozing in the back row. He motioned toward the man who had just arrived and moved his elbow back and forth a few times, as if to say, "Jab him one, will you?"

The man walked over to Phineas, who by this time was snoring loudly, and touched him on the shoulder. Phineas jumped up and mumbled:

Yahweh is my shepherd,
　I lack nothing.
In meadows of green grass he—

(Psalm 23:1–2)

Eleazar was grimacing and waving his arms while the other men kept singing the correct psalm. Two boys snickered and then laughed out loud. Eleazar shook his finger at them.

The first psalm finished, Eleazar motioned for Rabbi Jacob to start another. Jacob had a deep voice and loved to lead the singing. He began,

Shout for joy to Yahweh, all virtuous men,
praise comes well from upright hearts. . . .

(Psalm 33:1)

This one went much better. Everyone seemed to concentrate, even the two boys in the back. This psalm and another completed, the men took up the *Shemoneh Esreh,* the "Eighteen Benedictions." They bowed deeply and piously at appropriate moments as the long, repetitious litany continued.

The service was drawing to a close. "Some reading from the Scriptures and a brief teaching would make a nice conclusion," Eleazar thought. "Whom will I select?"

He surveyed his little flock. Each man stared down at the ground, knowing why Eleazar was looking them over. Each man but one, that is. The late arrival was looking eagerly at the leader. One could almost see the question written on his face: "May I read today, Master?"

Eleazar loved the young man—indeed, the entire congregation did. There was no one more devout, more pious, no one who was a better Jew.

"How can I refuse?" the old man thought. "This fellow is a blessing for us all. Still, I wonder if he's not too intense. He is as devoted to Yahweh as was David himself. Is that kind of attitude healthy? Oh, well, no one else seems interested."

The young man eagerly accepted Eleazar's nod of invitation. Rabbi Jacob and another man handed him a scroll, and the young man began to read:

The spirit of the Lord Yahweh has been
        given to me,
for Yahweh has anointed me.
He has sent me to bring good news to the
        poor,
to bind up hearts that are broken. . . .
                    (Isaiah 61:1)

The congregation was spellbound. They had heard him read before, but this time his earnestness and emotion filled the room like crackling rays of lightning. No one stirred when he had finished. Then, lifting up his head and looking around the room at the men, he said,

"This day these words have been fulfilled in your presence." (See Luke 4:21.)

(*The People of the Book,* by Anthony E. Gilles [Cincinnati: Saint Anthony Messenger Press, 1981], pages 165–167. Copyright © 1983 by Anthony E. Gilles. Used with permission of the author.)

1. What do you think is going through Jesus' mind as he reads from the Scriptures?

    _____

    _____

2. How do you imagine you would have felt and reacted had you been there to hear Jesus' proclamation?

    _____

    _____

    _____

3. How is this message relevant for us today?

    _____

    _____

    _____

4. Why is this story a fitting way to conclude a study of the Old Testament?

    _____

    _____

    _____

Appendices

Sample Test Questions

Sample test questions for this course and most other Saint Mary's Press high school courses are available online at the Saint Mary's Press Web site, *www.smp.org*. This secure site provides teachers with electronic files that contain the test questions found in the manual. (The answers appear in the manual only.) Saint Mary's Press offers these testbank files free of charge to any high school teacher who has purchased a classroom set of one or more of Saint Mary's Press textbooks. The testbank files can be easily accessed and modified within your preferred word-processing program.

Chapter 1: The Old Testament

True or False

_t_ 1. The Bible consists of both the Old Testament and the New Testament.

_f_ 2. Religious truth is the same as historical accuracy or scientific explanation.

_f_ 3. The Old Testament was written over a period of about fifty years.

_t_ 4. The Bible was created by a kind of collaboration of God with human beings.

_f_ 5. The best Scripture scholars always agree on their findings and theories.

_f_ 6. The purpose of Scripture study is simply that we might know a lot of things about the Bible and its theological meaning.

_t_ 7. The biblical period was about 1850 BC until about AD 100.

_t_ 8. God's Promise to Abraham is that his descendants would reveal the one God to the world and that they would be given the land of Canaan.

_t_ 9. Jerusalem was both a political and a religious capital.

_f_ 10. Prophets were able to convince the kings of Israel and Judah to stop their oppressive, idolatrous practices before the exile.

_f_ 11. Most of the Jews of the first century AD became Christian.

_t_ 12. Judaism looks for an unknown messiah to come.

_t_ 13. The Hebrew Scriptures have always been considered part of the sacred Scriptures of Christianity.

_t_ 14. The Catholic canon has a few texts that are not part of the Protestant or the Jewish canon.

Multiple Choice

Choose the *best* answer to complete each statement.

_d_ 1. The Bible is
   a. the Story of God's love for us
   b. the Word of God
   c. inspired by the Holy Spirit
   d. all of the above

_d_ 2. The New Testament
   a. replaces the Old Testament
   b. is the fulfillment of the Old Testament
   c. cannot be understood without understanding the Old Testament
   d. both *b* and *c*

_c_ 3. To say that the Bible is inspired by God means that
   a. everything in it is factually correct
   b. God dictated the words to the Bible writers
   c. God ensured that it contains all the truth that is necessary for our salvation
   d. all the people in the Bible are ideal models of who God wants each of us to be

_b_ 4. To understand what a biblical author meant, we need to
   a. merely read the words
   b. understand the circumstances in which the Scriptures were written and handed down
   c. reach at least a graduate level of theological education
   d. read at least five different Bible translations

_c_ 5. The God revealed in the Old Testament is
   a. angry
   b. unforgiving
   c. involved and active in human history
   d. impersonal

_a_ 6. The time period of the Creation falls into the category of
   a. prehistory
   b. history
   c. the biblical era
   d. ancient history

_d_ 7. At various times in their history, the Israelites were ruled by
   a. the Persians
   b. the Greeks
   c. the Romans
   d. all of the above

_d_ 8. Catholic teaching on Judaism is that
   a. Christians cannot attend Jewish worship services
   b. Christians are forever linked with the Jewish people
   c. God's Covenant and special relationship with the Jews still stand
   d. both *b* and *c*

Appendix 1

<u>d</u> 9. What types of writing are found in the Old Testament?
   a. laws
   b. prayers
   c. poems
   d. all of the above

<u>d</u> 10. The Hebrew Scriptures told the Jews of the Dispersion in their own language
   a. how best to live a faithful life in unfamiliar surroundings
   b. that their people still loved them
   c. that the God of their people would be with them always
   d. all of the above

<u>c</u> 11. The Catholic canon of the Old Testament consists of how many books?
   a. 17
   b. 28
   c. 46
   d. 53

Identification

Listed below are the major sections of the Catholic canon of the Old Testament. Match the appropriate letter to the numbered descriptions of the books or examples of stories that would be found in a particular section.

a. Pentateuch
b. historical books
c. wisdom books
d. prophetic books

<u>b</u> 1. Stories of Israel's conquest of the land of Canaan—including stories of Joshua, the judges, and Israel's first kings.
<u>c</u> 2. A collection of religious songs once attributed solely to David but now to a number of authors.
<u>a</u> 3. In the Jewish faith, these books are referred to as the Torah and are the primary scriptural authority in matters of belief and practice.
<u>d</u> 4. Haggai, Zechariah, Malachi, and Joel.
<u>a</u> 5. Stories of the Creation and Adam and Eve; the patriarchs and matriarchs; and Moses' leading the Israelites out of Egypt.
<u>c</u> 6. Job explores the problem of evil.
<u>d</u> 7. First Isaiah and Jeremiah warn Israel of coming disaster if it does not repent of its unfaithful ways.
<u>b</u> 8. A description of the breakup of the nation of Israel.

Matching

<u>a</u> 1. Another word for "covenant."
<u>e</u> 2. The listing of books of the Bible that were inspired by God and selected by the Church under his guidance.
<u>f</u> 3. The oral preaching of Jesus' followers, the Apostles, that has been handed down to the bishops and has been expressed in the Church's doctrine, teachings, and worship.
<u>b</u> 4. The Story of God's actions and the people's responses over many centuries.
<u>g</u> 5. Founders of the Jewish faith, like Abraham, Isaac, and Jacob.

a. testament
b. salvation history
c. Jesus
d. Ten Commandments
e. canon
f. Tradition
g. patriarchs

Appendix 1

k 6. The scattering of the Jews after the Romans' destruction of Jerusalem in AD 70.

h 7. The belief in one God, which the Israelites revealed to the world.

d 8. The Israelites' part of the Covenant with God was to keep the _____.

i 9. Moses leads the _____ and frees his people from slavery in Egypt.

j 10. This name means "I am the One who is always present."

c 11. Christians believe God's Promise to Abraham reached its fulfillment in _____.

l 12. The discovery of these in 1947 were a boon to Scripture scholars.

h. monotheism
i. Exodus
j. Yahweh
k. Dispersion (or Diaspora)
l. Dead Sea Scrolls

Essay

1. Write a letter to someone you love, to encourage their faith by sharing with them some aspect of the Story of God's love.
2. One of your friends insists that the Bible is not any harder to understand than any other book. "Take it at face value," she says. "The words aren't difficult, and there's no need for interpretation. God says what he means, and that's that." Do you agree or disagree with her perspective? Why?
3. "I'm Christian," says one of your classmates. "What difference does the Old Testament mean to me? Why should I study it? The New Testament is all that counts now." Write a response to this classmate.
4. Do you think the ancient Israelites had a sense that God was acting in their everyday life and history as a whole? Explain your answer.
5. What do you think the Hebrew Scriptures meant to the ancient Jews? What do they mean to us today?

Chapter 2: Beginnings

True or False

t 1. Sin is essentially refusing to acknowledge God as God and ourselves as dependent on him.

f 2. God sometimes creates suffering and injustice in the world.

f 3. Adam and Eve were tricked by the serpent, so they did not really have a free choice to sin or not.

f 4. God offers the first covenant to Adam and Eve.

t 5. The first part of Genesis explains why things went wrong in the world that God created to be good.

f 6. The authors of the story of Noah were primarily interested in figuring out the historical causes of the flood.

t 7. Abraham is considered the ancestor of Judaism, Christianity, and Islam.

f 8. The Israelites were often reminded that being chosen always means being more worthy.

t 9. Hagar emerges from the Genesis story more noble than the ancestral heroes Abraham and Sarah.

f 10. Rebekah believes Esau is destined to be heir to Isaac.

t 11. Jacob is renamed Israel after his encounter with the mysterious being.

_f_ 12. Jacob has special coats made for all his children.
_t_ 13. Joseph becomes governor of Egypt.
_t_ 14. Jacob is rewarded for his sacrifice of Benjamin by seeing all his sons reunited.
_f_ 15. Joseph fails to prepare Egypt for the famine.

Multiple Choice

Choose the *best* answer to complete each statement.

_b_ 1. Much of the Old Testament, including the Book of Genesis, was written down and put into final form around the time of
 a. Moses
 b. the Babylonian Exile
 c. King David's reign
 d. Jesus

_d_ 2. The first eleven chapters of Genesis
 a. tell the story of God's creation of the world
 b. set the stage for the story of God's relationship with Israel
 c. tell how sin entered the world and spread
 d. all of the above

_d_ 3. Through the Creation story, we learn that God wants us to
 a. preserve the environment
 b. be his slaves
 c. have life to the full and be happy
 d. both *a* and *c*

_c_ 4. The Creation story writer said God rested on the seventh day
 a. because he was tired after creating the universe
 b. because the number seven symbolized luck
 c. in order to emphasize the importance of keeping the Sabbath holy
 d. all of the above

_a_ 5. God created Adam and Eve to
 a. enjoy the garden and be intimate companions for each other
 b. name the animals
 c. work, even though it presented difficulties
 d. be equal to him

_d_ 6. The end of the Flood is marked with a rainbow that is
 a. a revelation that people of all colors must live in harmony
 b. a sign of God's love for all earth's creatures
 c. a promise that the world will never again be destroyed by flood
 d. both *b* and *c*

_b_ 7. The story of Babel shows how
 a. people came to have different languages
 b. sin has spread to affect even the behavior of nations
 c. people came to be dispersed
 d. both *a* and *c*

_b_ 8. God promises Abraham that he will
 a. never suffer if he remains faithful
 b. become a father of a multitude of descendants
 c. fully understand God
 d. become a famous governor

_d_ 9. Ishmael is
   a. a bedouin
   b. the father of the Arab peoples
   c. the ancestor of the Israelites
   d. both *a* and *b*

_a_ 10. In the story of Abraham's test the biblical writer wants us to focus on
   a. the faithfulness between Abraham and God
   b. the request of a harsh, unyielding God
   c. a trial only Abraham could pass
   d. learning how people can secure divine help

_c_ 11. This child of Isaac and Rebekah manages to gain the birthright of his firstborn twin.
   a. Benjamin
   b. Esau
   c. Jacob
   d. Laban

_d_ 12. Various Scripture translators have called the mysterious being who wrestles with Jacob
   a. a stranger
   b. a man
   c. an angel
   d. all of the above

_b_ 13. Israel means
   a. "one who has contended with suffering"
   b. "one who has contended with divine and human beings"
   c. "one who has contended with unfaithfulness"
   d. "one who has contended with God"

_d_ 14. Joseph's brothers
   a. deceive Jacob into thinking that Joseph has been killed
   b. sell Joseph to traders
   c. plot to kill him
   d. all of the above

_b_ 15. The Genesis stories show how God
   a. almost gave up on every patriarch
   b. worked with flawed humans to bring about his Promise
   c. offered forgiveness only to the worthy
   d. regretted creating the world

Matching

Listed below are the names of people in Genesis. Match the appropriate letter to the numbered descriptions of the people.

_b_ 1. One of this pair kills the other because of jealousy.

_i_ 2. He forgives his brothers for selling him into slavery.

_e_ 3. Abraham's concubine who conceives and bears Ishmael.

_a_ 4. They choose to rebel against the divine command that humans should not try to be equal to God.

a. Adam and Eve
b. Cain and Abel
c. Noah
d. Abraham
e. Hagar
f. Isaac
g. Jacob
h. Rebekah
i. Joseph

h   5. Isaac's wife.
c   6. This one man finds favor with God and is saved from destruction along with his family and animals.
g   7. A twin who is renamed Israel.
d   8. The father of biblical faith.
f   9. Abraham and Sarah's son.

Matching

c   1. A solemn promise.
e   2. Worshiping many gods.
h   3. The biblical ideal for marriage.
d   4. A number of ancient peoples of the Near East from whom the Israelites descended.
k   5. The meaning of *genesis*.
a   6. What Christians call the first sin of humankind.
i   7. Abraham and Sarah offer this to three strangers who represent God.
j   8. Day of rest for Jews.
f   9. God calls Abraham to lead his people to this land.
b   10. A city God destroys because of its wicked inhabitants.
g   11. The sign of God's covenant that identifies Abram's people as his people.

a. Original Sin
b. Sodom
c. covenant
d. Semites
e. polytheistic
f. Canaan
g. circumcision
h. monogamy
i. hospitality
j. Sabbath
k. beginning

Essay

1. The Jews during the exile needed to hear the liberating truth that God is in charge of everything in the world and will never abandon them. Why did they especially long to hear this message at that time? Who do you think could still benefit from learning that truth, and why?
2. A Babylonian woman and a Jewish man are caught in a turbulent thunderstorm. They seek shelter together and begin discussing what part supernatural forces have in natural events and disasters. Using the worldviews attributed to Babylonians and Jews in the text, write an imaginary conversation between these two people as each explains the storm.
3. A Catholic high school principal has been petitioned by some angry parents not to allow the teaching of evolution theory in biology courses, but to present the biblical understanding of how the world came about. One parent says, "If the Bible says God created the world in six days, I believe it. It's God's Word, and God doesn't lie. Why should you hide the truth from our children?" How might the principal respond to this question using the point of view of Catholic teaching?
4. Describe how sin spreads, first by recounting a biblical story and then by giving an example from your everyday life.
5. The authors of the story of Noah were most interested in teaching the powerful truth that whoever obeys God's Word will be saved. Are devout people necessarily saved from disaster? If not, what are they saved from?
6. Contrast two stories from Genesis to show how human arrogance brings disaster while God works wonders through a humble person.
7. Describe "Abraham's test." Do you think God ever asks us for a similar level of trust? Explain your answer.

8. Tell a story from Genesis in which deception plays a part in accomplishing God's purpose. Then describe an incident that involved deception in your own or another's experience. What effect did it have on the persons and their relationships?
9. Write a conversation that might have taken place between Jacob and the mysterious being during their all-night wrestling match.
10. Propose an argument either agreeing or disagreeing with this statement: Joseph, his brothers, and Jacob all grow in love from their experiences.

Chapter 3: Freedom

True or False

_t_ 1. The name Yahweh is interpreted within the scriptural text as "I am who I am."
_t_ 2. Scholars suggest that worship of the God named Yahweh was unknown before the time of Moses.
_f_ 3. Pharaoh consents to free the Israelites when Moses and Aaron first ask him.
_t_ 4. When striking down the firstborn of Egypt, the angel of God passes over the homes that have doorways smeared with lamb's blood.
_f_ 5. Miracles are always works of overcoming natural phenomena, like parting the sea.
_t_ 6. "Worshiping" popularity can be a kind of idolatry.
_f_ 7. In ancient times the individual's desires took precedence over the well-being of the family.
_t_ 8. Stealing can be defined as people with abundance not sharing with others who go without necessary food, shelter, or employment.
_t_ 9. Today the eighth commandment against "false witness" is understood to forbid all forms of lying.
_t_ 10. Some laws in the Book of the Covenant may seem unjust today.
_t_ 11. In the Old Testament, blood is the sign of life itself.
_t_ 12. The Covenant of Sinai surpassed all other covenants in the minds of the biblical editors.
_f_ 13. Moses is never allowed to see God.
_t_ 14. God accompanies the people of Israel as a cloud by day and as fire by night.
_t_ 15. At the time of Moses, Jews did not believe in personal punishment in an afterlife.

Multiple Choice

Choose the *best* answer to complete each statement.

_d_ 1. The Book of Exodus proclaims that the descendants of Abraham, Isaac, and Jacob were
a. freed by God from oppression in Egypt
b. formed by God into a chosen nation
c. bonded with God forever through the Covenant of Sinai
d. all of the above

b 2. The Exodus stories were collected and edited into the Book of Exodus
    a. just after the Exodus took place
    b. around the time of the Exile in Babylon
    c. close to the time Jesus was born
    d. none of the above

d 3. Moses
    a. is the pharaoh's biological son
    b. is raised by Pharaoh's daughter as an Egyptian prince
    c. grows up knowing he is really an Israelite
    d. both *b* and *c*

c 4. The final plague that Moses proclaims is
    a. the overrunning of the land by frogs
    b. the destruction of crops by hail and locusts
    c. death for the firstborn of Egypt
    d. serious illness that afflicts both cattle and people

b 5. The Catholic use of unleavened bread in Communion is rooted in
    a. the Egyptian sacred meal
    b. the Jewish custom of serving only unleavened bread during Passover season
    c. Moses' meal after encountering the burning bush
    d. a practical decision because unleavened bread stays fresh longer

d 6. The Israelites' crossing of the Sea of Reeds was
    a. the most miraculous historical event ever
    b. an event to impress the Israelites
    c. the best way to get even with the Egyptians
    d. the work of the saving God

d 7. Idolatry can be understood as
    a. making a god out of something that is not God
    b. worshiping another person
    c. worshiping things that represent gods
    d. all of the above

Appendix 1

a 8. Observing the Sabbath
    a. helped the Jews preserve their religious identity during the exile
    b. was always celebrated by Jews on Sunday
    c. was a way to honor one's parents
    d. was an excuse not to work

a 9. The fourth commandment originally addressed
    a. adults and sought to protect aging parents
    b. children and required their obedience to parents
    c. those who used God's name irreverently
    d. anyone who worshiped false gods

c 10. At the time of the Exodus, the purpose of the fifth commandment was to
    a. prevent stealing
    b. denounce anger, contempt, and vicious gossip
    c. lessen the violence arising from hating and taking the law into one's hands
    d. none of the above

<u>d</u> 11. Adultery
- **a.** in the time of the ancient Israelites was punishable by death
- **b.** occurs when a married person has sexual relations with someone other than the marriage partner
- **c.** occurs when unmarried persons have sexual relations
- **d.** all of the above

<u>d</u> 12. Slavery
- **a.** was a universal practice in the ancient world
- **b.** has always been a violation of human rights
- **c.** was clearly prohibited by the Book of the Covenant
- **d.** both *a* and *b*

<u>b</u> 13. At Sinai God proclaimed for all time that
- **a.** Christians were expected to do more than just follow the Ten Commandments
- **b.** the people of Israel were his people
- **c.** the Jews would always be victorious in battles
- **d.** the Israelites would experience exile repeatedly in different forms

<u>d</u> 14. After Moses sees the people worshiping the golden calf, he
- **a.** refuses to accompany them any further
- **b.** angrily breaks the tablets of the Law, confronts Aaron, and orders the idolaters slain
- **c.** intercedes with God on the people's behalf, begging God to forgive them and accompany them
- **d.** both *b* and *c*

<u>a</u> 15. Which of the following is *not* one of the thirteen attributes of God revealed to Moses?
- **a.** friendly
- **b.** merciful
- **c.** gracious
- **d.** slow to anger

Matching

<u>d</u> 1. The name of God, which the Jews prefer not to pronounce out of reverence, revealed to Moses.

<u>g</u> 2. Moses' brother, who fashions a golden calf.

<u>j</u> 3. The mountain where God gives Moses the Ten Commandments.

<u>i</u> 4. A ritual meal that celebrates the Jews' freedom from slavery in Egypt.

<u>a</u> 5. A title for God, meaning "the Lord."

<u>b</u> 6. Moses' sister, who with Moses sings a canticle praising God for the victory over the Egyptians.

<u>e</u> 7. The food the Israelites depended on as their "daily bread" in the wilderness.

<u>c</u> 8. Another name for the Ten Commandments.

<u>h</u> 9. The container for the stone tablets of the Law.

<u>f</u> 10. The Promised Land.

- **a.** Adonai
- **b.** Miriam
- **c.** Decalogue
- **d.** Yahweh
- **e.** manna
- **f.** Canaan
- **g.** Aaron
- **h.** ark of the Covenant
- **i.** seder
- **j.** Sinai

Essay

1. Briefly describe the parallels between the experiences of the people of the Exodus and of the exilic and postexilic Jews. Imagine that you are an exiled Jew. What significance would the Exodus stories have for you?
2. A doubting friend of yours says she would do anything God asks, so long as she knew for certain he was doing the asking. Tell her a story from the Book of Exodus about someone who believed himself to be in God's presence and communicating with God, but was still not eager to follow his command. What were some of this person's excuses, and what was God's reaction?
3. The human heart is hardened by flinging itself against the will of the loving God. Think of a person from the Book of Exodus whose heart became hardened, and describe how that happened. Then name a character from a book, a movie, or a television show whose heart became hardened. Explain the circumstances that led to this.
4. Write a brief story about the effect an idol has on its worshiper's life.
5. The ninth and tenth commandments both reveal a profound understanding of the path of sin. Create a diagram to describe this path, using a particular sin as an example. Explain whether you think that intent to do wrong can be as sinful as the deed itself.
6. The Israelites regarded the Ten Commandments and other laws not as burdens that dragged them down, but as mutual understandings that enabled people to live in freedom and peace. Do you agree with this viewpoint? Explain why or why not.
7. Recall in writing a story of infidelity from the Book of Exodus, including the circumstances that led up to the infidelity. What was God's reaction? Could a similar situation occur today? Explain your answer.
8. Your friend says "the God of the Old Testament" is angry and vengeful, but the God that Jesus describes is compassionate, like the father in the story of the prodigal son. Using the Book of Exodus, build a case that "the God of the Old Testament" is also portrayed as compassionate.

Chapter 4: The Law

True or False

_t_ 1. Many laws in Leviticus, Numbers, and Deuteronomy address situations that the Israelites did not experience until long after their desert wanderings.
_t_ 2. Much of the language Christians have used to describe how Jesus Christ redeemed the world comes from the Book of Leviticus.
_f_ 3. Leviticus reminds us that holiness is simply a matter of going through all the right prayers and rituals.
_t_ 4. The ancient Israelites commonly assumed that natural disasters were punishments from God.
_f_ 5. God allows Moses and Aaron to enter Canaan.
_f_ 6. Biblical scholars are almost certain that Moses actually preached the sermons that make up most of the Book of Deuteronomy.
_t_ 7. A number of the historical books of the Bible were written or edited by the Deuteronomists.

Multiple Choice

Choose the *best* answer to complete each statement.

  d   1. The whole collection of laws from Exodus through Deuteronomy is called
- **a.** the Mosaic Law
- **b.** the Law
- **c.** the Law of Moses
- **d.** all of the above

  b   2. The Book of Leviticus can be thought of as
- **a.** a history of the Israelites' desert wanderings
- **b.** a handbook of instructions for Israel's worship
- **c.** a book about the Ten Commandments
- **d.** a prayer book, or spiritual guide

  a   3. In a sacrificial ritual, an animal's blood signified
- **a.** life itself
- **b.** the presence of God
- **c.** evil
- **d.** hopelessness

  d   4. Community worship was central in the Israelites' lives because
- **a.** it expressed who they were
- **b.** it bound them together as one family of faith
- **c.** Jews were not allowed to worship alone
- **d.** both *a* and *b*

  b   5. The Holiness Code in Leviticus is a collection of teachings that
- **a.** focus on worship in itself
- **b.** show how true worship is expressed in a person's everyday life
- **c.** have nothing to do with worship
- **d.** apply only to priests

  b   6. Where does the Book of Numbers get its title? From
- **a.** the mathematician who wrote it
- **b.** the census mentioned in the first part of the book
- **c.** the emphasis the authors placed on numerical accuracy throughout the book
- **d.** both *b* and *c*

  a   7. In the Book of Numbers, who challenges Moses' authority?
- **a.** Miriam and Aaron
- **b.** Jacob
- **c.** Levi
- **d.** Joshua

  c   8. Why did God punish Moses and Aaron so harshly after they berated the people as rebels? Because
- **a.** Moses and Aaron had continually sinned against God
- **b.** God didn't agree that the people were rebellious
- **c.** Moses and Aaron did not show forth God's holiness in how they treated the people
- **d.** both *a* and *b*

<u>d</u> 9. What words does Balaam have for the king of Moab?
   a. a prediction that the Israelites will fall to the Moabites
   b. a scolding for putting his faith in a soothsayer
   c. a premonition that the king will soon die
   d. a blessing for Israel

<u>b</u> 10. Who becomes the Israelites' new leader as they prepare to enter Canaan?
   a. Jacob
   b. Joshua
   c. Aaron
   d. Josiah

<u>d</u> 11. The Deuteronomists
   a. were probably part of Josiah's reform movement
   b. composed the Book of Deuteronomy
   c. believed the exile was inevitable because the people continued to defy God
   d. all of the above

Identification

Listed below are the books of the Bible that spell out more precisely how Israel is to keep the Covenant. Match the appropriate letter to the numbered examples of what can be found in that book.

a. Leviticus
b. Numbers
c. Deuteronomy

<u>b</u> 1. This book tells of Israel's wandering in the wilderness on the way to Canaan.
<u>c</u> 2. Moses recounts the giving of the Law.
<u>a</u> 3. The Holiness Code is contained here.
<u>a</u> 4. This book includes teachings on how to live out the meaning of the Israelites' worship in their relationships.
<u>c</u> 5. This book is the last book of the Pentateuch, which brings the Israelites to the brink of the Promised Land.
<u>b</u> 6. This book contains many stories about jealousy, rebellion, and greed.

Matching

<u>d</u> 1. The Day of Atonement, celebrated by Jews as the holiest day of the year.
<u>h</u> 2. A time when debts are canceled, and those who have lost property are given an opportunity to redeem it.
<u>a</u> 3. A scroll inscribed with verses of the Shema that many Jews fasten to their doorpost.
<u>c</u> 4. Priests in ancient Israel were members of this tribe.
<u>e</u> 5. The situation of Jews living in foreign lands away from Jerusalem and their Temple.
<u>i</u> 6. Balaam's oracle refers to this coming from Jacob.
<u>f</u> 7. The Promised Land.

a. mezuzah
b. phylacteries
c. Levi
d. Yom Kippur
e. Dispersion
f. Canaan
g. Shema
h. jubilee
i. star
j. Deuteronomy

 b 8. Two small, square leather boxes in which verses of the Shema are kept and which are worn by Jews on their heads and arms.
 j 9. A Greek word meaning "second law."
 g 10. This prayer has been called the essence of Judaism.

Essay

1. Imagine that you are a Jew in ancient Israel. Your neighbor tells you that he is holy because he always observes the proper prayers and rituals. However, you notice that he takes all the harvest for his own family and often mistreats people. Using teachings from Leviticus, explain to him what true worship and true holiness constitutes.
2. When a person's relationship with God is damaged through sin, how does he or she go about repairing it? How did the ancient Israelites do it?
3. Tell a story from the Book of Numbers of how God provides, and compare it to an example of his providence that you are familiar with.
4. Israel was made up of people who were, like Christians today, sinful. Recall a story from the Book of Numbers that shows how sin hinders a community's journey. How does the community get back on its way again?
5. Like the Israelites who were afraid to enter Canaan, many people fear a new situation, either because of the unknown or, as in the Israelites' case, because of thinking the negatives outweigh the positives. Write a short story, ballad, or rap about someone whose faith and trust in God makes her or him willing to risk trying something new.
6. Which of these sayings do you think applies better to the attitude of the Israelites wandering in the wilderness: The grass is always greener on the other side, or Absence makes the heart grow fonder? Why?
7. Give some examples of how the Book of Deuteronomy shows great sensitivity to the poor and the oppressed. Do you think the laws regarding justice in Deuteronomy are being followed in our society today? Explain.
8. What is the Shema? How does it express what the Jews' life as God's people is all about?
9. How do you think the story of Israel would have differed from the Torah's account if the Israelites had remained unwaveringly faithful to God?

Chapter 5: The Land

True or False

 t 1. The Deuteronomic history serves as a self-examination for the Israelites in exile.
 t 2. Joshua represented everything that Israel was supposed to be—completely faithful to God.
 f 3. The biblical writers portrayed the Canaanite prostitute Rahab as an unworthy betrayer at odds with God's purposes.
 f 4. The Israelites almost drown when crossing the Jordan River to enter Canaan.
 t 5. The events at Jericho may have some connection to a liturgical ritual.
 f 6. No person or animal inhabiting Jericho survived the Israelites' siege.

_t_ 7. In the centuries before the exile, Israelites sometimes engaged in Canaanite practices, such as visiting temple prostitutes and sacrificing children to the gods.

_t_ 8. The Israelites suffered defeat at Ai.

_f_ 9. The writer of the book of Joshua accurately claimed that the Israelites conquered Canaan quickly.

_f_ 10. The judges were nobles who also exhibited particularly noble behavior.

_t_ 11. Gideon enrages the townspeople by destroying an altar to Baal that the Israelites built.

_t_ 12. The stories about Samson convey the truth that God was with the Israelites.

_f_ 13. Samson ultimately conquers the Philistines.

_t_ 14. Because she is a Moabite, Ruth is excluded by a law in Deuteronomy from membership among the Israelite community.

Multiple Choice

Choose the *best* answer to complete each statement.

_c_ 1. The Books of Joshua, Judges, and Ruth tell stories about
   a. the Israelites' experiences in Egypt
   b. Moses' leading the Israelites out of Egypt and receiving the Law
   c. the beginnings of the Israelites' life in the Promised Land
   d. Saul and David

_a_ 2. The biblical books called the Deuteronomic history include
   a. Joshua, Judges, 1 and 2 Samuel, and 1 and 2 Kings
   b. Deuteronomy, Josiah, and Chronicles
   c. Deuteronomy, Joshua, and Ruth
   d. Judges, Chronicles, and Maccabees

_d_ 3. What did the Deuteronomists do for the people of Israel?
   a. gave them hope for the future
   b. helped them turn the disaster of the exile into a time of transformation
   c. helped them recognize that the exile was not their fault
   d. both *a* and *b*

_b_ 4. Israel's exile was the result of
   a. God's suspending the Covenant because Israel was extremely unfaithful
   b. the Israelites' ignoring the Law of Moses and rejecting God's love
   c. God's encouraging the Babylonians to conquer the Israelites
   d. both *a* and *c*

_d_ 5. The theme repeated again and again in the Book of Joshua's accounts of amazing victories is that
   a. the Israelites' arrival in Canaan was a gift from God, not something they accomplished on their own
   b. God would remain on the Israelites' side fighting for them in their struggle to claim the Promised Land
   c. the Israelites were unworthy to enter Canaan and would later pay for their unfaithfulness
   d. both *a* and *b*

d 6. As the Israelites prepare to storm Jericho, they
    a. circle the city seven times
    b. blow rams' horns
    c. call for seven days straight to the city's inhabitants to repent
    d. both *a* and *b*

b 7. Stories of brutal warfare in the Book of Joshua are
    a. intended to give us moral direction about war
    b. not intended to give us moral direction about war
    c. only fictional accounts that carry no theological meaning
    d. proof that God approves of armed battle

c 8. The point of the sun standing still until Joshua and his army had overcome the local kings is that
    a. God is often obedient to human beings
    b. it was actually scientifically impossible and suggests the entire account is fictional
    c. the Israelites' victory was a gift from God
    d. none of the above

b 9. This number of tribes in Israel later became symbolic for Christians as well.
    a. twenty-one
    b. twelve
    c. seven
    d. three

d 10. The purpose of the Joshua account is
    a. theological
    b. historical
    c. to show that God was with Joshua and that Canaan was his gift to the Israelites
    d. both *a* and *c*

a 11. The Book of Judges
    a. might better be called the Book of Deliverers
    b. is mainly concerned with legal matters
    c. is an account of God's and others' judgments that Israel's infidelities are beyond redemption
    d. was written by Israel's equivalents of lawyers

a 12. Who from the Book of Judges killed Sisera after offering him hospitality?
    a. Jael
    b. Deborah
    c. Delilah
    d. Barak

c 13. What was the point in God's asking that Gideon scale down his army? Because
    a. too many Israelite soldiers would be killed
    b. Gideon wasn't up to commanding such a large force
    c. the Israelites might credit their triumph to their own might, not to God's power
    d. the Midianite army was so small that a large Israelite army was simply unnecessary

Appendix 1

<u>b</u> 14. After Gideon's army's victory, Gideon
    a. agrees to be king
    b. creates a cultic object to celebrate
    c. dies within a week due to the stress of battle
    d. consults God about everything he does

<u>c</u> 15. How does Samson die?
    a. The Philistines execute him.
    b. Delilah kills him while he is asleep.
    c. He is killed by the collapse of the Philistine temple, which he caused.
    d. He dies of natural causes as an extraordinarily old man.

<u>d</u> 16. Why might the Deuteronomists have listed Samson among the judges?
    a. to marvel at the kind of people God can make use of
    b. to boost the spirits of the exiles who needed to hear larger-than-life exploits
    c. to remind the exiles of how their nation, though blessed, had become morally weak
    d. all of the above

<u>d</u> 17. The purpose of the Book of Ruth was to
    a. teach how God could create a blessed ending out of a difficult situation
    b. emphasize the difficulty of life in Israel
    c. explain how it came about that King David had a Gentile great-grandmother
    d. both *a* and *c*

<u>a</u> 18. Ruth has a right to glean in Boaz's field because
    a. the Law requires that gleanings be left for the poor
    b. her distant relationship to Boaz entitles her to do so
    c. anyone is entitled to glean
    d. foreigners had such special privileges in Israel

Matching

Listed below are the names of persons from the Book of Judges and the Book of Ruth. Match the appropriate letter to the numbered descriptions of the people.

<u>b</u> 1. Gideon's son, who murders all but one of his brothers after Gideon's death.
<u>c</u> 2. Nicknamed Jerubbaal, this person leads Israel to victory over the Midianites.
<u>g</u> 3. Known for great strength, this person starts the Israelites' resistance to the Philistines.
<u>e</u> 4. A Moabite widow, she pledges herself to the God of Israel in order to help a family member.
<u>a</u> 5. Referred to as both a judge and a prophet, this person is also a magistrate of the tribe of Naphtali and accompanies Barak in leading an army against Sisera.
<u>f</u> 6. A generous farmer who marries Ruth.

b. Abimelech
c. Gideon
d. Naomi
e. Ruth
f. Boaz
g. Samson

  d 7. She urges her daughters-in-law not to accompany her back to Israel because of the misery that surely awaits them there and helps one of them get a new husband.

a. Deborah

Matching

  e 1. The deep peace of God.

  c 2. A practice in which conquerors destroy everything in a conquered town and take nothing for their own.

  a 3. The offering of refuge and aid to the persecuted and homeless, a practice established by the Israelites that remains a universal custom.

  f 4. The Israelites renewed the Covenant here just before Joshua died.

  b 5. A tribal leader through whom God delivers the people from destruction.

  d 6. A man consecrated to God from birth and forbidden to cut his hair or consume strong drink.

a. sanctuary
b. judge
c. ban
d. Nazirite
e. shalom
f. Shechem

Essay

1. Write a poem, a song, or a short story about a gravely upsetting experience that helps someone begin to turn their life around. Then compare this experience to the Jews' experience of exile.
2. God sometimes chooses the most unlikely persons to accomplish God's purposes in the world. Give an example of this from the Book of Joshua.
3. Write your reaction to this statement: *For the Israelites Canaan was just a place to live.*
4. Explain how the practice of the ban and violent warfare could be justified by scriptural writers as God's will.
5. Reflect in writing about the difficulty a person, perhaps you, can have in holding nothing back in his or her devotion to God. Then recall a story from the Book of Joshua that illustrates the consequences of not doing so.
6. Briefly compare Joshua's character to Samson's. Then tell which one is still a role model for today's society. Why?
7. Is the Canticle of Deborah meant to glorify violence? Explain your answer.
8. Tell the story of a man from the Book of Judges who might have been great if he had used his gifts to do good. What message does his story have for you personally?
9. The Jews long debated the question of whether it was right or good that a Gentile be welcomed by marriage into the community of Israel. How did the Book of Ruth shed light on this question?
10. What core biblical message do the Books of Joshua, Judges, and Ruth share? Explain your answer by giving at least two examples.

Chapter 6: The Kings

True or False

_f_ 1. By the end of the era of the judges, Israel was united as one people under God's Law.

_t_ 2. God tells Samuel to warn the Israelites of the troubles a king could bring, but to go ahead and give them a king if they still want one.

_t_ 3. The term *Israel* has numerous meanings.

_f_ 4. Saul hates David from the moment they meet.

_t_ 5. Saul's children give their loyalty to David.

_t_ 6. Despite David's failings, the Scripture writers repeatedly hold him up as a model of faithfulness to God.

_t_ 7. David's trust in God is mixed in with some heavy-handed tactics to further his own purposes.

_t_ 8. Saul gives David's wife, Michal, to another man.

_f_ 9. David responds to his rivals' deaths with feelings of great relief.

_f_ 10. The Hebrew word *messiah* and the Greek word *christos* have different meanings.

_t_ 11. The early Christians saw the Davidic Covenant as fulfilled in Jesus Christ.

_t_ 12. The Books of Kings were written to remind the exiles in Babylon that it was the people, not God, who broke the Covenant.

_t_ 13. Solomon worshiped at "high places," or outdoor sanctuaries, frowned on by the Deuteronomists.

_t_ 14. The scriptural writers probably exaggerated the number of proverbs and songs that Solomon wrote.

_f_ 15. God is pleased with Solomon's reign because Solomon remained wise and faithful throughout his life.

_f_ 16. A prophet tells Jeroboam that God would have him lead Judah in the south if he follows God's ways.

Multiple Choice

Choose the *best* answer to complete each statement.

_d_ 1. The Books of Samuel and the beginning of the First Book of Kings
   a. describe the time of Israel's transition to nationhood
   b. tell stories of Saul, David, and Solomon
   c. tell stories of Joshua, Samuel, and the Maccabees
   d. both *a* and *b*

_b_ 2. The Deuteronomists believed that
   a. the Israelites should have a king
   b. only God is the king of Israel
   c. a king would unite Israel and help it gain more territory
   d. both *a* and *c*

_d_ 3. After Saul becomes king, he is
   a. a model king
   b. anxious, instead of trusting
   c. unfaithful to God
   d. both *b* and *c*

__c__ 4. David's place of origin was
   a. Jerusalem
   b. Hebron
   c. Bethlehem
   d. Nazareth

__c__ 5. David
   a. never has an opportunity to kill Saul
   b. is closely related by blood to Saul
   c. could have killed Saul easily at one point, but spares him
   d. both *a* and *b*

__a__ 6. The ghost of Samuel prophesies that
   a. Saul and his sons will perish in a battle with the Philistines
   b. Saul will die in battle, but his sons will survive
   c. the Israelites will defeat the Philistines in battle
   d. both *b* and *c*

__d__ 7. What was David's greatest feat(s)?
   a. unifying the Israelite tribes
   b. ending the Philistine threat
   c. building the Temple at Jerusalem
   d. both *a* and *b*

__d__ 8. Why was Jerusalem an ideal choice for Israel's capital?
   a. As a Canaanite city, it had never belonged to any one of the twelve tribes, so accusations of favoritism could not be made.
   b. It was ideally located in territory between the northern and the southern tribes.
   c. Its weather was the most ideal in all the territory, and its situation on a major trade route assured its economic success.
   d. both *a* and *b*

__b__ 9. The Davidic Covenant is God's promise that
   a. David will never suffer
   b. David's royal line of descendants will endure forever
   c. God will keep David free of sin because he has proved so faithful
   d. both *a* and *c*

__a__ 10. Many Jews in Palestine at the time of Jesus believed that
   a. a messiah was to come from the line of David
   b. the Messiah had already come
   c. King David was the Messiah
   d. both *b* and *c*

__d__ 11. David
   a. fails to recognize Absalom's treacherous intentions
   b. refuses to punish Amnon
   c. refuses to punish Saul's family
   d. all of the above

__d__ 12. Solomon
   a. introduces forced labor and taxation to provide supplies for government officials
   b. divides the land into twelve new districts, ignoring tribal boundaries
   c. forms an elite group of administrators
   d. all of the above

<u>b</u> 13. What happens when in a dispute between two women over a child Solomon calls for a sword to divide the child between them?
  a. The child dies.
  b. The true mother gives up her claim to the child.
  c. The women flee in fear.
  d. The mothers agree that a third party should care for the child.

<u>c</u> 14. Solomon designs the Temple based on
  a. the model of Heaven, revealed by the prophets
  b. the model of Israel's previous temples
  c. Canaanite models
  d. none of the above

<u>a</u> 15. Because of Solomon's idolatry, his line loses the throne and all the tribes but
  a. Judah
  b. Naphtali
  c. Manasseh
  d. Benjamin

Matching

Listed below are the names of people in stories from the Books of Samuel and the First Book of Kings. Match the appropriate letter to the numbered descriptions of the people.

<u>b</u> 1. A farmworker who was the first king anointed by Samuel but turns out to be unfaithful.

<u>h</u> 2. A priest and judge who leads the Israelites and warns them against having a king.

<u>m</u> 3. If this man hadn't been of the house of David, Jesus might not have been born in Bethlehem.

<u>a</u> 4. A priest at the shrine of Shiloh who is Samuel's mentor.

<u>i</u> 5. Saul's eldest son, whom Abner originally made king over the northern tribes.

<u>k</u> 6. He kills Amnon for raping Tamar and betrays his father, David.

<u>f</u> 7. Saul's son and David's loyal friend.

<u>d</u> 8. Secretly anointed king by Samuel, he is publicly anointed king over all Israel at age thirty.

<u>l</u> 9. The surviving son of Jonathan, he tries to take away the throne from David.

<u>j</u> 10. David's firstborn son who rapes his half-sister Tamar.

<u>g</u> 11. To cover up his adulterous affair with Bathsheba, David arranges for the death of this man, Bathsheba's husband.

<u>e</u> 12. A prophet who plays an important role in the lives of both David and Solomon, he tells David to postpone building the Temple.

<u>c</u> 13. David's son by Bathsheba, he succeeds David as king.

a. Eli
b. Saul
c. Solomon
d. David
e. Nathan
f. Jonathan
g. Uriah
h. Samuel
i. Ishbaal
j. Amnon
k. Absalom
l. Mephibosheth (or Meribaal)
m. Joseph

Essay

1. Imagine you are an exiled Jew. What sorts of questions would gnaw at you? Does the Deuteronomic history offer any answers?
2. Writing from the hindsight perspective of a Deuteronomist, debate the pros and cons of Israel's becoming a nation "like other nations" (1 Samuel 8:20).
3. Briefly recount a story from the First Book of Samuel about God calling someone who at first doesn't recognize it is him. Then tell whether you think that failure to recognize God's call (at least initially) commonly occurs in people's lives today. Explain your answer, giving an example if possible.
4. Throughout the Bible God chooses the lowliest and least likely people to accomplish his purposes. Give at least one example of this from the First Book of Samuel. Then reflect in writing on why God would make such choices. In other words, why wouldn't God pick stronger, more virtuous people?
5. Recall the story of a deep friendship in the First Book of Samuel. What makes it such a remarkable friendship? What qualities of friendship do you consider important?
6. Use examples from David's life to illustrate what you think was his most outstanding quality. Then describe his weaknesses. How could a person with such grave flaws be revered through the ages as a model of faithfulness?.
7. Imagine that you have discovered King David's evil deed. Confront him by telling a parable—either Nathan's or one that you make up. How does God deal with repentant sinners like David—and us?
8. Give an example of how Solomon exercised his wisdom.
9. Explain the effect of Solomon's reign on Israel. Be sure to reflect on why the building of the Temple marked the beginning of Israel's downfall.
10. Both King David and King Solomon sinned grievously, yet their reigns are regarded quite differently. What lessons do you think their lives had for the exiles in Babylon?

Chapter 7: The Prophets

True or False

_t_ 1. The northern tribes end up rejecting Rehoboam because he was an oppressive ruler like his father.
_f_ 2. The capital city of the northern kingdom of Israel was Jerusalem.
_f_ 3. The nonwriting prophets of the northern kingdom were Amos and Hosea.
_t_ 4. Ahab's greed for a vineyard eventually results in the killing of Naboth.
_t_ 5. After Elijah dies, a belief arose that he would return to announce the coming of the Messiah.
_f_ 6. Samaria is the capital of the southern kingdom.
_t_ 7. Amos has visions of Israel's final fate.
_f_ 8. God tells Hosea and Gomer to name their children after Israel's patriarchs.
_t_ 9. For the most part, Judah's kings were as bad as the kings of the north.

t 10. Isaiah emphasizes the majesty and glory of God.

f 11. God tells Isaiah in the Temple that he is to open the ears and eyes of the people to his message.

t 12. *Immanuel* means "God is with us."

t 13. Isaiah prophesies not only defeat for Jerusalem but also hope after the exile.

f 14. Micah points to Bethlehem as the place from which the Messiah-king will come.

t 15. The Assyrians have a reputation as warmongers.

Multiple Choice

Choose the *best* answer to complete each statement.

a 1. Which of the following is a nonwriting prophet?
   a. Nathan
   b. Amos
   c. Hosea
   d. Isaiah

c 2. Which of the following is a writing prophet?
   a. Elisha
   b. Samuel
   c. Micah
   d. Elijah

b 3. Who carries on David's royal line in the south?
   a. Jeroboam
   b. Rehoboam
   c. Omri
   d. Elisha

c 4. What speaks to Elijah of God's presence at Horeb?
   a. a powerful wind
   b. an earthquake
   c. a gentle breeze
   d. a fire

c 5. Elijah appears after his death at
   a. the birth of Jesus Christ
   b. the baptism of Jesus Christ
   c. the Transfiguration of Jesus Christ
   d. the Crucifixion of Jesus Christ

d 6. Elisha
   a. multiplies loaves of bread
   b. raises a child from the dead
   c. cures Naaman of leprosy
   d. all of the above

b 7. Amos
   a. resents the rich because they have so much more than he does
   b. is angered by and condemns Israel's disregard for God's law
   c. is a rich prophet who can relate to the people he preaches to
   d. believes Israel is on the right track

 a   8. Hosea
      a. takes Gomer back after a separation
      b. divorces Gomer and remains celibate the rest of his life
      c. divorces Gomer and marries someone else
      d. supports a death sentence for Gomer because of her infidelity

 b   9. From Solomon's death to the Babylonian Exile, Judah's kings were
      a. from a variety of families
      b. direct descendants of King David
      c. chosen by the leaders of the northern kingdom
      d. both *a* and *c*

 a 10. First Isaiah spoke to the people
      a. before the Babylonian Exile
      b. during and at the end of the Exile
      c. after they returned to Judah from exile
      d. around the time of Jesus' birth

 a 11. Fearful of the Assyrian threat, Judah
      a. joins a coalition of neighboring states to stave off the empire
      b. begins building an army to attack Assyria
      c. becomes a vassal of Assyria and pays it tribute
      d. puts all its trust in God through repentance and prayer

 d 12. What was Isaiah's response to the question posed in the Temple, "Whom shall I send?" (Isaiah 6:8)?
      a. "My brother, Judah."
      b. "I wish I were worthy."
      c. "Anyone but me."
      d. "Here am I; send me!"

 c 13. Isaiah's oracle about the birth of Immanuel was interpreted at the time as a passage about
      a. Jesus Christ's Incarnation
      b. a coming messiah
      c. a perfect Davidic prince who would rule Judah in an age of peace and justice
      d. both *a* and *b*

 b 14. The Assyrian army waiting to storm Jerusalem
      a. successfully conquered the city the next day
      b. was stricken by an angel of the Lord and retreated
      c. killed half the city's inhabitants
      d. both *a* and *c*

Sentence Completion

1. *Elijah* has the prophets of Baal killed after their god proves powerless.
2. It is said that a flaming chariot took *Elijah* to Heaven.
3. *Elisha* carries on the mission of his mentor, Elijah.
4. The northern kingdom of Israel fell to the *Assyrians* in 721 BC.
5. The longest and most influential of the prophetic books, the Book of *Isaiah*, is usually recognized as falling into three parts.
6. Micah imagines the day when nations "shall beat their swords into *plowshares*" (Micah 4:3).

Appendix
1

Matching

Match the appropriate letter of the names below to the numbered descriptions of the persons and groups.

<u>d</u> 1. The greatest of Judah's prophets, this well-educated person had a vision of God in the Temple at Jerusalem.

<u>g</u> 2. A movement of peace activists in the United States.

<u>b</u> 3. One of the favorite saints of modern Catholicism, she lived a loving but quiet life in a Carmelite monastery in the late 1800s before dying at age twenty-four.

<u>e</u> 4. As king of Judah, he destroys the pagan shrines his father, Ahaz, erected and insists that sacrifices be made only in the Jerusalem Temple.

<u>c</u> 5. The descendants of the Israelites who remained in the north after Samaria's collapse.

<u>a</u> 6. The cofounder of the Catholic Worker Movement, a leading voice of advocacy for justice today.

<u>f</u> 7. This prophet's sympathy for poor people came from his own experience of poverty.

a. Dorothy Day
b. Thérèse of Lisieux
c. Samaritans
d. Isaiah
e. Hezekiah
f. Micah
g. Plowshares

Essay

1. Describe the role of a prophet. What part did prophets play in general among the Israelites? Are prophets still among us today? Give a brief example.
2. By telling their stories, describe the actions of two pagan women in the First Book of Kings. What meaning do these stories have for you?
3. A friend of yours, Jennifer, who works with troubled children is feeling discouraged, thinking that she can do little to repair all the damage already done to them. She complains that she is even beginning to lose faith, not having a sense of God's presence and strength, which she needs to sustain her in this challenging volunteer job. Using a story about Elijah, encourage Jennifer and point to where God might be acting in her life.
4. A beloved neighbor of yours is killed in a drive-by shooting. Explain why a loving God would allow such evil to occur, especially to someone who is innocent, faithful, and so good.
5. Write a paragraph either agreeing or disagreeing with this statement: *The main point of Elisha's miracles, and Jesus' miracles later, was to impress the crowds.* Do you think those miracles are any more miraculous than a medic reviving a heart attack victim today? Why or why not?
6. In what way were the prophets all alike? Explain whether their message is still relevant today, giving examples in your answer.
7. Amos is the preacher at your church today. Report on what he says to the assembly about worship practices.
8. Explain how Hosea's experience with Gomer is a parable for Israel.
9. Why were the Jews so prejudiced against the Samaritans?
10. Write a contemporary story or song that has the same message as the Vineyard Song.
11. Do you think God was pleased with Isaiah's response to his vision of God in the Temple? Why or why not?

12. Give examples to support or oppose this statement: *The Judahites in Isaiah's time became complacent and did not sincerely place their trust in God.*
13. Describe a person (real or fictional) who lives his or her life in the way God requires, according to Micah.
14. Does anyone listen to prophets? Give some examples of the effect prophets have had over time.

Chapter 8: The Exile

True or False

_t_ 1. Josiah's reforms help slow down Judah's slide to ruin.
_t_ 2. Josiah, as well as several pre-exilic prophets, inspired the Deuteronomists.
_f_ 3. Habakkuk did not believe people should question God.
_f_ 4. Jeremiah is eager to become a prophet, flattered that God should choose him.
_f_ 5. Jerusalem is destroyed in the first exile in 597 BC.
_t_ 6. The exile was a time of religious renewal for the Jewish community.
_t_ 7. The Book of Baruch ridicules the idols that surround the Jews in other lands, underlining that the only god is the Lord.
_f_ 8. Ezekiel remained behind with the Judahites after Jerusalem fell.
_t_ 9. During the Babylonian Exile, the Jews were not allowed to practice their religious rituals in any public way.
_f_ 10. Most of the Jews exiled in Babylon returned to Jerusalem after they were freed.
_t_ 11. Christians see a prophetic image of Christ in the suffering servant.
_t_ 12. In Jesus' time millions of Jews lived throughout the Roman Empire.

Multiple Choice

Choose the *best* answer to complete each statement.

_d_ 1. Manasseh, son of Hezekiah,
    a. continues his father's reforms
    b. bows to the Assyrian gods
    c. is the grandfather of Josiah, one of Judah's great reformers
    d. both *b* and *c*

_b_ 2. Nahum
    a. calls Judah to repentance
    b. calls Judah to hope
    c. prophesies that God will use Babylon to purify Judah
    d. predicts that Judah will become corrupt again

_d_ 3. More than any other prophet, Jeremiah communicated God's message through
    a. his words and oracles
    b. his own life of suffering and struggle
    c. pantomime
    d. both *a* and *b*

<u>d</u> 4. The Temple is called "a den of robbers" in the Book of
    a. Matthew
    b. Lamentations
    c. Jeremiah
    d. both *a* and *c*

<u>a</u> 5. Jeremiah tells the people that the Lord is
    a. the only god
    b. the only god who mattered, superior to all the other gods
    c. one of three gods, the one who created the world
    d. one of many gods

<u>b</u> 6. Jeremiah urges the people of Judah to
    a. fight Babylon for their king and country
    b. go willingly into exile in order to be purified
    c. become vassals of Babylon
    d. become allies of Babylon and conquer other peoples

<u>d</u> 7. God tells Jeremiah that when the people return from exile,
    a. they will be made anew as God's beloved
    b. they will go back to their same broken relationship with God
    c. God will make a new Covenant with them
    d. both *a* and *c*

<u>c</u> 8. Ezekiel's gifts were
    a. writing and poetry
    b. great physical prowess
    c. drama, symbol making, and storytelling
    d. both *a* and *b*

<u>b</u> 9. What is *not* part of Ezekiel's call to be a prophet? He
    a. sees a chariot drawn by four winged creatures and a being of light on a throne above the creatures
    b. sees a boiling cauldron tipped on a hearth in the north
    c. is told to eat a scroll containing words of woe
    d. is instructed to be silent until bidden to speak

<u>a</u> 10. Ezekiel
    a. dies in exile
    b. returns to Jerusalem with his people
    c. helps rebuild the Temple
    d. both *b* and *c*

<u>c</u> 11. Second Isaiah prophesied
    a. more than a century before the Exile
    b. just before the Exile began
    c. toward the end of the Exile
    d. more than a century after the Exile

<u>a</u> 12. The exiles were
    a. made to stay in Babylon
    b. treated as slaves
    c. forced to labor for the Babylonian Empire
    d. all of the above

_d_ 13. What passage from Second Isaiah is used to describe John the Baptist in the Gospels?
    a. "He reduces princes to nothing."
    b. "He shall run and not be weary."
    c. "He marches valiantly against his foes."
    d. "A voice cries out: / 'In the wilderness prepare the way of the LORD.'"

_b_ 14. What new concept did Second Isaiah introduce to Israel in the songs of the suffering servant?
    a. Israel will bring salvation to the world by being a glorious nation.
    b. Israel will bring salvation to the world through its willingness to suffer for others' sake.
    c. Israel should welcome suffering because it signifies God's favor.
    d. All suffering is a punishment for sin.

Matching

_c_ 1. Leaders of a movement that called the people back to the Covenant.

_h_ 2. A collection of five hymns of grief composed shortly after Jerusalem's fall.

_d_ 3. Though its setting is the exile, this book was meant to nurture the faith of the later Jews of the Dispersion and encourage them to return home.

_b_ 4. He hears God speak through him that God will replace the people's hearts of stone with hearts of flesh.

_j_ 5. King Josiah's son, a contemptible monarch.

_a_ 6. This king of Persia, called "God's anointed," overcame the Babylonians and, in 538 BC, set the exiles free.

_e_ 7. The most influential Jewish writing other than the Hebrew Scriptures.

_g_ 8. Chapters 40–55 of Isaiah, which aim to raise the people's hopes.

_i_ 9. Described in Second Isaiah, an innocent man who suffers greatly.

_f_ 10. The Greek translation of the Old Testament and today the oldest complete version in existence.

a. Cyrus
b. Ezekiel
c. Deuteronomists
d. Book of Baruch
e. Babylonian Talmud
f. Septuagint
g. Book of Consolation
h. Book of Lamentations
i. suffering servant
j. Jehoiakim

Essay

1. Write a description of how a prophet, either from biblical times or the modern day, "comforts the afflicted and afflicts the comfortable."
2. Why were Zephaniah's words about the kind of people who would become God's remnant shocking to the Temple-going citizens of Zephaniah's day? Are those words still shocking today? Why or why not?
3. Should we question God? Answer this question the way Habakkuk would; then provide your own perspective.
4. Why did the Judahites ignore Jeremiah's and Ezekiel's messages? Do you think the same thing could happen today? Explain your answer.
5. In what ways was Jesus' life like Jeremiah's?

6. One of your neighbors has been sentenced to serve time in prison on drug charges and is greatly despairing for his future. Tell your neighbor a story from Jeremiah that will comfort him by giving him hope.
7. Explain how the new Covenant prophesied by Jeremiah differed from the Sinai Covenant. Is the new Covenant the same as a person's conscience? Explain.
8. Name two things that Ezekiel shared in common with Jeremiah. Then describe two ways they were different.
9. Discuss how something that is difficult or sorrowful could possibly be described as "sweet."
10. Describe one of Ezekiel's dramatic performances and the message intended by it. Then create a brief pantomime for a prophet today and spell out its message.
11. In what way does Ezekiel's vision of the dry bones bring hope to the exiles and to Christians through the centuries?
12. How did the exile change Ezekiel's relationship with the people of Jerusalem? Give an example from your own life or the life of someone you know in which someone sharing a difficult situation with someone else changed their relationship.
13. Imagine you are an exiled Jew in Babylon. Describe your life there, including your religious practices and customs.
14. How can suffering bring salvation? How would Second Isaiah answer? What is your answer?
15. Recall some images from Second Isaiah that tell us God is compassionate and tender. Then come up with your own image of God.
16. By describing the effect of the Dispersion on the Jews throughout history, explain how faith can endure through a variety of circumstances.

Chapter 9: The Remnant

True or False

t   1. The author of Chronicles was not concerned with Israel's scandals, wars, or wealth.

t   2. Persian rulers halted the rebuilding of the Temple for eighteen years.

f   3. The Samaritans were regarded as inferior by the Jews of the north.

t   4. Third Isaiah sees things going downhill rapidly after the exiles return.

f   5. The New Testament contains no more than a dozen references to Zechariah.

f   6. The wealthy and the poor work harmoniously together until Jerusalem's walls are completely rebuilt.

f   7. Nehemiah has no enemies.

t   8. We first hear about Ezra in the Book of Nehemiah.

t   9. Judaism has survived because it is centered in the Jewish Bible.

t 10. Some of the later books of the Bible were originally written in Greek because so many Jews did not understand Hebrew.

f 11. All the Jews during the Greek domination were faithful to their old ways, allowing no concession to Greek thinking or customs.

t 12. Antiochus IV eventually orders all Jews to abandon their religion under penalty of death.

t 13. By 164 BC the Jews had taken back control of the Jerusalem Temple.

_t_ 14. Christians have always regarded the promise of the coming reign of "one like a son of man" in the Book of Daniel as Jesus Christ.

_f_ 15. Apocalyptic literature is simple and clear, making it easily understood by everyone.

_f_ 16. The Jerusalem Temple, destroyed in AD 70, was rebuilt about a century later.

Multiple Choice

Choose the *best* answer to complete each statement.

_c_ 1. The two Books of Chronicles were written
 a. before the Exile
 b. during the Exile
 c. after the rebuilding of the Temple
 d. a century before Jesus' birth

_c_ 2. The Chronicler criticized and condemned
 a. David
 b. Solomon
 c. kings who came after Solomon and led Israel into infidelity
 d. all of the above

_b_ 3. What was the returned exiles' response to the Samaritans' offer to help build the Temple? The exiles
 a. gratefully accepted the offer
 b. rejected the offer
 c. told the Samaritans they would consider the offer and eventually accepted it
 d. none of the above

_d_ 4. Which of the following is *true* fasting, according to Third Isaiah?
 a. not eating for a day
 b. freeing the oppressed
 c. sheltering the homeless
 d. both *b* and *c*

_d_ 5. Referring to a passage from Third Isaiah, this person is reported by Luke to have said, "Today it 'is fulfilled in your hearing'" (4:21).
 a. Ezra
 b. Solomon
 c. Paul
 d. Jesus

_c_ 6. What event from Jesus' life reminds us of an image from Zechariah?
 a. baptism in the Jordan River
 b. the temptations in the desert
 c. the riding of a donkey into Jerusalem
 d. the rising from the dead

_a_ 7. The Book of Malachi depicts
 a. faith at its lowest in Jerusalem
 b. faith at its peak in Jerusalem
 c. blameless priests who cannot seem to turn the people from their unfaithful ways
 d. faithful people whose priests offer inadequate sacrifices

<u>d</u> 8. Why was rebuilding Jerusalem's walls important? The walls
   a. symbolized the outlines of Judaism's identity
   b. provided a sense of security to Jerusalem's inhabitants
   c. kept the city's inhabitants contained in a small place
   d. both *a* and *b*

<u>d</u> 9. Nehemiah
   a. sealed Jerusalem's gates during the Sabbath
   b. had the Jews who had married foreign women beaten
   c. banished unfaithful Jews from the city
   d. both *a* and *b*

<u>b</u> 10. Ezra's greatest gift to Judaism was his
   a. military prowess
   b. preaching the Law, or the Torah
   c. financial astuteness
   d. psychological insight

<u>b</u> 11. The Persians _____ Ezra's reforms.
   a. opposed
   b. tolerated and supported
   c. questioned
   d. both *a* and *c*

<u>d</u> 12. The problem of Greek domination in Judea was that
   a. at times Greek rulers punished Jews for practicing their religion
   b. the Greek lifestyle and philosophy lured many Jews away from their own traditions and faith
   c. Greeks never stopped openly persecuting Jews
   d. both *a* and *b*

<u>d</u> 13. Belief in resurrection appears in the Book of
   a. Nehemiah
   b. Maccabees
   c. Daniel
   d. both *b* and *c*

<u>c</u> 14. This man and his family managed to achieve a degree of independence for Judea.
   a. Eleazar
   b. Joel
   c. Judas Maccabeus
   d. Epiphanes

<u>d</u> 15. The stories and visions in the Book of Daniel
   a. are set in Babylon at the time of the Exile
   b. are set in Jerusalem during the time of Greek rule
   c. address the situation of the Jews under Greek rule
   d. both *a* and *c*

<u>a</u> 16. Daniel's visions and the Book of Revelation are prime examples of
   a. apocalyptic literature
   b. mystery writing
   c. science fiction
   d. biographical writing

Matching

Listed below are books of the Bible. Match the appropriate letter to the numbered descriptions of these books.

_d_ 1. The shortest book in the Bible, a one-chapter attack on Edom.

_b_ 2. Intends to get across God's universal love for all peoples through the satirical story of a mean-spirited prophet.

_f_ 3. A history of the Jewish revolt against the Greek rulers.

_e_ 4. Filled with code so that Greek oppressors couldn't understand its meaning.

_a_ 5. Explains how a foreign woman came to be the great-grandmother of King David.

_c_ 6. Focuses on a plague of locusts that ravages the land, symbolizing God's judgment on the people's continuing infidelity.

a. Ruth
b. Jonah
c. Joel
d. Obadiah
e. Daniel
f. First and Second Maccabees

Matching

_f_ 1. The period after the exiles returned to Jerusalem.

_b_ 2. A priest and scribe from Babylon who led a religious renewal in Jerusalem about a hundred years after the exiles returned to Judah.

_a_ 3. A grandson of King Jehoiachin and governor of Judah, he and the high priest Joshua led the returned exiles in building a new Temple in Jerusalem.

_d_ 4. The notion that God's love for Israel will make it a "light to the nations" (Isaiah 49:6), ultimately bringing together all people under his Reign.

_g_ 5. A prophet who encourages the exiles to get going again on rebuilding the Temple in order to preserve the people's faith.

_i_ 6. This prophet, whose pen name means "my messenger," tells the people to tithe.

_c_ 7. The governor of Judah and a model public servant, he called for the rebuilding of Jerusalem's walls.

_j_ 8. In Nehemiah's time, the quickest way to weaken a people's religious commitment.

_e_ 9. This Greek ruler conquered the Persian Empire in 330 BC.

_h_ 10. This feast, also called the Festival of Lights, has its origins in the celebration that followed the rededication of the Temple after the Greeks had defiled it.

a. Zerubbabel
b. Ezra
c. Nehemiah
d. universalism
e. Alexander the Great
f. restoration
g. Haggai
h. Hanukkah
i. Malachi
j. intermarriage

Essay

1. Why was setting up spiritual boundaries important for the Jews after the Exile? Reflect on the spiritual boundaries in your own life.
2. How do the Books of Chronicles differ from the other scriptural histories of Israel, such as the Books of Samuel and Kings? Does inaccuracy affect a book's validity? Explain your perspective.
3. By the time the exiles started back to Judah from Babylon, they were pumped full of hope and excitement. Write a conversation between two exiles, discussing the prophecies and their own feelings and observations as they arrive in Jerusalem.
4. Why was the Temple important to the Jerusalem community after the Exile? What is the importance of worship spaces today?
5. Compare the messianic vision of First Zechariah with that of Second Zechariah. Do you think either vision was actually borne out? Explain your answer.
6. Build an argument for or against this statement: *Nehemiah and Ezra were overly rigid men who promoted intolerance and whose policies were ineffective.*
7. Why didn't Eleazar take advantage of the opportunity he was given to escape execution? Give another example of a person or group who placed integrity and the common good before self-interest. Reflect in writing on the effect such an action has on society.
8. The strategies of resistance against the Greeks described in the Books of Maccabees and the Book of Daniel are quite different. Tell which strategy you think was best and why.
9. Standing up for what is right and for faith in God can lead to persecution and suffering. So what does the author of Daniel mean when he says through his stories that God will save the righteous from harm? Do you believe the author is right? Why or why not?
10. Write about a fictional crisis in your school or neighborhood using apocalyptic writing.

Chapter 10: Wisdom and Wit

True or False

<u>t</u> 1. Biblical wisdom literature grew out of a kind of writing that flourished in non-Jewish cultures of the ancient Near East, especially in Egypt.

<u>f</u> 2. According to Proverbs, the reward for a virtuous life is a happy afterlife.

<u>t</u> 3. The Book of Proverbs portrays God's wisdom as a woman.

<u>t</u> 4. Qoheleth came to the conclusion that life was a mystery he could not solve.

<u>f</u> 5. Solomon was the author of the Book of Wisdom.

<u>t</u> 6. Unlike most Jewish wisdom literature, Sirach is deeply concerned with the history of Israel, its heroes, and its institutions.

<u>t</u> 7. For both Jews and Christians, the mutual love of the bride and groom in the Song of Songs was an image of God's love for and passionate devotion to Israel.

<u>t</u> 8. Modern Scripture scholars have determined the Books of Tobit, Judith, Esther, and Jonah to be fictional tales that inspire courage and faith.

<u>f</u> 9. Jonah is eager to carry out his mission of prophesying to the Ninevites.

Multiple Choice

Choose the *best* answer to complete each statement.

_b_ 1. The goal of the biblical teachers of wisdom was to
   a. make Jews the most knowledgeable of all peoples
   b. inspire moral integrity
   c. cultivate judges for Judea
   d. both *a* and *c*

_a_ 2. What literary device is typically used in biblical wisdom sayings?
   a. stating the same wise truth in two ways
   b. alliteration
   c. irony
   d. analogy

_d_ 3. Catholic Tradition has often read the passages on wisdom in the Old Testament as related to
   a. Eve
   b. Abraham
   c. David
   d. Mary, the Mother of God

_d_ 4. The Book of Job helps us understand that
   a. God often initiates human suffering, especially for sinners
   b. God is in charge, loving us through even our darkest moments
   c. the mystery of life is too great for us to grasp
   d. both *b* and *c*

_a_ 5. Which of the following ideas is *not* found in Ecclesiastes?
   a. "Where were you when I laid the foundation of the earth?"
   b. "For everything there is a season, and a time for every matter under Heaven. . . ."
   c. "All is vanity!"
   d. "Nothing is new under the sun."

_b_ 6. Sirach depicts wisdom as
   a. a king like Solomon
   b. a woman who was with God at Creation
   c. an angelic poet
   d. a saintly priest

_c_ 7. The alternate name for the Book of Sirach is
   a. Wisdom
   b. Ecclesiastes
   c. Ecclesiasticus
   d. Wisdom of Solomon

_a_ 8. The Song of Songs is a book
   a. of love poems
   b. of teachings about wisdom
   c. about music
   d. about a famous singer

_c_ 9. The wisdom offered by the Song of Songs is
   a. those who toil for justice will ultimately triumph
   b. the just will be rewarded in this life
   c. love can overcome death
   d. money isn't everything

_a_ 10. Which of the following books had an author who showed familiarity with the folktale called "The Grateful Dead"?
a. Tobit
b. Judith
c. Esther
d. Jonah

_d_ 11. How does Judith save her people? By
a. surrendering to Holofernes
b. rallying the Israelites to attack the Assyrians under cover of night
c. becoming Holofernes' wife
d. deceiving Holofernes

_b_ 12. The author of Judith emphasized that Judith
a. relied more on her own powers than on God
b. trusted completely in God
c. was wrong to engage in immoral conduct
d. both *a* and *c*

_d_ 13. The purpose of the Book of Esther is to
a. praise the goodness of God, who saved the Jews from annihilation
b. explain the origin of the feast of Purim
c. show how the faithfulness of Haman was rewarded
d. both *a* and *b*

_b_ 14. Jonah is _____ when God forgives the Ninevites.
a. pleased
b. angry
c. vindicated
d. not at all concerned

_d_ 15. Judaism's three main branches—Orthodox, Reform, and Conservative—all
a. share belief in the one God
b. hold the same moral truths revealed in the Torah
c. observe the same ritual and dietary laws
d. both *a* and *b*

Matching

Listed below are story books in the Old Testament. Match the appropriate letter to the numbered descriptions of the books.

_c_ 1. A story about a timid queen who risks her life to save her people from Haman's savage plot to slaughter them.

_a_ 2. A wisdom tale about a noble and faithful elder who remains steadfast in the face of personal disaster and is rewarded with blessings.

_d_ 3. A humorous satire intended to show that God's mercy extends to all.

_b_ 4. A tale of a courageous woman who defies all stereotypical notions of "how women are supposed to be," saving her people from the Assyrian army with wit and charm.

a. Tobit
b. Judith
c. Esther
d. Jonah

Matching

_c_	1.	The dilemma of why the good suffer and the wicked prosper in this life.	**a.** Raphael
_f_	2.	He ran a school for scriptural study and Jewish wisdom in Alexandria, Egypt.	**b.** John Henry Newman
_a_	3.	This angel helped both Tobit and his son Tobias.	**c.** problem of evil
_e_	4.	A Hebrew word meaning "fit" or "proper"; food prepared this way follows Jewish dietary laws.	**d.** Hasidim **e.** kosher
_g_	5.	A Jewish feast that celebrates Esther's triumph.	**f.** Jesus ben Sirach
_b_	6.	A convert to Catholicism who became a cardinal in nineteenth-century England.	**g.** Purim
_d_	7.	A mystical movement (whose name means "pietism") within Orthodox Judaism.	

Essay

1. Most of the sayings in the Book of Proverbs do not mention God. The Song of Songs does not mention God. Why, then, did these books end up in the Bible?
2. Your best friend's mother was killed suddenly when a drunk driver hit her car. Contrast how the Book of Proverbs and the Book of Job would explain why it happened and what part God played in it. For extra credit reflect on what John Henry Newman might have to say about it.
3. How did Greek thought influence the Jewish author of the Book of Wisdom? Do you think this influence shed more light on the problem of evil? Why or why not?
4. Sirach suggests that wisdom often tests us with difficulties. Tell what good can come out of such difficulties through a story. It can be a true-life story, a story of your own creation, or one you have read or heard.
5. The Books of Tobit, Judith, Esther, and Jonah were told during the centuries after the Babylonian Exile to inspire courage and faith in times of trial. Summarize one of these stories, tell how you think it helped the people hearing it in ancient times, and how it still speaks to us today.
6. Write both sides of a debate on this question: Is it morally acceptable to take immoral actions for a good cause?
7. The Book of Jonah ends with God asking Jonah, "Should I not be concerned about Nineveh, that great city, in which there are more than a hundred and twenty thousand persons who do not know their right hand from their left, and also many animals?" (Jonah 4:11). How do you think Jonah would have answered? What is the message the Book of Jonah has for us today?
8. Using examples from the biblical books you studied in this chapter, answer one of the following questions: Can the depth of God's wisdom be understood by any single point of view? What does it mean to be a wise person? What is the meaning and purpose of life?

Chapter 11: The Psalms

True or False

_f_ 1. Psalms have been central to Jewish worship since biblical times, but did not become important to Christian worship until the Middle Ages.

_t_ 2. Many psalms express more than one sentiment, but most psalms focus predominantly on one sentiment.

_f_ 3. Scholars believe King David wrote about half of all the psalms.

_t_ 4. The Psalms were originally set to music and meant to be sung in public worship, in some cases along with certain liturgical actions.

_t_ 5. Over four weeks' time, almost the entire Psalter is prayed during the liturgy of the hours.

_f_ 6. The Psalms use mostly abstract language.

_f_ 7. To feel negative emotions and bring them to God is as sinful as acting on those emotions.

_f_ 8. The Psalms usually end with the psalmist expressing disappointment in God's response to a complaint.

_t_ 9. Psalms of thanks and praise are similar to each other and often overlap.

_f_ 10. The ancient Jews believed that only bad people entered Sheol after death.

Multiple Choice

Choose the *best* answer to complete each statement.

_b_ 1. The Psalms' taglines
  a. identify each psalm as being written at the time of the event referred to
  b. remind us of the events in biblical history that could have prompted such prayers
  c. refer to the psalmist's experience alone
  d. both *a* and *c*

_c_ 2. How many psalms are in the Book of Psalms?
  a. 50
  b. 100
  c. 150
  d. 200

_c_ 3. This line from Psalm 137, "Sing us one of the songs of Zion" (verse 3), recalls this time in the lives of the Israelites:
  a. Samuel's reign
  b. Josiah's reign
  c. the exile in Babylon
  d. the Second Temple

_a_ 4. When Christianity and Judaism split, Christians
  a. continued to have their own service of the word modeled on the Jewish service
  b. developed a worship service totally different from the Jewish service
  c. quit reading the Hebrew Scriptures in order to focus on the New Testament
  d. both *b* and *c*

_d_ 5. Why are the Psalms easy to remember? They
    a. rhyme
    b. include much repetition
    c. express the same idea in two contrasting ways
    d. both *b* and *c*

_d_ 6. The psalms of lament
    a. sometimes convey shocking emotions
    b. voice the deep pain people are suffering
    c. recall God's mercy, kindness, and power
    d. all of the above

_d_ 7. Psalms of praise
    a. come from an attitude of humility
    b. tend to focus on a particular request that God answered
    c. tend to focus on the goodness, power, and majesty of God
    d. both *a* and *c*

_a_ 8. Which of the following attitudes characterizes a psalm of praise?
    a. "I feel wonder and awe at all I see."
    b. "What you see is what you get."
    c. "Life is not worth living."
    d. "People are strange."

_d_ 9. What themes come up repeatedly in the psalms of praise?
    a. God's wonderful deeds and goodness to people again and again
    b. the beauty and intricacy of all creation, which God brought into existence and sustains with love
    c. the difficulty of life and the mystery of why evil exists in the first place
    d. both *a* and *b*

Identification

Listed below are the three major types of psalms. Match the appropriate letter to the numbered examples of the types of psalms.

a. psalms of lament
b. psalms of thanks
c. psalms of praise

_b_ 1. "What shall I return to the LORD / for all his bounty to me?" (Psalm 116:12).
_a_ 2. "With your faithful help rescue me / from sinking in the mire; / let me be delivered from my enemies / and from the deep waters" (69:13–14).
_b_ 3. "O LORD my God, I cried to you for help, / and you have healed me" (30:2).
_a_ 4. "My God, my God, why have you forsaken me?" (22:1).
_c_ 5. "Clap your hands, all you peoples; / shout to God with loud songs of joy" (47:1).

Matching

<u>e</u> 1. The official daily prayer of the Catholic Church; also called the Divine Office.

<u>b</u> 2. The first part of the Mass during which the Bible is read aloud to the community.

<u>a</u> 3. One of the elements found in most psalms of lament.

<u>c</u> 4. A shadowy underworld where the ancient Jews believed people went after death.

<u>d</u> 5. This is read or, preferably, sung after the first Bible reading at Mass.

a. plea for help
b. liturgy of the word
c. Sheol
d. responsorial psalm
e. liturgy of the hours

Essay

1. Select a psalm from the Bible. Use your imagination and tell what experience in the psalmist's life might have prompted the psalm. Then tell how this psalm applies to your own life experience.
2. Describe how psalms are used in Jewish and Christian worship today. Why do you think the Psalms are particularly suited to both individual and communal prayer?
3. Write a psalm describing God's power, using the same literary qualities used in the Psalms.
4. Build an argument supporting or opposing the following statement: *Psalms of lament do nothing but whine to God, who tires of hearing people's complaints.*
5. Why is it important that the Psalms express such uncensored feelings to God? Isn't God offended by such talk?
6. Explain how a psalm can open us to God's loving transformation.
7. Describe who the "enemies" might be in the psalms of lament. Then tell how each might be overcome.
8. Would it be appropriate to pray a psalm of thanks even when we are not feeling grateful? or a psalm of lament when we are feeling great? Explain why or why not.
9. Write a short story or poem that sheds light on what it might mean to be brought up from Sheol by the Lord.
10. How could the Psalms be a "school" of prayer for us?

APPENDIX 2

Suggestions for Effective Teaching

Most teachers have a firm background in pedagogical techniques. The points that follow here are simply reminders of general guidelines for leading group activities and discussions. Even the experienced teacher benefits from reviewing the basics that make the difference between success and failure in the classroom.

General Principles Regarding Class Sessions

1. After the students have read a section of the student text, make sure they understand its main points. Obviously, for meaningful class discussion to take place, the students must grasp the basic content of the text. Simply ask if anyone has questions about what the author has explained, whether any words or definitions were not clear, and so on. Or for another and perhaps more effective approach, begin the session by asking questions about the main points of the section. (Review questions of this kind are found at the end of each section in the student text.) Also, the possibility of a quiz can provide an incentive for the students to read and understand the assigned material.

2. Spend time determining in which areas and to what extent students disagree with the student text. Such disagreement on the part of the students should be not only allowed but encouraged. As the teacher you must discover where differences lie and which topics need greater attention and discussion. Once students are convinced that disagreement is allowed, they will usually express their opinions more freely.

3. Discussion between peers plays a particularly important role in this course. Studies show that peer interaction, especially when one group disagrees with another, does more to alter or shape a student's views than similar interaction with authority figures like parents or teachers. For that reason, encourage debate whenever significant differences of opinion are involved. You can both guide and participate but should never dominate such debates.

4. It is always beneficial to focus on the real world of the students, on the life situations they actually face. Theorizing on issues that your students seldom if ever encounter will cause the students to lose interest quickly. However, it is important to distinguish between *theorizing* on the issues and *teaching the facts* about the issues. As the facts are being conveyed, most students come to discover how we are all part of the issues at hand—a major discovery that can motivate them to learn more and to become part of a solution.

5. **On sensitive issues no student should be forced to speak if she or he prefers not to do so.** Do not hesitate to invite and encourage students to participate in discussion. Make it clear, though, that the students can simply say that they prefer not to comment.

6. **Begin each session with time for review and reports. Try to include prayer, however brief, in each session. Conclude each session with a summary, assignments if any, and dismissal.**

7. **View the course as one more step toward mature faith on the part of the students.** Do not expect that this course will result in a profound sense of commitment to the Catholic faith and moral vision for your students, although it might. Rather the intent of the course is that the students review and reflect on the Scriptures and in particular the Old Testament with a fresh perspective and the honest sense of searching that is appropriate to adolescents. If you have achieved that, you have succeeded in teaching the course. The rest is up to God and to the individual student.

Assigned Reading of the Student Text and the Scriptures

Throughout the text students are directed to read corresponding passages from the Old Testament. It is critical that students have a Bible available to them during class and for homework assignments so they can fully experience the intent of this course. You will notice that full references to the sources quoted in the text are not given within the body of the text. They can be found in the acknowledgments on page 300 at the back of the text, arranged by the text page number on which the quote appears. Generally the acknowledgments are listed in the order in which the quotes appear in the text. In some cases, however, the first mention of a source lists all the pages on which that source was used.

Leading Discussions

Discussion as a learning technique may refer to a teacher-centered discussion involving an entire class or to the placement of students in small groups or pairs. Naturally, guidelines for effective discussion vary depending on the size of the group involved.

The following are general guidelines applicable to both large- and small-group discussion.

1. **Discussion is primarily a reaction to some stimulus.** The students need something real and tangible to discuss. In this course the readings, reflection activities, student handouts, interviews, group exercises, and so on, are intended to stimulate discussion. A discussion will be only as effective as the activity that motivates it.

2. **Discussion works only if the students are interested in, excited about, and knowledgeable about the topic.**

3. **Specific questions are more effective than vague ones in stimulating discussion.** For example, rather than asking, "What do you think of the video we just viewed?" you could ask, "What is one important point this video made?"

4. **A discussion should have a definite time limit.** Let the students ask for more time if necessary.

5. **Let each student have a chance to talk.** Be on the lookout for signs that a student wants to say something. However, do not put undue pressure on those who are shy or introspective; you will only make them more reluctant to participate if you do.

6. **Do not mistake silence for disinterest.** Sometimes students will have nothing to say simply because the material is too fresh or because they need more time to think about it. Though silence can be frustrating and can cause tension, it is often this very tension that will spark a response later.

7. **Establish a principle in the classroom that students must demonstrate an understanding of a concept or another student's point of view before agreeing or disagreeing with it.** This principle promotes learning over debating, encourages open-mindedness, and engages students in critical thinking.

8. **Be clear with the students from the beginning of the course that all discussions are intended to be open to the honest thoughts and questions of all.** Students should not feel anxious about expressing ideas that are contrary to Catholic teaching or students' perceptions of the teacher's opinion. At the same time, it is critical for the students to understand that the purpose of discussion is to help unfold a greater sense of what is objectively true.

9. **Your role as teacher is to lead the discussion, clarify issues, and summarize or highlight points.** Be careful not to dominate the discussion with your opinions, reactions, or personal stories. These should be used sparingly and with the intention of stimulating student discussion or summarizing points.

10. **Close the discussion with a summary of the main points raised.**

Directing Activities

1. **Make sure you understand thoroughly the purpose of each activity.** A given activity could be used to bring out any number of points; be sure that you know precisely where you want to go with the experience.

2. **Work through the activity yourself before leading it.** Take some time to go through the whole activity, imagining what the experience will be like. In cases when a student handout will be used, photocopy the handout and complete it, reacting not only as an individual but also as you think the students will react.

3. **Have all materials required for the activity available and ready for use.** Do not let an inadequate number of handout copies or some other minor problem ruin the entire experience.

4. Try to set the appropriate mood before conducting the activity. For example, if silence during an activity is critical, set a quiet tone even before introducing it.

5. Explain the directions thoroughly and then re-explain them. Ask questions to be sure that your students understand what to do—for example, "Dave, how about describing the second step?" But do not get trapped by overexplaining. Too many details can so influence a group's response that nothing will be gained from the exercise.

6. Always stress the need for cooperation in group activities. Emphasize that cooperation is necessary to complete the activity *and* to make it enjoyable.

7. When an activity is going to bring strong feelings to the surface, be sure to allocate some extra time. These feelings need to be processed at the end of the activity.

8. Move immediately into discussion or processing at the end of an activity. Catch the moment.

9. Be patient with yourself and with group activities. Group activities do not always work out as planned. Some students come out with unexpected conclusions; others react apathetically. In either case, do not become discouraged. Analyze the situation and make any adjustments in the activity that are required.

Research Projects and Class Reports

Ideas for research topics are listed for many of the major concepts in this course. Select those topics that you think will interest your students and for which information is readily available. This is a wonderful opportunity to assist the students in developing research skills, especially to access the vast amount of information available via the Internet and other information technologies.

Assign the research projects and their due dates well ahead of time. This means that before covering a given chapter in class, you will have to know which research projects you want to assign. One way to plan for research projects is this: At the beginning of the semester, go through the entire teaching manual and mark research projects that you want students to do. Then make a tentative schedule for the presentation of reports—maybe two a week. Individual students can sign up on this schedule to do one or two reports for the semester.

Each report should be written as an essay but also delivered orally to the class. Encourage the students to deliver the oral reports like speeches, using principles of good public speaking, such as speaking loudly and clearly, being familiar with the material so they do not stumble over parts of it, maintaining eye contact with the class, and so on. Whenever possible the students should include visual aids to enhance their presentations. Oral reports will not only contribute valuable information to your class but also provide opportunities to practice these principles of public speaking.

Guest Speakers

Guest speakers can add an enjoyable dimension to your course. Because guest speakers tend to take up a full period, you probably cannot afford to schedule too many guest presentations. You will need to familiarize yourself with all the possible topics for guest speakers (or panels of speakers) suggested in this manual and choose those that you think your students would appreciate most; then try to line up the guest speakers before or early in the semester.

Be sure to prepare your students with some background about each speaker and the topic. It may be helpful to introduce the topic the class period before the speaker presents and have the students write questions that interest them about the topic. Collect these and use them if needed during the discussion that follows the presentation.

Make time after the presentation for the students to process what they heard.

Role-Plays and Choral or Dramatic Readings

Many passages and stories from the Bible can be effectively dramatized in class. Students can take parts in a role-play or one student can do a dramatic reading or the whole class can take parts for a choral reading. This manual makes some suggestions about how to arrange particular stories or passages as choral or dramatic readings, but you can add many more such activities if you wish. To do so follow these steps:
1. Select a relevant story or passage that can be dramatically presented.
2. Assign parts to the players for a role-play, or to groups for a choral reading. For the first couple of presentations, carefully select the better readers in class for individual parts.
3. If necessary instruct the participants about the background of the story or passage.
4. Tell your players or readers to highlight or clearly mark the passages for which they are responsible.
5. Before the "performance" set the tone. Introduce the story or passage and remind the class that the players or readers are taking parts—they are acting.
6. After the performance take time to discuss the story or passage with the class. Find out how the players or readers felt when they were in character.

The stories of the Bible were meant to be heard. They come from an oral tradition of many centuries. Students should become used to hearing the word as well as reading it.

In the role-plays suggested throughout this manual, the students may improvise the words according to what they know from reading the story. They can be encouraged to adapt the story to modern times, a technique that can be enlightening and fun.

Prayer in Class

Prayer can be a vital way to foster hope, celebration, and joy. Structuring a brief period of prayer or reflection into every class meeting, along with occasional prayer services on a larger scale, is ideal. This manual contains several ideas in each chapter for prayer activities, but it is best to encourage prayer experiences that come out of the life of the class.

Students should prepare and lead prayer experiences as much as possible. Such experiences may range from a thought for the day to full-fledged thematic prayer services or eucharistic celebrations. Whatever the format, these need to be authentic, to come from the students' hearts. Allowing students a good deal of freedom in organizing prayer—rather than mandating particular formats and themes—encourages authenticity.

Maps

Several map exercises are suggested in this manual, and maps appear in the student text. Refer to these maps frequently. Working with and referring to maps helps students develop skills and knowledge in geography, an area that many of our young people need to work on. See appendix 3, "Additional Resources," for suggestions of Bible atlases.

Interviews

Interviews included as activities in this manual are intended to broaden the students' perspectives about various issues. The students will need plenty of notice for each interview assignment in order to set up an appointment, formulate questions, and so on.

Here are some guidelines for students as they prepare for an interview:
- Before anything else, make sure that you know the main questions that you want answered. Write down all the questions you wish to ask, then number them from the most important to the least important. In this way if you run out of time, you will at least have covered some of the most important information about the topic.
- Set up a mutually agreeable time to meet with the person you are going to interview. Remember, the interviewee is doing you a favor, so be flexible about a time for meeting.
- Arrive on time and come prepared for the interview. Have your questions written down and a notebook and at least two pens for writing down responses. Being prepared will help you relax.
- During the interview ask your questions and listen carefully to the responses. Take brief notes while you listen. Ask follow-up questions; sometimes people need a little encouragement to say more.
- Do not interrupt the speaker, and do not get into an argument with him or her. Your job is to report accurately what the speaker thinks, even if you disagree. A good interviewer gets people to talk; if you seem to be objecting to what the speaker says, he or she might clam up.
- Immediately after the interview, using your notes, write out everything that you remember the person saying. Use your questions as an outline for your report. The responses are the body of the report. At the end of the paper, you may wish to add some of your reactions to or reflections about the interview.

In some cases an interview will be the springboard for class discussion; in other instances the written reports of the interview will be handed in to you. You will probably think of additional ways to use interviews.

Flash Cards

The names of a tremendous number of people, places, and events fill the Old Testament. To help your students remember all these names, require that they make flash cards. On one side of a card, they should write the name of a person, place, or event that they are studying; on the other side, they should summarize in a phrase or sentence any related information they need to know. These flash cards will come in handy when the students review for tests.

Tests

Appendix 1 contains a bank of tests for each chapter of the student text. Objective and essay questions are included. You should pick questions from them to supplement tests of your own making. Test questions for this course and all other Saint Mary's Press high school courses are available online for downloading. Call 800-533-8095 for information about this resource.

APPENDIX 3

Additional Resources

Achtemeier, Paul J., gen. ed. *Harpercollins Bible Dictionary.* New York: Harper-Collins, 1997.

Bergant, Dianne, and Robert J. Karris, gen. eds. *The Collegeville Bible Commentary.* Collegeville, MN: Liturgical Press, 1992.

Berit Olam: Studies in Hebrew Narrative and Poetry. Collegeville, MN: Liturgical Press, 1996–2007.

Binz, Stephen J. *Introduction to the Bible: A Catholic Guide to Studying Scripture.* Liturgical Press, 2007.

Brown, Raymond E. *Responses to 101 Questions on the Bible.* New York: Paulist Press, 1990.

Brown, Raymond E., Joseph A. Fitzmeyer, and Roland E. Murphy, eds. *The New Jerome Biblical Commentary.* Englewood Cliffs, NJ: Prentice-Hall, 2000.

———. *The New Jerome Biblical Handbook.* Collegeville, MN: Liturgical Press, 1992.

Brueggemann, Walter. *Theology of the Old Testament: Testimony, Dispute, Advocacy.* Minneapolis, Augsburg Fortress, 2005.

Campbell, James P. *The Stories of the Old Testament: A Catholic's Guide.* Loyola Press, 2007.

Carvalho, Corrine L., PhD. *Encountering Ancient Voices: A Guide to Reading the Old Testament.* Winona, MN: Saint Mary's Press, 2006.

Charpentier, Etienne. *How to Read the Old Testament.* New York: Crossroad, 1982.

Childs, Brevard. *Old Testament Theology in a Canonical Context.* Minneapolis: Augsburg Fortress, 1989.

Cooke, Joan E., SC. *Hear, O Heavens and Listen, O Earth: An Introduction to the Prophets.* Collegeville, MN: Liturgical Press, 2006.

Gilles, Anthony E. *The People of the Book.* Eugene, OR: Wipf and Stock Publishers, 2001.

Hiesberger, Jean Marie, ed. *The Catholic Bible: Personal Study Edition.* New York: Oxford University Press, 2007.

Holladay, William Lee. *Long Ago God Spoke: How Christians May Hear the Old Testament Today.* Minneapolis: Fortress Press, 1995.

Hoppe, Leslie J., OFM. *Priests, Prophets and Sages: Catholic Perspectives on the Old Testament.* Cincinnati: St. Anthony Messenger Press, 2006.

Jenkins, Simon. *The Bible from Scratch, Catholic Edition.* Winona, MN: Saint Mary's Press, 2006.

John of Taize. *The Pilgrim God: A Biblical Journey.* Washington, DC: Pastoral Press, 1986.

Kohlenberger, John R., III, ed. *The Concise Concordance to the New Revised Standard Version.* New York: Oxford University Press, 1993.

Libreria Editrice Vaticana. *Catechism of the Catholic Church: Second Edition.* United States Catholic Conference (USCC), trans. Washington, DC: USCC, 2003.

Madrid, Patrick. *Does the Bible Really Say That? Discovering Catholic Teaching in Scripture.* Servant Books, 2006.

McKenzie, John L. *Dictionary of the Bible.* New York: Macmillan, 1995.

Mills, Mary. *Images of God in the Old Testament.* Collegeville, MN: Liturgical Press, 1998.

O'Connell-Roussell, Sheila. *Saint Mary's Press® Essential Bible Dictionary.* Winona, MN: Saint Mary's Press, 2005.

Ralph, Margaret Nutting. *"And God Said What?" An Introduction to Biblical Literary Forms.* Mahwah, NJ: Paulist Press, 2003.

———. *Discovering Old Testament Origins: The Books of Genesis, Exodus, and Samuel.* Mahwah, NJ: Paulist Press, 2002.

———. *The Bible and the End of the World: Should We Be Afraid?* Mahwah, NJ: Paulist Press, 1997.

Rohr, Richard, and Joseph Martos. *The Great Themes of Scripture: Old Testament.* Cincinnati: Saint Anthony Messenger Press, 1987.

Saint Mary's Press® College Study Bible and *Saint Mary's Press® College Study Bible CD-ROM.* Winona, MN: Saint Mary's Press, 2007.

Sink, Susan. *The Art of the Saint John's Bible: A Reader's Guide to Pentateuch, Psalms, Gospels and Acts.* Collegeville, MN: Liturgical Press, 2007.

The Catholic Youth Bible®, Revised. Winona, MN: Saint Mary's Press, 2005.

The Collegeville Bible Handbook. Collegeville, MN: Liturgical Press, 1997.

Vatican Council II. *Dogmatic Constitution on Divine Revelation (Dei Verbum).* Council document, November 18, 1965.

Teaching Resources

Harpur, James, and Marcus Braybrooke. *The Collegeville Atlas of the Bible.* Collegeville, MN: Liturgical Press, 1999.

Marmouget, C. Rosemary. *Scripture Alive: Role-Plays for Youth.* Winona, MN: Saint Mary's Press, 1997.

O'Connell-Roussell, Sheila, and Terri Vorndran Nichols. *Lectionary-Based Gospel Dramas for Advent, Christmas, and Epiphany.* Winona, MN: Saint Mary's Press, 1997.

———. *Lectionary-Based Gospel Dramas for Lent and the Easter Triduum.* Winona, MN: Saint Mary's Press, 1999.

Schroeder, Carrie J. *Saint Mary's Press® Old Testament Companion CD-ROM: Understanding Key Scripture Passages.* Winona, MN: Saint Mary's Press, 2008.

Singer-Towns, Brian. *The Bible: Power and Promise.* Winona, MN: Saint Mary's Press, 1997.

The Catholic Youth Bible® Triple Challenge CD-ROM. Winona, MN: Saint Mary's Press, 2005.

The Collegeville Bible Handbook. Collegeville, MN: Liturgical Press, 1997.

Theisen, Michael. *Ready-to-Go Game Shows (That Teach Serious Stuff), Bible Edition.* Winona, MN: Saint Mary's Press, 2001.

———. *Ready-to-Go Game Shows (That Teach Serious Stuff), Catholic Teachings and Practices Edition.* Winona, MN: Saint Mary's Press, 2002.

———. *Ready-to-Go Scripture Skits . . . That Teach Serious Stuff.* Winona, MN: Saint Mary's Press, 2004.

———. *Ready-to-Go Scripture Skits . . . That Teach Serious Stuff: The Sequel.* Winona, MN: Saint Mary's Press, 2005.

Tamberino, Tony. *Scripture Sessions on the Old Testament Student Workbook* and *Leader's Guide.* Winona, MN: Saint Mary's Press, 2006.

Other Bible Resources

Biblical Journeys Map Pack. Winona, MN: Saint Mary's Press, 2001.

Calderone-Stewart, Lisa-Marie. *Know It! Pray It! Live It! A Family Guide to "The Catholic Youth Bible®."* Winona, MN: Saint Mary's Press, 2000.

Dreier, Gary. *Saint Mary's Press® Essential Quick Charts: Bible Basics.* Winona, MN: Saint Mary's Press, 2007.

_____. *Saint Mary's Press® Essential Quick Charts: Salvation History.* Winona, MN: Saint Mary's Press, 2007.

Frank, Harry Thomas, ed. *Atlas of the Bible Lands.* Maplewood, NJ: Hammond, 1977.

Gardner, Joseph L. *Reader's Digest Atlas of the Bible: An Illustrated Guide to the Holy Land.* Pleasantville, NY: Reader's Digest, 1981.

Haas, David. *Prayers Before an Awesome God: The Psalms for Teenagers.* Winona, MN: Saint Mary's Press, 1998.

Kurtz, Dennis, Michaela Hedican, and Judy Kramer. *Day by Day with People of the Bible.* Winona, MN: Saint Mary's Press, 2007.

Scripture from Scratch. Cincinnati: Saint Anthony Messenger Press. For more information about this four-page monthly periodical covering topics on the Scriptures, and a list of available articles, call 800-488-0488.

Singer-Towns, Brian, and Lisa-Marie Calderone-Stewart. *Bringing Catholic Youth and the Bible Together.* Winona, MN: Saint Mary's Press, 2000.

The Bible in History Timeline Poster. Winona, MN: Saint Mary's Press, 2001.

The Collegeville Bible Time-Line. Collegeville, MN: Liturgical Press, 1993.

Music

Ancient Echoes: Music from the Time of Jesus and Jerusalem's Second Temple. San Antonio Vocal Arts Ensemble. Schiller Park, IL: World Library Publications, 2002.

Glory and Praise. Vols. 1–3. Phoenix, AZ: North American Liturgy Resources, 1977, 1980, 1982.

Pray Your Heart: Contemporary Songs from the Psalms. Oregon Catholic Press, 2001.

Psalms for the Church Year. Vols. 1–8. Bedford Park, IL: GIA Publications.

Scripture Themes and Popular Music: Year 2001. Santa Rosa, CA: Cornerstone Media, Inc., 2001. Distributed by Saint Mary's Press, Winona, MN.

The Passover Celebration: A Haggadah for the Seder. Chicago: Liturgy Training Publications (LTP).

We Are Fire! Companion Songs for "The Catholic Youth Bible®." Comet Records, 1999.

Ten Commandments for Catholic Bible Study Groups

Matthias Neuman

The last fifteen years have witnessed a marvelous rediscovery of the Bible by Catholics in the United States. Some twenty years ago the Second Vatican Council strongly encouraged the Catholic people to read the Scriptures regularly as nourishment and direction for their lives of faith. The response began slowly, picked up with a rush, and has increased steadily. Spirituality movements like the charismatic renewal and Cursillo as well as parish renewal programs (e.g., RENEW) helped to stimulate the initial stages. From those beginnings, regular Bible study and scriptural prayer groups sprang up, flourished under their own momentum, and now show no signs of slacking off.

But though this renewal has spiritually enriched the lives of many Catholics, several problems invariably arise that create anxieties and inner turmoil. Some individuals remain fearful and uncertain about reading the Bible. They can remember many past warnings about inaccurate interpretations: only the official Church can and should interpret the Bible! Still others discover passages, customs, and language hard to understand or with which they directly disagree: "Is the Bible correct in everything it says?" Then there are those who are profoundly shocked by sexual passages or the blatantly immoral practices of venerated biblical figures. For those who respond in these ways, the rediscovery of the Bible frequently presents as many troubling aspects as spiritual riches. The problem is compounded if the individual or study group has no resource person to consult.

From a scholar's perspective, these problems in reading the Bible are understandable and probably inevitable. It is not an easy task to interpret the Bible at face value, even those passages that seemingly cause no immediate problems. The books of sacred Scripture reflect cultures and religious backgrounds vastly different from those of our twenty-first century.

The presuppositions of the writers and intended readers of an ancient desert society diverge radically from those of a modern urban or suburban society. These presuppositions include religious expectations, views of self and society, norms of morality, familial customs, and so on. Deriving a fairly accurate meaning from a biblical text isn't accomplished by simple goodwill and fervent prayer.

Simply put, Bible reading may be called a *religious skill*. People need to learn the basics of that skill and practice it before they will be able comfortably to utilize the whole Bible as an authentic source for healthy spiritual development. The skill of Bible reading includes a number of fundamental points that have been worked out for centuries in the Catholic Christian tradition. In the following *ten commandments* I have tried to present these main points in succinct form, with a little further explanation. My hope is to help individuals and groups to continue reading the Bible as a means of personal spiritual enrichment, but to do so with more confidence and insight about the religious meanings in the Scriptures.

1. The Bible is the Word of God because it is the Church's book.

To call the Bible the Word of God or the Word of the Lord as we do so often in public worship tends to give it a certain divine aura. It comes "from God" as a message to us! Yet the proper meanings of this phrase need clarification. The Bible did not just drop out of the sky with a return address marked "Heaven." The two "testaments" are collections of quite *divergent writings specifically chosen* by the Christian Church at a particular point in time. That selection process was lengthy, taking place from approximately AD 170 to 390.

In that two-hundred-year process some books were accepted (e.g., the pastoral Letters to Timothy and Titus) and others were not, even though they were written at about the same time (e.g., the Letter of Clement to Corinth). Some writings were put on the list, dropped off, then put on again (e.g., the Revelation of John, the Letter to the Hebrews). Other writings were on some lists, then finally dropped (e.g., the Didache). The Bible is called the Word of God because it was selected and accepted by the Christian Church as expressing something important about God's plan for us and about the beginnings of the Christian Church. Therefore it is crucial to know the purposes that the Christians of the second to the fourth centuries saw in these writings. It is in those reasons and purposes especially that we must seek the authentic foundation for understanding in what specific way the Bible is the Word of God.

2. The Bible is "inspired by the Holy Spirit" because the Church believes that a special truth from God can be found in those writings.

The Catholic Christian tradition has generally confessed a divine origin to the Bible through the doctrine of Inspiration. This view can be traced back to a teaching found in one of the writings of the Christian Scriptures: "All scripture is inspired by God and profitable for teaching, for reproof, for correction, and for training in righteousness, that the man of God may be complete, equipped for every good work" (2 Tim. 3:16–17). This teaching about Inspiration gradually developed into two doctrines: (a) that God is in some way the "author" of the Bible, and (b) that there is a special truth or Revelation in these writings.

The first issue is this: in what way can we call God the Holy Spirit the author of these writings when they were obviously written by Paul or Luke or Ben Sirach? For some time in Christian history, people thought that God "dictated" the biblical books word for word to the human writer.

But this view of Inspiration ultimately collapses against one of the most fundamental principles of Catholic Christian theology—that because of the divine-human mystery in Jesus Christ, all Christian beliefs need to be understood in a similar dual valuation of both humanity and divinity. The Word of God took on that fullness of humanity in Jesus Christ. That central belief became the model and example of how God interacts with human beings in all circumstances.

To transfer this divine-human model to the case of biblical inspiration means that God did exert some influence in the process of writing these books (and so can be called "author"), but that influence did not remove the individual characteristics of the actual human writers of the biblical texts. Some authors write clearly, others confusedly. Some are pessimistic, others optimistic. Some reflect Greek customs, others Hebrew. For the Catholic Christian tradition, the Second Vatican Council clearly spelled out this intertwining of God as author and the human writers as full composers:

> To compose the sacred books, God chose certain men who, all the while he employed them in this task, made full use of their powers and faculties, so that, though he acted in them and by them, it was as true authors that they consigned to writing whatever he wanted written, and no more. (*On Divine Revelation,* no. 11)

The second major implication of the teaching on Inspiration is that the biblical writings contain a special revelation of truth. If God is the author of Scripture, then he must have a special religious truth to convey to us. But this truth is not always directly evident. The human writers all bring their own intentions and feelings into the act of writing. When Paul hoped that his Galatian opponents would castrate themselves (Gal. 5:12), he didn't necessarily express a wish God directly inserted into his mind. We must acknowledge his own anger and frustration also coming into play. But what is that special religious truth the Bible possesses?

3. The revealed truth of the Bible is found in what the various writers wished to express about the meaning of faith itself.

The reason why the Christian Church accepted these particular books—which make up what we now call the Hebrew Scriptures and the Christian Scriptures—is because they told the story of the origins and earliest development of the Christian faith. Every book in the Bible expresses some aspect of the struggle to know what faith is, what one believes about God, how one lives by faith, or what faith asks of us. The Bible can be called the Word of God, not because every single word and phrase was dictated by God, but because it tells the true and authentic story of how Christian faith came into existence and continues to the present. The story of faith was and is regarded by Catholic Christians as the model, the challenge, and the inspiration for all following generations of believers. It is a "truth for our salvation."

This means that in every biblical writing readers ought to seek to grasp the precise faith experience present in and behind the words. Faith-meaning remains the key that leads us into the revealed truth of the Bible. We are taught the ups and downs, the ins and outs, of living with faith. In that sense the Bible always remains a permanently revealed truth for the Christian believer.

To get to the faith-meaning of a particular writing like Paul's Letters to the Corinthians, the Book of Job, or the Gospel of Mark, we should know the mind and intention of those authors as best we can. For example, Paul, reflecting the style of faith and worship that emerges from a pluralistic and urban community, offers guidelines and teaching. Job delves into the struggle to believe in God's goodness when connected with so many failures in life.

What is the main point they were trying to say about faith in God? That's the truth we should be seeking—a constant guide for how we should live by faith. The teaching of the Catholic Church is stated clearly in the Second Vatican Council's decree *On Divine Revelation:*

Appendix 4

We must acknowledge that the books of Scripture, firmly, faithfully and without error, teach that truth which God, for the sake of our salvation, wished to see confided to the sacred Scriptures. (No. 11)

4. Thou shalt not believe everything in the Bible.

The faith-meaning in each writing remains the essential truth of the Bible. Other factors like geographical, botanical, or historical narration are not covered by the guarantee of inerrancy. The various books in the Hebrew and Christian Scriptures reflect vastly different cultures and time periods; the writers use the available historical, cultural, and scientific knowledge of their time to express their views. Much of this material may be inaccurate according to present knowledge, and it isn't really essential to faith, for example, how far Jericho is from Jerusalem.

Moreover, in 1893 Pope Leo XIII said very clearly in the encyclical *Providentissimus Deus* that "inerrancy did not pertain to matters of physical science or nature." The divine truth of the Bible does not reside in every insignificant detail but in the pattern of how people relate to God and God relates to people. That's what Christians read the Bible to discover.

It is also important to recognize that the Bible contains a great variety of different kinds of written expressions to make its points (see no. 7 in this article). Catholics have been encouraged to study and to learn to recognize these different types of writing (e.g., history, poetry, wisdom sayings, gospels) to be better able to grasp the kind of faith-teaching within them.

Finally, and perhaps most controversially, people must recognize that there are some few passages in the Bible that the Church has not accepted as representing an accurate view of Christian faith. These cause the most trouble for the ordinary reader (e.g., the bloodbath in Josh. 8:20–25; the unforgivable sin in Mark 3:29). Even though these passages do express a point about faith and faith activity, they are contradicted and "overruled" by other passages. When one stumbles on one of these sections, some help will probably be needed to clarify the issue.

5. Thou shalt not take one passage from the Bible and make it an absolute.

In the past (and sometimes even today,) when people thought that each word of the Bible was dictated by God, they could decide disputes, name towns, or solve personal problems by randomly opening a Bible and blindly pointing to some passage on a page. "Let God's Word decide!" Such a tactic betrays a serious misunderstanding of the phrase *Word of God,* and the faith it tries to illuminate.

A similar tactic is used by some people today: they land upon one particular passage in the Bible and make it into an absolute statement: "You just aren't a New Testament Christian if you don't speak in tongues." "Only those churches with only bishops and deacons are authentically Christian." In a similar way, ordinary readers can get upset when they read about the unforgivable sin (Mark 3:29); they wonder what it is and worry whether they might have done it by accident.

An important principle of interpretation always needs to be remembered in such cases. One text alone does not make a permanent Christian belief about faith; we must be attentive to the unity of the entire Scripture. Often one opinion may be canceled by a contrasting view. For example, the notion of the unforgivable sin is sharply countered by Jesus' words about the incredible mercifulness and forgiveness of God, and by the admonition to forgive seventy times seven (Matt. 18:21–22).

Because of these differences and contrasts the reader of the Bible must avoid making an absolute of any single passage and always consider the whole of the Scriptures. Again the decree *On Divine Revelation* of Vatican II makes this point a basic aspect of the skill of Bible reading:

> Attention must be devoted to the content and unity of the whole of Scripture, taking into account the Tradition of the entire Church and the analogy of faith, if we are to derive their true meaning from the sacred texts. (No. 12)

6. Thou shalt not be surprised at finding different opinions in the Bible.

Some of the preceding points may make some people stop for a moment: How can there be differing opinions in Scripture? Isn't that like saying that God contradicts himself? Not really, if we recall some of the basic principles already enunciated. First we remember that God speaks through and in the literary expressions of the human authors. Second, the religious truth of the Bible does not extend to everything the Bible says, but only that truth which speaks of faith ("for our salvation"). To these we must add a further notion—that the various writings of the Bible were composed over a thousand-year period and in many different circumstances.

Here one must remember that the unity or the whole of Scripture is important because within that thousand-year history we can see a very clear development of religious attitudes and convictions about faith. And development clearly implies change. For example, many of the early wisdom writings clearly affirm that individuals' sufferings are the result of their personal sins; but a later wisdom writing, the Book of Job, disputes this point; and the Gospel of Luke through the words of Jesus denies it (Luke 13:1–5).

Just as we should not take the early wisdom writings as an absolute, so we ought not expect complete unanimity in all faith convictions. We acknowledge the gradual deepening of religious truth through history and recognize that God's Revelation comes to us in human steps. "The same Holy Spirit constantly perfects faith by his gifts, so that Revelation may be more and more profoundly understood" (*On Divine Revelation*, no. 5).

When one finds a particular passage that seems strange or even shocking, one should not make an immediate judgment to reject it. Remember that there exists a history of struggling with faith in the biblical writings, and make an effort to learn more about the Bible's complete view on the issue.

7. Thou shalt learn something about the history and literary background of the various books of the Bible.

If God fully used the human writers and their various abilities—their intentions, language, and ways of expression—then it is crucial to know some fundamental facts about the particular book one is reading. For example, reading the prophecy of Isaiah or the Gospel of Mark one should know, as far as possible, what was the time and place of its composition; who was the author and to whom was he writing; what were the setting, the problems, and the occasion of the book; and whether the author was using a particular style of expression.

The last point is especially important. Writers have different ways of expressing their convictions—a historical narrative, poetry, a prophetical genre, a visionary writing, or even fiction. Again the decree *On Divine Revelation* encourages Catholic readers to recognize the fact "'that truth is differently presented and expressed in the various types of historical writing, in prophetical and poetical texts,' and in other forms of literary expression" (no. 12). What is the truth that the writer really wishes to express?

If we don't recognize the different literary forms, we run the danger of making serious faulty judgments. One example that frequently bothers

Christians is the parable of the eleventh-hour laborers, in which Jesus tells of the vineyard owner who hires workers at the third, sixth, ninth, and eleventh hours and then gives them all the same wages (Matt. 20:1–16). People get upset because they interpret the parable as some kind of social justice teaching on equal salaries. However, the parable as a literary form is intending to make only one particular point—that God's generosity far exceeds any human generosity. It has nothing to do with contemporary wage scales or job seniority.

If a Catholic Bible study group decides to focus on some particular sections or writings of the Bible, it would be well to have a member of the group first do a little reading on the background of the book. There are two standard biblical commentaries that provide adequate background material. They are *The Jerome Biblical Commentary* (Englewood Cliffs, NJ: Prentice-Hall, 1968) and the *Interpreter's One-Volume Commentary on the Bible* (Nashville: Abingdon, 1971). Every parish library should have one or both of these, as well as other materials, available to provide some resources for Bible study. If not, then requests should be made of the pastor and parish committees to obtain such sources.

8. Read the Bible regularly to stimulate and nourish personal faith.

Bible reading is a religious skill and, like any skill, it does take some practice. Again the Second Vatican Council strongly encouraged all Catholics to read (and pray) the Bible regularly, for "it can serve the Church as her support and vigor, and the children of the Church as strength for their faith, food for the soul, and a pure and lasting fount of spiritual life" (*On Divine Revelation*, no. 21). Catholic Bible study and prayer groups are indeed fulfilling one of the Church's most direct suggestions when they meet to read, reflect, and pray over the Holy Scriptures.

If we recognize the background and context of the biblical author's expression of faith, then we can say that the reading of the Bible places us into an ongoing history of faith. We become part of that search for faith that inspired those writers of long ago. As we pore over the Gospels, Letters, and Prophecies, we search to find their perduring patterns of faith: how they imaged God, how they understood God's commands, how they explained the presence of evil, and so on. These are faith issues still very much alive in the hearts of all believers. The biblical writings become a guide and source for our own process of faithful living.

9. The Bible serves as a "religious conscience" for the Church and the individual believer.

Some biblical scholars refer to the Bible as the conscience of the Church; that is, it calls the Christian community back to an awareness of its true foundations. To hear the Bible read becomes a brief "back-to-the-basics" course in Christian living and faith. Frequently these basics clash quite openly with attitudes and practices that have crept into Christian living. We can feel uneasy, and rightfully so, as the Scriptures point out the pathways and pitfalls of the Christian journey of faith. We should. The Bible functions precisely as a religious conscience, prodding us to judge, purify, and develop both our ways of believing and the contents of our belief. It is good to feel uncomfortable before God's Word, which is sharper than a two-edged sword (Heb. 4:12).

10. The Bible does not remove the responsibility of the reader to make conscientious and responsible decisions about faith.

Saint Bernard once described the *inspiration* of the Bible as the result of an inspired reader interpreting an inspired text. Even though Christians believe the Bible to be the authentic Word of God, this conviction in no way cancels out the belief that God's Holy Spirit also works in our hearts and lives to make us aware of God's will. The Bible does not absolutely answer all religious questions. The skill of Bible reading still requires us to use the human intellectual abilities God bestows on us and illuminates through the empowering Spirit.

The process of articulating a faith-meaning for our lives in the twentieth century merely continues the struggle, the purifying, the give-and-take process that the writers of the Bible bear witness to. No matter how clear a text may seem, there always remains the responsibility of the reader patiently and lovingly to examine its implications of a life of Christian faith today.

Indeed a Bible study group may be one of the best places to explore, share, and deepen the faith-meaning of a particular text. To listen to other people's understandings, to reconsider one's own, and to pray together constitute legitimate steps toward the clarifying of God's Word in our lives. It remains my hope and prayer and the major intent of this article that Catholic Bible study groups will devote themselves ever more assiduously to developing the skill of Bible reading. May the above "commandments" guide them along that path!

Appendix
4

This article appeared in *PACE* 16, October 1985, pages 20–24.

APPENDIX 5

Inspiration: God's Word in Human Words

George Martin

What do we mean when we say that the Bible is the inspired Word of God? Some Catholics and other Christians may carry with them an image of God whispering into the ear of the writer, or an angel dictating God's words to a dutiful scribe. Moreover, we often use the word *inspired* to talk about a piece of music or a work of art: "Beethoven was inspired when he composed his Fifth Symphony"; "Michelangelo's Pieta is an inspired sculpture."

Beethoven and Michelangelo were certainly gifted as few others were, and one way to express this is to say that they were inspired artists. While these artists used God-given gifts to achieve new heights of artistic expression, the inspiration of Scripture is a different reality. We do not reverence the Bible because it is great literature but because it contains the Word of God.

Many portions of the Bible are in fact literary masterpieces: the poetry of Isaiah's prophecies deserves ranking with the poetry of Shakespeare's sonnets. But Isaiah was inspired in a way that Shakespeare was not. Even if Isaiah had been a wretched poet, his prophecies would still be the Word of God. Even if Luke or Paul were poor spellers, their writings would still be the Word of God.

What makes the inspiration of Isaiah, Luke and Paul something quite different from the inspiration of Beethoven, Michelangelo, and Shakespeare? The best place to begin to answer this is the Bible itself. In the Second Letter to Timothy we read: "From infancy you have known the sacred scriptures, which are capable of giving you wisdom for salvation through faith in Christ. All scripture is inspired by God and is useful for teaching, for refutation, for correction, and for training in righteousness, so that the one who belongs to God may be competent, equipped for every good work" (2 Timothy 3:15–17).

Timothy is told that Scripture is *theopneustos*—a Greek word whose literal meaning is "God-breathed." When this verse was translated into Latin, the translator used the equivalent Latin phrase *divinitus inspirata*. So in Latin as well as Greek, Scripture is described as "God-breathed." Our English word *inspired* comes from the Latin word *inspirare,* so when we say that Scripture is inspired, we too are saying that Scripture is "God-breathed." But what does it mean to say that the Scriptures are breathed by God? There has been much discussion of this question through the centuries.

Some early Church Fathers understood "God-breathed" quite literally. One of them, Athenagoras, wrote of the Spirit making use of the authors of Scripture "as a flautist might blow into a flute." Others, such as Jerome, thought of the inspiration of Scripture in terms of the Holy Spirit dictating words which human authors set down in writing.

These explanations, while easy to understand on a literal level, have not passed the test of theological scrutiny through the centuries. Hence the understanding of inspiration that has prevailed in the Catholic Church dates back to Augustine, who said that God was the author of Scripture. But we know God didn't sit down with quill, typewriter, or word processor. Just how God is the author of Scripture requires further exploration.

God and Humans as Co-authors

The most important Church teaching on inspiration is that of the Second Vatican Council, the *Dogmatic Constitution on Divine Revelation (Dei Verbum)*. Its own words deserve our reflection:

> "Those divinely revealed realities which are contained and presented in sacred Scripture have been committed to writing under the inspiration of the Holy Spirit. Holy Mother Church, relying on the belief of the apostles, holds that the books of both the Old and New Testaments in their entirety, with all their parts, are sacred and canonical because, having been written under the inspiration of the Holy Spirit (cf. Jn. 20:31; 2 Tim. 3:16; 2 Pet. 1:19–21; 3:15–16), they have God as their author and have been handed on as such to the Church herself. In composing the sacred books, God chose men and while employed by Him they made use of their powers and abilities, so that with Him acting in them and through them, they, as true authors, consigned to writing everything and only those things which He wanted. Therefore, since everything asserted by the inspired authors or sacred writers must be held to be asserted by the Holy Spirit, it follows that the books of Scripture must be acknowledged as teaching firmly, faithfully, and without error that truth which God wanted put into the sacred writings for the sake of our salvation" (*Divine Revelation, 11*).

The bishops of the Second Vatican Council packed a lot of meaning into these words. They clearly affirm that the books of the Bible were written under the inspiration of the Holy Spirit, and that therefore in a real sense God is their author. But they also teach that God made use of human authors in the composition of the Bible, and that these human authors functioned as "true authors."

That is important. The human authors who gave us the writings contained in the Bible were not unthinking instruments of the Holy Spirit, like a flute is the unthinking instrument of the one who plays it. Nor did the human authors of Scripture merely write down words dictated by the Holy Spirit. No, the human authors of Scripture wrote as true authors.

For example, they may have done careful research before they began to write. Luke tells us that he "investigated everything carefully from the beginning" before he began to write his "orderly account" of the gospel events (see Luke 1:3). They also wrote for distinctive audiences. Thus Luke's account is a little different than Mark's or Matthew's, while John's account is very different than any of the other three Gospels. The Holy Spirit inspired the human authors to write in such a way that the differing needs of their audiences were met.

And that is the mystery of the inspiration of Scripture: at one and the same time both God and humans were its authors. This mystery of inspiration is akin to another mystery of our faith, the mystery of the Incarnation. Just as Jesus Christ was both fully human and fully divine, so too Scripture has human writers as its authors and God as its author. Neither reality of authorship diminishes the other, anymore than the two natures of Christ diminish each other.

Reading the Bible as God's Word

Both the human and the divine dimensions of the authorship of the Bible have implications for how we read and understand the Bible, for the flip side of inspiration is interpretation. We must try to understand what the human authors intended to convey when they wrote, in order to understand the inspired sense of Scripture. The Fathers of Vatican II insist that we must "carefully investigate the meaning the sacred writers intended" (*Divine Revelation, 12*).

Arriving at the meaning intended by the human authors requires the same kind of study that is necessary to understand any writing that comes from ancient times and cultures. We must pay attention to the type of writing (or "literary form") being used; we must understand what is said in its historical context. This is necessary in order to understand what the biblical authors intended to convey, which is the inspired sense of Scripture.

There can be a fuller meaning to a text of Scripture, beyond that intended by the human author, and passages can be interpreted in a spiritual as well as a literal sense. But any fuller meanings or spiritual senses should be rooted in the meaning intended by the inspired author. There are no shortcuts to understanding the inspired meaning of Scripture, which bypass the human dimension of its authorship.

Pope John Paul II offered advice to Catholics who seek to understand the inspired authorship of the Scriptures. To understand the Bible, he said, we must "start with the concern to understand the meaning of texts with all the accuracy and precision possible and thus, in their historical cultural context." He continued:

> "A false idea of God and the incarnation presses a certain number of Christians to take the opposite approach. They tend to believe that, since God is the absolute Being, each of his words has an absolute value, independent of all the conditions of the human language. Thus, according to them, there is no room for studying these conditions. However, that is where the illusion occurs and the mysteries of scriptural inspiration and the incarnation are really rejected, by clinging to a false notion of the Absolute" *(address on April 23, 1993).*

Neglecting either the divine or the human dimensions of Scripture means denying the true nature of biblical inspiration. To treat the Bible as a collection of merely human words is an obvious denial of the inspiration of Scripture. But it is no less a denial of inspiration to treat the Bible as a disembodied Word of God uttered from the heavens without any human component.

A Love Letter from God

To read the Bible as God's Word, we must grapple with the meaning intended by its human authors. But we are not reading merely human words. Our goal is to hear God's Word in the words of the human authors of Scripture. We read Scripture to encounter the God who reveals himself through its words. Søren Kierkegaard, a nineteenth century Lutheran theologian, compared reading Scripture to receiving a love letter written in a language one did not understand. The one who received the letter would sit down with a dictionary and painstakingly translate it word by word. When asked whether he was reading a letter from his beloved, he would reply, "Are you out of your head? Do you think this is reading a letter from my beloved! No, I sit here toiling with a dictionary in order to get it translated. If you call that reading, you mock me. I will be soon finished with the translation, and then I shall read the letter from my beloved. That is something absolutely different."

In Kierkegaard's analogy, studying Scripture and striving to understand what its human authors intended when they wrote is like translating a love letter. It is another step to then read Scripture as God's Word, as a love letter from God. When reading a love letter, one sets aside all distractions and simply concentrates on the one who wrote the letter and what that person is saying. There is a time for biblical study, and there is a time to set the commentaries aside and simply listen to the one who speaks through the "God-breathed" words of Scripture.

This article appeared in *Scripture from Scratch,* July 1994.

The Ten Commandments: Sounds of Love from Sinai

Alfred McBride, OPraem

Whatever happened to the Ten Commandments in religious education? Have we totally forgotten them? Did they really only become the Ten Suggestions? Should parents despair that their children will never encounter these moral guides?

Relax. The Ten Commandments are more alive than ever because now they are seen not just in terms of the sins they forbid, but also the values they espouse. Moses heard the sounds of love as well as the cadences of the law when he went to Sinai. Divine love created us as a people of faith and provided us with ten core values that show us how to love.

The key to the richest understanding of the Commandments is covenant, which is a love bond between God and us. Love liberates the human person. The Ten Commandments propose ten statements of liberty *from* attitudes and behaviors that undermine love. The decalogue liberates us *for* the acquisition of attitudes that enhance love. Far more than being restrictive laws, the Ten Commandments are liberating values as well as loving directives for our moral lives. Look, then, at each commandment in this light.

I. Believe in the real God.

"I, the Lord, am your God. You shall not have other gods beside me" (Dt. 5:6–7).

The First Commandment invites us to faith in the real God, who is a God of love. Many of us possess a diminished view of God. Maybe it's the *"eye in the sky"* deity policing our behavior. Some think of God as the *Superparent*. The son of a Jewish mother and a Catholic father put it this way, "I have the worst of both worlds, Jewish guilt and Catholic neurosis." This would be a guilt-producing God. Others view God as *Mr. Clean*, urging us to be spiritual "Danny or Denise Dusters," forever vacuuming our souls to make sure there are no wrinkles in our obsessively perfect lives.

Laid-back, passive types view God as a modern *wimp* who has replaced the Pale Galilean of Victorian times. People who see God this way prefer a limp, value-free divinity who vaguely loves us and makes no demands upon us.

Finally, still others think of God as *Rambo,* a muscular, patriotic deity who confirms the role of religion as a major supporter of militaristic adventures. These persons may have little interest in God as a humble and loving savior.

These five diminishments are false gods. The real God watches us to guide us to happiness, offers us forgiveness to wash away our sins, seeks the company of the imperfect and walks with us on our journey, cares deeply about what will enhance our worth and dignity—and fosters our freedom to grow in virtue. The First Commandment liberates us from faith in too small a god and frees us for a lifelong faith journey in a God who loves to be with us.

The First Commandment teaches us that our first moral task is not just a gloomy responsibility to avoid this or that, but a call to a life of *gratitude before the real God of loving graciousness.* It teaches us to begin our moral life with a God of love and to make our life a responsive song of love that echoes the sounds of love from Sinai.

II. Reverence the sacred.

"You shall not take the name of the Lord, your God, in vain" (Dt. 5:11).

The Second Commandment invites us to search for signs of the sacred in the midst of life and develop an attitude of reverence. Moses found the sacred at the burning bush and symbolized his reverence by taking off his shoes. When we appreciate the sacredness of God, we also acquire a reverence for ourselves, others, and the environment.

The best translation for this Commandment is, "You shall not make *wrong use* of God's name." Of course, we should not utter God's name carelessly or irreverently. Nor should we use it to justify wars, slaughter enemies, brutalize heretics and impose unjustified political and ecclesiastical power on others.

The right use of God's name is to recognize God's power and loving presence in the sacred aspects of existence: in the human person, in relationships, in the universe. Religion offers us visible signs of the sacred, above all in the person of Jesus, as well as in the Church and the sacraments.

We will appreciate these obvious signs of the holy more effectively when we also look for signs of the sacred in our everyday world. Notice, for example, the feeling of the holy in our desire for *order.* When a mother tells a frightened child, "It will be all right," she implies there is a divine order behind everything.

Other feelings can be signs of the sacred. We can find the holy, for example, in *playfulness*—a quality of God's own Spirit. A heavy, serious-minded world needs to play more, to experience the joy of release from being too solemn in God's presence. *Hope* moves us beyond the imprisonment of the present into a life that is eternal. To bring hope to the aches and bruises of the human heart is to discover the eternal. Even God's judgment can open up an experience of the sacred—not to justify vengeance but to awaken a sense of *justice* that points to God's all-embracing love for each of us.

Lastly, we can find God in *humor,* which shakes troubles from our shoulders and lifts up our hearts into the heart of the one who joyously lives forever. These five signs of the sacred in the world around us offer us a path to reverence and to appreciating the sacred aspects of human existence. That is the liberating purpose of the Second Commandment.

III. Take time off to pray and play.

"Take care to keep holy the sabbath day" (Dt. 5:12).

On a mellow Sunday in southern California, a young bachelor said, "Surfing was great this morning. Now I'm driving to the mountains to ski. Church can't compete with this." In one sense this "happy hedonist" hews closely to the intent of the Third Commandment. God said, "I worked six days. I'm going to rest on the seventh." Relaxation is one purpose for the Sabbath. The Sabbath reminds us to rest in the knowledge that God is behind all things—a knowledge that brings deep personal peace.

The biblical Sabbath remembers both *creation* and *covenant.* In recalling *creation,* it summons us to rest from our labors and think of the Creator. In remembering *covenant,* the Sabbath calls us to take time with God in a prayerful communion of love.

The Jewish Sabbath closes the week, while the Christian Sunday, remembering Easter, begins the week. On the Christian Sunday, the Church invites us to the Eucharist where we show gratitude to God (the true meaning of the word *Eucharist*) and assimilate anew the grace of salvation from sin. We can then resolve to implement God's Kingdom of love, justice, and mercy in the world and prepare for Christ's final coming.

Rabbi Abraham Heschel offers positive advice regarding the Sabbath from three viewpoints. 1) *Meditate on the Creator behind the creation.* The Sabbath tells us there is someone beyond workdays, earth management and civilization-building. 2) *Get in touch with eternity.* The Sabbath is a day in which eternity can be felt inside of time. If we never experience it here, can we do it hereafter? 3) *Commune with the Holy.* We are space people during the week, filling up the world's space with our products. But time is invisible, like a melody, closer to the spirit. Spend Sabbath time with God. Take time to pray and play on the Sabbath as the Third Commandment would lead us to do.

IV. Support family values in changing times.

"Honor your father and mother" (Dt. 5:16).

The original intention of the Fourth Commandment touched precisely on the loving care of aging parents by their adult children. Nomadic societies were often tempted to leave aging and sick parents behind to die when the tribe moved on. Biblical people, however, did not act like some of their nomadic neighbors. They honored their aging parents and took care of them.

The graying of America presents many problems for the adult children of aging parents, due to extended life spans, rising medical costs, and severe stress on their growing families. These "sandwich families" feel strain as they try to raise their children on a squeezed household budget. Yet, happily, today's adult children provide more care to more elderly parents over longer periods of time than ever before. They are perfectly in tune with the liberating value of the Fourth Commandment, even as one must admit that some adult children abuse and abandon their parents.

This Commandment also is concerned with the stability of family values, particularly in the light of training children. This means helping growing youth to understand their responsibilities to their parents and family members. Rapid cultural change makes this a far more demanding challenge than was the case in simpler times. Rising divorce rates, the increase of single-parent families, of both parents working, of child-care centers, of costs for available housing, of the impact of TV, drugs and alcohol are major signs of such change. Families need the fullest possible support of the Church, the government, businesses and other families if they want family values, as upheld by the Fourth Commandment, to truly flourish.

V. Cherish the life of your neighbor.

"You shall not kill" (Dt. 5:17).

In the Fifth Commandment, God asks us to renew our belief in the sacredness of life and the love which sustains it. So long as love of God, self and others is experienced and practiced, life has a chance. It crowds out the destructive impulses that beget anti-life behavior. This liberating value of the Fifth Commandment can free us from war, murder, genocide, terrorism, abortion, euthanasia, and a host of other forms of mayhem that humans inflict on one another.

The destructive impulse—evidenced by hatred, envy, jealousy and violent behavior—appears early in one's life and should be promptly addressed by a lifelong education in creativity, non-violence and love. Love is the closest experience we have to the act of creation. Love does not murder life. Love wants to produce, sustain, and care for it. Some speak of love as a seamless garment that wraps its creative protectiveness around life from conception to natural death. Love urges us to be pro-life at every turn.

The Fifth Commandment reminds us that life-cherishing love should be the guiding light in solving the multitude of moral problems that arise in issues of life and death. Love is meant to make the world safe for life.

VI. Wear the ring of fidelity.

"You shall not commit adultery" (Dt. 5:12).

The primary aim of the Sixth Commandment is fidelity to God, self, and others, a fidelity meant to liberate us from adulterous infidelity and other forms of sexual unfaithfulness. Perhaps no other commandment so vividly dramatizes the covenant dynamic of love and fidelity—ratified at Sinai and fully realized in the saving act of Christ who loved us faithfully until death.

The covenant fidelity of husband and wife is the major concrete illustration of what this Commandment is all about. Hence the proper context of this Commandment is the sanctity of marriage, the sacredness of the person, and the importance of a permanent marital relationship based on love and committed to the begetting and nurturing of children. Human love grows best in a stable, secure relationship.

Romantic passion gives the initial signal for fidelity. People in love have an instinctive inclination to bind themselves with promises. Thousands of love songs echo the pledges of constancy. "Darling, I will love you forever." Once into the marital relationship, when romantic emotion may have subsided, the spouses can discover a new reason for fidelity, namely, the affirmation of each other's worth and dignity. Fidelity assumes a new and more profound purpose, the lifelong pleasure of lavishing creative love on the beloved, enabling each partner to become more truly the image of God who rests in the heart of the marriage.

This Commandment is neither anti-sex, nor anti-body. In fact it wants to protect sexuality and truly let it flourish. Sexual sharing, in turn, is meant to enhance the total commitment to love. The body is a friend of the human person, showing to the spouses the unique image of God in each other, each being a shrine of the Holy Spirit who has made this body a temple.

Thus the positive force of the Sixth Commandment ministers to fidelity and the maximum human and spiritual growth of the spouses, liberating them from the forces of divorce and the compulsive search for sexual forms of infidelity that fall short of what God intended for one's human potential.

VII. Be trustworthy and respect others' rights.

"You shall not steal" (Dt. 5:19).

The Seventh Commandment celebrates the value of trust that is the basis of honesty and justice. A safe home and neighborhood arise from people who trust each other. A just society originates when the poor trust that their dignity and human rights will be respected. God has entrusted creation to us in the hope we shall not exploit it.

Regrettably, trust is in short supply these days. People have experienced too many assaults on their trusting natures. Mugged, burglarized, cheated, pick-pocketed, bribed, shortchanged, conned, and flim-flammed, people give up on trust. Nonetheless, God gave us a covenant dream of a peaceful society based on trust and challenges us to make it a reality.

Laws and surveillance systems are useful but insufficient. The value of trust needs to be instilled in the character of every human being. God offers us spiritual strength to make this possible. Trustful living requires community building, the experience of honest people, and the restoration of a spiritual outlook.

This Commandment also calls us to work for social justice. A trustful society demands a just social order for the poor, the weak and the outcast. This means both immediate relief for the homeless and the suffering as well as changing the laws, customs, and structures that keep people poor—in effect, stealing from them.

Finally, this Commandment urges us to take responsibility for the environment. The rape of the earth is another form of stealing, an injustice wrought on the human family and on the productivity of creation. God asks us to make trust, justice, respect for human rights, and environmental responsibility our top priorities. Our faith response should be a fervent yes.

VIII. Tell the truth with love.

"You shall not bear dishonest witness against your neighbor" (Dt. 5:20).

The Eighth Commandment opens us to the value of truthful living. The age of information floods the world with facts. Propagandists can manipulate the facts to deceive us. We need the protection of a truthful society in order to be free from such control. Liars murder more than truth. They kill souls and can cause physical death. Hitler taught that the big lie works better than the small one. He used lies to control his people and destroy Jews. Lying is an enemy of sound human relations.

Yet lying seems to be as American as apple pie. Spouses lie to each other. Children lie to their teachers. Commercials often deceive us. Some doctors use euphemisms to avoid telling patients the real state of their health. Some lawyers shroud the truth in technicalities. Watergate and the Iran-Contra affair mocked the truth.

But true love means telling the truth. It is a test of character for the person. The truth makes a person feel free. The process of becoming a free person by living truthfully takes a lifetime. It is worth the effort.

IX. Practice chastity.

"You shall not covet your neighbor's wife" (Dt. 5:21).

The Ninth Commandment brings us to the value of chastity, which is state-of-the-heart morality (and it applies to your neighbor's husband, too). Many people confuse chastity with celibacy. Chastity is not the absence of sex, but the presence of a clean heart that leads to the proper use of sexuality. Married people and celibates should both be chaste. Chastity should be as present in the act of sex as it is in those who are unmarried or who have vowed to abstain from sex.

Chastity deals with heart language more than with bodily behavior. It is about attitudes—like not exploiting others or treating them as objects, as happens in the case of pornography, which mocks the beauty and sacredness of sexuality. That is what Jesus meant when he taught that one could commit adultery in the heart—through lust—even though no sexual act had occurred. Heart language is decision language. It deals with motives and intentions. The Ninth Commandment celebrates the value of a clean heart and the pure intention. It seeks to liberate us from lust and the exploitation and human destruction it causes.

X. Replace greed with the joy of giving.

"You shall not covet your neighbor's goods" (Dt. 5:21).

By diverting human energy away from avarice, the Tenth Commandment asks us to enjoy the considerable pleasures of giving. It celebrates the words of Saint. Francis, "It is in giving that we receive." It inspires the generosity of heart that causes the giver to be as happy as the receiver. In an age when audiences give standing ovations to shamelessly greedy billionaires (as dramatized in the film *Wall Street*), this Commandment is exceedingly relevant. In a time when hundreds of millions of our brothers and sisters are starving, this Commandment asks us for an attitude that gives a "preferential option for the poor."

The Tenth Commandment teaches us to exchange the desire to hoard with the desire to seek the true well-being of others. It wants to liberate our hearts from greed and open them to giving our time, talent and treasure for the good of others. Throughout history, the human family has sensed that the unrestrained love of money is the root of all evil. Christian generosity creates an environment of goodness. As Jesus himself taught, "It is more blessed to give than to receive" (Acts 20:35). A peaceful world can only be built on the truth that generosity is better than greed.

This article appeared in *Catholic Update*, September 1989.

ACKNOWLEDGMENTS

The scriptural quotation on page 294 is from the New American Bible with revised New Testament and Revised Psalms. Copyright © 1991, 1986, and 1970 by the Confraternity of Christian Doctrine, Washington, D.C. Used by the permission of the copyright holder. All rights reserved. No part of the New American Bible may be reproduced in any form without permission in writing from the copyright owner.

All other scriptural quotations in this book are from the New Revised Standard Version of the Bible, Catholic Edition. Copyright © 1993 and 1989 by the Division of Christian Education of the National Council of the Churches of Christ in the United States of America. All rights reserved.

The teacher prayers in this book are adapted from various selections in *Taste and See: Prayer Services for Gatherings of Faith,* by Jacqueline Syrup Bergan and S. Marie Schwan (Winona, MN: Saint Mary's Press, 1996). Copyright © 1996 by Saint Mary's Press. All rights reserved. Used with permission of the author.

The four functions of myths listed on page 9 are from *The Power of Myth*, by Joseph Campbell with Bill Moyers (New York: Doubleday, 1988), page 31. Copyright © 1988 by Apostrophe S Productions, Inc., and Alfred van der Marck Editions.

The excerpt on pages 9–10 is from *The Art of Biblical Narrative,* by Robert Alter (New York: Basic Books, 1981), pages 23 and 32. Copyright © 1981 by Robert Alter.

The excerpt by John H. Westerhoff on page 10 is from "Contemporary Spirituality: Revelation, Myth and Ritual," in *Aesthetic Dimensions of Religious Education,* edited by Gloria Durka and Joanmarie Smith (Ramsey, NJ: Paulist Press, 1979), page 23. Copyright © 1979 by Gloria Durka and Joanmarie Smith.

The quotation on page 13 is from *Stories of Faith,* by John Shea (Chicago: Thomas More Press, 1980), page 89. Copyright © 1980 by John Shea.

The quotations on handout 1–B, handout 5–B, and handout Epilogue-B are from *The People of the Book,* by Anthony E. Gilles (Cincinnati: Saint Anthony Messenger Press, 1981), pages 3–4, 37–38, and 165–167, respectively. Copyright © 1983 by Anthony E. Gilles. Used with permission of the author.

The psalm on handout 4–B is from *Psalms Anew: In Inclusive Language,* by Nancy Schreck and Maureen Leach (Winona, MN: Saint Mary's Press, 1986). Copyright © 1986 by Saint Mary's Press. All rights reserved. Used with permission of the authors.

The quotation by W. M. Thomson on page 192 is from *The Student Bible,* edited by Philip Yancey and Tim Stafford (Grand Rapids, MI: Zondervan, 1986), page 787. Copyright © 1986 by Zondervan.

The excerpts on pages 217–218 are from *Praying the Psalms,* by Walter Brueggemann (Winona, MN: Saint Mary's Press, 1993), pages 14–17, 49–53, and 58–60, respectively. Copyright © 1993 by Saint Mary's Press. Used with permission of the author.

Handout 1–C is adapted from and appendix 4 is from "Ten Commandments for Catholic Bible Study Groups," by Matthias Neuman, in *PACE* 16, October 1985, pages 20–24.

Appendix 5, "Inspiration: God's Word in Human Words," by George Martin, is from *Scripture from Scratch,* July 1994. Copyright © 1994 by St. Anthony Messenger Press, 1615 Republic Street, Cincinnati, OH 45210; 800-488-0488. All rights reserved. Used with permission of the author.

Appendix 6, "The Ten Commandments: Sounds of Love from Sinai," by Alfred McBride, OPraem, is from *Catholic Update,* September 1989. Copyright © 1989 by St. Anthony Messenger Press, 1615 Republic Street, Cincinnati, OH 45210; 800-488-0488. All rights reserved. Used with permission of the author.

During this book's preparation, all citations, facts, figures, names, addresses, telephone numbers, Internet URLs, and other pieces of information cited within were verified for accuracy. The authors and Saint Mary's Press staff have made every attempt to reference current and valid sources, but we cannot guarantee the content of any source, and we are not responsible for any changes that may have occurred since our verification. If you find an error in, or have a question or concern about, any of the information or sources listed within, please contact Saint Mary's Press.